# PSYCHIC WARS

For Thomas, Marco and Oliver

# PSYCHIC WARS

## PARAPSYCHOLOGY IN ESPIONAGE – AND BEYOND

### ELMAR R. GRUBER

BLANDFORD

A Blandford Book
First published in the English language
in the UK in 1999 by Blandford

A Cassell Imprint

Cassell plc
Wellington House
125 Strand
London WC2R 0BB

www.cassell.co.uk

Distributed in the United States by Sterling Publishing Co., Inc.,
387 Park Avenue South, New York, NY 10016-8810

A Cataloguing-in-Publication Data entry for this title is available and
may be obtained from the British Library.

ISBN 0-7137-2762-4

Translated from the German by Helmut Bögler
Designed and typeset by Richard Carr
Printed and bound in Great Britain by MPG Books Ltd,
Bodmin, Cornwall

# CONTENTS

# Part 2

### CONTEMPORARY PSI RESEARCH
#### Towards a New Understanding of Reality

# Part 3

## A SELF-AWARE UNIVERSE? SILENT REVOLUTION IN THE PSI LABORATORIES

# PROLOGUE

Encounters with the inexplicable have always challenged human imagination. Reports of extraordinary anomalies in connection with human consciousness have come down to us from all cultures and eras and from all levels of society. These anomalies, which are normally associated with terms such as 'paranormal', 'mystical' and 'spiritual', form an integral part of human experience.

The field of science that has dedicated itself to the study of such phenomena has had to fight a long battle against both the gullible proponents of anything 'supernatural' and those who reject out of hand anything that is paranormal. It has survived all the controversies with undiminished vigour and is on the verge of establishing an indispensable place for itself within the new science of consciousness, possibly the last remaining uncharted terrain of human knowledge.

If you have never heard of AC, AMP, ganzfeld or DMILS or of EFHB and CRV, it may be because recent developments in the exploration of the paranormal have passed you by. You are not alone. They have passed many people by, because psi research has increasingly withdrawn from the public stage and, in so doing, may have entered into a third and decisive phase.

In its early days parapsychology was the domain of amateurs and hobby researchers. Later on, during the heyday of the great pioneers, it seemed as if it were at least likely to achieve partial acceptance by the 'hard' sciences. Nonetheless, a large part of the research conducted remained in the hands of interested laymen. During the last two decades, however, psychic research has expanded into areas that can be dealt with only by those who have undergone appropriate scientific training. Current research is mainly concerned with complicated scientific theories and with experiments that the layman cannot understand.

Some people may regret that there are no longer any of those sensational experiments that for so long characterized parapsychology and whose exploitation by the media contributed so greatly to the suspicion with which it was widely regarded. The change, however, marked the beginnings of a breakthrough, which has been based not on the uncritical reporting of the extraordinary effects achieved by psychics but on unreported progress in areas that are very different from those that might have been expected. Recent research has focused on scientific attempts to decode the strange interactions between mind and matter at the most basic levels. Unobserved by many, this research has been carried out in recent years. The days when psychic research was laughed at as a pseudo-science lie in the past.

This development occurred within only a decade of the deaths of the fathers of psi research. The era of these pioneers, who had established parapsychology as a science – albeit each in a different way and with varying degrees of success – came to an end within a very short period in which the great and famous names disappeared. The first to die was Joseph Banks Rhine (1895–1980), the founder of quantitative–statistical research at the Institute for Parapsychology in Durham, North Carolina. One year later, in the Netherlands, Wilhelm H.C. Tenhaeff (1894–1981), who had brought together psychoanalysis and parapsychology, died. The next to die was Rhine's wife, Louisa Ella Rhine (1891–1983), who had won praise for her analysis of spontaneous experiences. Next was the founding father of German parapsychology, Hans Bender (1907–91), the founder of the Institute for Border Areas of Psychology and Mental Hygiene in Freiburg. Finally, the leading Italian parapsychologist and psychoanalyst Emilio Servadio (1904–95) died. These personalities had been of decisive influence, and their research achieved national and international acclaim. Their individuality and the passion they were able to inspire in many of their students were irreplaceable, but their place in the laboratories was filled. There, the basic changes had taken place that now permit innovative psi researchers to raise their eyes to the ultimate frontiers: the high-tech machine of tomorrow, which reacts directly to the interaction between mind and matter.

Today, the traditional sciences have begun to show respect for the new parapsychology and increasingly to open the pages of their journals to articles on parapsychology. Now one can find them in such established journals as *Foundations of Physics*, *Physical Review*, *American Psychologist*, *Psychological Bulletin*, *Statistical Science*, *Brain and Behavioral Sciences* and *Perceptual and Motor Skills*. They document the achievements of the new psi research and its integration into established fields of knowledge. The changing attitude of prominent critics also underlines this trend. They were forced to recognize that experiments had achieved a high quality and the results could no longer be rejected out of hand.

In the eyes of scientists, parapsychology no longer needs to prove that the phenomena it investigates actually exist. It can now concentrate on the questions of how such phenomena are to be understood, categorized and applied in practice. For parapsychologists, who were formerly chiefly occupied with attempting to justify the existence of their research, this is a quantum jump. Now all their energies can be concentrated on attempting to understand the phenomena.

In an official report on modern psi research, the respected statistician Jessica Utts, professor at the University of California at Davis, wrote: 'The statistical results of the studies examined are far beyond what is expected by chance. Arguments that these results could be due to methodological flaws in the experiments are soundly refuted ... It is recommended that future experiments focus on understanding how this phenomenon works and on how to make it as useful as possible. There is little benefit to continuing experiments designed to offer proof.'[1]

These developments are still being ignored by large segments of the general public, even though interest in the extraordinary and uncanny continues to flourish. Television stations strive to outdo each other with programmes about fantastic phenomena and series based on the borderline between fact and fiction. Both fear of and hope for extraordinary paranormal abilities are being nourished.

In fact, the extraordinary is at work throughout the world, not in the form of spectacular phenomena but invisibly, as a silent, inconspicuous exchange between mind and matter. This might not sound like much, but it is no less than a revolution in our understanding of consciousness and its action in the world. What we may regard as chance is actually not chance at all. Chance has its own hidden organization, and this organization is called psi. Psi is part of the way in which nature is organized.

In this book I have attempted to provide an insight into the new fields of study that psi research has shaped for itself and into the work being carried out in the laboratories of creative scientists and their unusual, complex experiments. I have also attempted to explain the ways in which these scientists think, and the importance of the results they have achieved. Until now only experts have been able to appreciate why these findings are so sensational, because the effects observed are small – infinitesimal, even – when compared with the impressive cases that gained parapsychology its spurious popularity. And yet, at the very time that the evidence for these celebrated cases is slowly evaporating and many astonishing phenomena have been found to have natural explanations, it is the largely unreported results of laboratory research and the hardly detectable anomalous influences on electronic machinery and living systems that today make psi appear to be a scientifically proven fact.

I have compiled the most recent and exciting, but largely unknown empirical results. There are insights not only into American and European laboratories, but also into the formerly closed world of the recent massive efforts in this field by Russian, Chinese and Japanese researchers. The book also includes, however, information about the top secret programme that was initiated by the CIA in the early 1970s – a secret US government programme that supported research in this field for more than 23 years at a cost of more than $20 million. This work was entrusted to non-parapsychologists, mainly physicists, who, supported by government money, discovered many new approaches to research that led to important innovations in this field.

Their assignment had been completely pragmatic, however: psi was to be developed as a means of espionage. Some of the hitherto secret documents have now been released to the public, and these reveal the importance achieved by psychic research in the power game of the world's most powerful nations. The documents also show the successes and limitations in the practical application of psi.

I am fortunate that during my career as an active psi researcher I have been friends with those scientists who led the secret psi project and with many of the psychics with whom they worked. These friendships have enabled me to look behind the alleged results and fantastic claims and have made it possible for me to document the true story of the psi spies, their rise, their success and their decline.

Modern psi research includes new terms. I have used these in this book as well as the more traditional terminology. Although I explain these new terms and concepts whenever they first appear, there are several that recur repeatedly, and these require a brief definition.

Psi is the collective term for all paranormal phenomena. It includes extrasensory perception as well as psychokinesis. In *extrasensory perception* (ESP) information is gained by means that cannot be explained. In *psychokinesis* (PK) matter is influenced by means that cannot be explained. ESP includes *telepathy* (the exchange of information between individuals without the help of the normal senses), *clairvoyance* (the gaining of information about remote objects or situations without its transmission by the normal senses) and *precognition* (the gaining of information about future events without this having been gained by normal means).

In addition to these common terms, parapsychology itself is defined as the science of *anomalous mental phenomena* (AMP). Extrasensory perception is also called *anomalous cognition* (AC). Because laboratory research in the field of psychokinesis concentrates mainly on micro-effects within so-called stochastic (random) systems, two terms are commonly preferred for the description of these effects: *anomalous perturbation* (AP) and *mind–matter interaction* (MMI). Psi phenomena are termed 'anomalous' because they consist of anomalies within our current scientific and psychological concept of the world at large. Anomalies are inexplicable, but nonetheless real, phenomena. Anomalous phenomena have nothing in common with abnormal phenomena, a term that indicates behaviour that departs from a norm, particularly in a pathological sense.

A new term has, within only a few short years, come to replace the traditional designation for extrasensory perception: *remote viewing* (RV), which is defined as seeing or perceiving from a distance.

Anomalous cognition is being investigated by two experimental methods: forced choice and free response. Under the *forced-choice* method the selected image out of a range of already known images, which have been mixed at random, must be 'guessed'. The original format for this test was introduced at the Institute of Parapsychology, Durham, North Carolina, by J.B. Rhine in the 1930s. He used cards bearing the symbols of a cross, a circle, waves, a square and a star. A deck of 25 cards consisted of five cards of each symbol. The person being tested had to 'guess' the sequence of the cards. If they succeeded in correctly naming the cards at a rate significantly above chance, this was taken as an indication that they possessed paranormal abilities.

In contrast to this, the *free-response* method works with unknown targets, such as pictures, objects or places, thus permitting a free response to whatever impressions come to mind. In recent years the free-response method has become increasingly popular because it permits a better study of the mechanisms of psi.

When experimental results are subsequently analysed statistically, the first thing we have to determine is whether a given effect has occurred at all. To do so it is necessary to examine whether the result is 'significant'. Significance is the term that is used to describe whether a given result has reached a certain level above or below chance expectation and is, therefore, no longer regarded as a chance result but as caused by some variable. A result is normally called significant when there is a probability of at least 95 per cent that the result reflects some form of real influence.

When two values need to be compared, their correlation is determined. The correlation provides a measure of their interconnection, and a high correlation means a close interconnection. If one value rises while the second value also rises, we are dealing with a positive correlation. A negative correlation can also reflect a systematic interconnection between two values. There is, for example, a negative correlation between age and the ability to react: the older a person becomes, the more their ability to react decreases.

When I speak of 'psi signals', 'psi radar' and so on, I use these as figurative terms only to identify processes whose nature is still largely not understood. And when I speak of 'consciousness' I do not use the term as the opposite of unconscious psychological processes, but to describe the totality of the mental–spiritual means of expression of a human being.

# Part I

## INTELLIGENCE SERVICES AND PARAPSYCHOLOGY

### The History of Remote Viewing and the Psychic Spies

'I never liked to get into debates with sceptics,
because if you didn't believe that remote viewing
was real, you hadn't done your homework.
We didn't know how to explain it, but we weren't
so much interested in explaining it as in determining
whether there was any practical use to it.'

*Major General Ed Thompson*[2]

# Chapter One

# PARANORMAL REARMAMENT

## OCCULT PRACTICES AND THE MILITARY

In Menlo Park, to the south of San Francisco, in the high-tech belt of Silicon Valley, where computer and software companies with already legendary names have realized the modern version of the American dream, there is a unique research establishment: the Stanford Research Institute, better known as SRI International. There, 2700 scientists and their laboratories, which are full of the most up-to-date and most elaborate analytical equipment, stand ready to carry out research. The institute abounds with Nobel laureates and illustrious names. The SRI works for governments and enterprises from all over the world, and it maintains several branches in the United States, Europe and Asia. It offers everything from basic research in the natural sciences to advising governments and high-tech companies on matters of strategy. In 1995 the revenues of the 'think tank' amounted to $320 million, half of which came from governmental funds. Traditionally, one of the main sources of revenue is military research, including the development of new weapons and high-tech devices for military use. In this flagship of American science, the name of the game is applied research. There is no place for dreamers.

No one would have suspected that there was a laboratory at the SRI for such a controversial and seemingly out-of-place science as parapsychology. Nevertheless, for almost a quarter of a century parapsychological research was conducted within the walls of the SRI. The subject under study was not whether psi existed or not, but a solution to the problem of how it could be developed to the level of practical application, or, to be exact, to the level of military application with the end result of penetrating the Iron Curtain through the use of psi.

On 28 November 1995, before an audience numbering in the millions, Robert Gates, a former director of the CIA (Central Intelligence Agency), admitted on ABC television's *Nightline* programme that his agency had initiated the psi research programme at the SRI in 1972. The research had been undertaken in order to analyse the paranormal threat posed by the Soviet Union and to catch up with the Soviets in this area. The programme was to be discontinued.

Since then many sensational and paranoid stories have appeared in the media. Former members of the project have sold their stories to the highest bidder, while psychic research itself has become doubly suspect, first, because of the accusation that it was carried out for military purposes, and second, because of the snide remark that nothing came of it except hot air. Why else would the intelligence services have closed the psi file? Why indeed?

The weirdest myths and theories have been circulating about the SRI programme of psychic research for the intelligence services and military authorities. Nevertheless, it ranks among the most interesting chapters in the history of the science of anomalous mental phenomena, previously known as parapsychology, and an assessment of the work that was undertaken is worth the effort since it took place during a time when the old science of parapsychology was undergoing a change. The research done at the SRI contributed to this change, and this contribution should not be underestimated.

Like war itself, which, despite the apparently rational and controlled will to destroy, remains a basically irrational business, strategic thinking by the military has always made room for clairvoyance and precognition. In ancient times the 'soothsayers' in the confidence of great military leaders were elevated to the level of mystic prototypes. In Homer's *Iliad* the seer Calchas leads the ships of the Achaeans to Troy. Like Helen on the Trojan side, he hears 'the voices of the immortal gods'. In later times matters became less exalted and took place within more 'earthly' dimensions. But only a few decades ago, the Nazi amalgamation of racial mythology and a fascination with astrology still made possible the waging of an 'occult' war. In the spring of 1942 at the suspect 'Pendulum Institute' in Admiral von Schroeder Street in Berlin, the Ministry of War gathered together a group of woolly-headed enthusiasts for the occult, pendulum-wielders, dowsers, astrologers and psychics. The intention was to copy the British, who were allegedly employing pendulums to identify the positions of German submarines. A lieutenant commander in the German Ministry for the Navy became convinced that it was possible to tune in to certain emanations by means of a pendulum, and he made up his mind to discover the appropriate pendulum technique to achieve this. The 'emanations' from the hulls of the submarines were to be located on sea charts. The way these meetings were conducted with typical German thoroughness belongs to the more absurd chapters of history. There were ridiculously precise rules about how to dress, how to sit and how to hold the pendulum. When nothing came of it, the sea charts were laid on copper plates in the forlorn hope of achieving some sort of magic-physical increase in the effect.[3]

In the United States two decades later some people became convinced that comparable efforts were being made behind the Iron Curtain, and they feared for national security. How could psi be used in the service of the Soviet military?

For ideological reasons, for many decades parapsychological research in the former Soviet Union had taken a different direction from that in the West. In Russia the materialistic view of the world left no scope for the spiritual dimension that parapsychology was investigating. Despite this, parapsychology achieved universal recognition much earlier than in the West. In February 1922 the Russian Congress of the Association of Natural Sciences issued a positive opinion on the research conducted in this field by a certain Bernard Kazhinsky. The significance of this fact cannot be overstated. In the United States it would be the equivalent of the recognition of psychic research by the American Institutes of Mental Health, something that is still quite improbable even today.

In 1919 Kazhinsky had undergone a decisive paranormal experience in connection with the death of a close friend. This had led him to devote himself to research on the human nervous system and how it was able inexplicably to react to stimuli that the known senses could not detect. This was the beginning of a research programme that was, in concept, remarkably different from western parapsychological tradition. In the West the assumption was that psi had to be a trait primarily explainable in terms of psychology, but Kazhinsky believed it had to be a biological component, an undiscovered sensory organ or at least a predisposition in the structure of the organism.[4]

Kazhinsky's concept led to research being carried out in the Soviet Union that was strongly orientated towards neurophysiology and biology. Its pre-eminent proponent was to become the physiologist Leonid Vasiliev, and in the 1920s Vasiliev's books, articles and presentations formed the ideological foundation for Soviet parapsychological research.[5] The gist of his theory was that the experimental factors of telepathy should be investigated from a physiological – that is, a material – point of view, so that they could not be exploited by the proponents of 'religious superstition' – that is, from an idealistic point of view.

In an elegant experiment on 'mental suggestion' conducted during this period Vasiliev proved that people could be influenced telepathically over great distances, even if they were screened to protect them from known electromagnetic waves. This concept of distant influence has remained the key theme of Russian research to the present, and it was the reason the Americans finally felt obliged to initiate an analysis of its potential threat.

It was only at the end of the 1960s, however, that the US intelligence services became really nervous. The extent of Soviet research led to great consternation, particularly since it had been believed that there was no place for paranormal phenomena within the official materialistic doctrine. No one was aware that the research in question did not contradict materialistic convictions in any way because it was being conducted on the same level as the natural sciences, particularly biology.

## PSYCHIC ARMS RACE BETWEEN THE WORLD POWERS

Even before the 1960s the US intelligence services had flirted with the idea of applying psi, but clearly the urgency of undertaking research had not been appreciated. Thanks to the Freedom of Information Act it became possible in 1981 to look at secret files, which reveal that only a few years after the end of the Second World War the CIA had recommended investigating extrasensory perception. A memorandum dated 7 January 1952 states: 'If, as now appears to us established beyond question, there is in some persons a certain amount of capacity for extrasensory perception (ESP), this fact, and consequent developments leading from it, should have significance for [a] professional intelligence service.'[6]

We do not know if the 1952 project was ever realized, but we do know that in the same year J.B. Rhine, America's leading parapsychologist, and his 'crown prince', John Gaither Pratt (1910–79), travelled throughout Europe on a secret mission for the US government. Included in the party was Richard Lowrie, the project leader at the US Corps of Engineers' research and development laboratory at Fort Belvoir, Virginia, and the man responsible for the project. The delegation was supposed to investigate the possibility of extrasensory abilities in animals and their military application.

Also in 1952, at a secret meeting at the Pentagon, Andrija Puharich (1918–95), a physician, gave a presentation entitled 'Report on the

Possible Applications of Extrasensory Perception in Psychological Warfare', and a year later he gave a talk on telepathy to the air force and another on the biological foundations of extrasensory perception at the Army Chemical Center. Puharich's view of the world was a strange mixture of parapsychology, occultism and science fiction. Through a medium, he was in contact with 'the Nine', allegedly the greatest brains in the universe. In his book *The Sacred Mushroom*[7] he expounded the theory that psycho-active substances in certain kinds of mushrooms were parts of a 'key to eternity'. In the 1970s Puharich became famous through his 'discovery' of Uri Geller.

Former CIA agent Victor Marchetti tells the most incredible stories from the early 1960s. Colonel Oleg Penkovsky was one of the CIA's most valuable contacts on the other side of the Iron Curtain until he was found guilty of treason and executed in 1963. According to Marchetti, this did not deter the CIA from attempting to continue to contact Colonel Penkovsky – meanwhile truly 'on the other side' – with the help of a medium who was supposed to get the dead agent to reveal secret information. Apparently the medial contact completely satisfied the CIA. Marchetti states that they saw no reason to discontinue this rather unorthodox – even for parapsychologists – method of gathering information.

Around 1967 the Americans learned that the Soviets were financing 14 research institutes with an estimated $500 million a year in order to advance their version of parapsychological research. What could have persuaded the Soviet Union to support such an uncertain field of science so intensively? It sounds like irony, but the reason was – a newspaper article!

The USS *Nautilus* was the world's first nuclear-powered submarine. According to French sources, when she undertook her first cruise under the ice cap of the North Pole in 1959, successful telepathic card guessing experiments were carried out between a member of the crew and a research institute belonging to the Westinghouse Electric Corporation in Friendship, Maryland. It was known that Westinghouse was engaged in telepathic experiments and that Bell Telephone Laboratories had considered such experiments but then rejected them. Communications with a submerged submarine posed an insurmountable problem for standard means of transmission. An enterprising reporter had simply tied the two pieces of unrelated information together and forged them into a sensational story. His report led to one of the strangest chain reactions in recent history.

Vasiliev spoke fluent French. His main contacts with the West were through the Institut Métapsychique International in Paris. Raphael

Kherumian, a well-known member of the institute, collected the reports in the French press on the alleged *Nautilus* experiments and sent them to his friend Vasiliev. The Soviets were shocked by the Americans' lead and immediately began enormous efforts to initiate militarily applicable psychic research.

At a conference in Moscow in 1968 western scientists were deliberately confronted with the successes of this research. They were shown the exciting experiments in psychokinesis conducted by Nina Kulagina, and even permitted to 'smuggle' a copy of the film to the West.[8] The Russian parapsychologist Eduard Naumov reported to the conference that the Red Army had successfully 'repeated' the *Nautilus* experiments. These and many even less verifiable – and therefore all the more spectacular – stories were collected in a book by Sheila Ostrander and Lynn Schroeder,[9] and the book, in turn, set off nervous reactions among Americans about the psi advances of the Soviets.

Until the late 1960s the intelligence services had periodically reviewed the work of parapsychologists, but they based their judgements on analyses by non-parapsychologists and sceptics, who always advised against getting involved in this uncertain science. When a leading Soviet scientist gave a presentation about research in borderline sciences in his country at an obscure conference at Big Sur, California, the alarm bells sounded. Suddenly everybody saw the investigations into 'mental suggestion' and 'remote influencing' in the context of 'telepathic remote control' and brain-washing, and fear of the enemy superpower had been enriched by a new concrete threat, the 'mental attack'.

The new information about developments in applied psychic research in the Soviet Union electrified the US intelligence services. Almost overnight they did an about-face and the pressure was on to catch up the alleged Soviet lead as quickly as possible.[10]

What convinced the United States of the need to take up psychic research was not only the rumours about the Soviet Union's alleged advances in this field but also the fact that this research is not expensive – indeed, compared to the costs of modern weapons, it is ridiculously cheap. And if the enemy superpower was actually capable of telepathically influencing the personnel of an intercontinental missile silo from a great distance – as a report by the Defense Intelligence Agency (DIA, the intelligence service of the US army) assumed – then it was all the more urgent to protect the expensive hardware by cheap countermeasures. Because the DIA knew: 'The major impetus behind the Soviet drive to harness the possible capabilities of telepathic communication, telekinetics and bionics [is] said to come from the Soviet military and the KGB.'[11] The report closes with the claim that the Soviets were far in advance of the United States in this field.

Without question, this DIA report from 1972 is an impressive sociological curiosity. The scenes of psychic attacks by an army of Soviet clairvoyants and psychokinetic mediums that it projects can hardly be surpassed in their naïvety. The report continues: 'Soviet efforts in the field of psi research, sooner or later, might enable them to do some of the following: (a) Know the contents of top secret US documents, the movements of our troops and ships, and the location and nature of our military installations. (b) Mold the thoughts of key US military and civilian leaders at a distance. (c) Cause the instant death of any US official at a distance. (d) Disable, at a distance, US military equipment of all types including spacecraft.'

Such views must have been astounding, unless you happened to be a parapsychologist, who knew that such scenarios belonged in the realm of science fiction. Laboratory results were producing a very different picture. Psi was emerging as an extremely weak signal that could easily be interfered with, and it was clear that its controlled application was possible only with a very high rate of error. Nevertheless, parapsychology, a science that had notoriously suffered from lack of funds, was highly delighted that the US government was seriously considering giving it a financial shot in the arm. And an assessment such as that contained in the DIA report was bound to speed up decisions at the highest political level. It is quite possible that some parapsychologists in the United States deliberately supported some of the rumours about Soviet advances in psychic research simply to keep the money coming.

In those days US government circles entertained hopes of being able to apply paranormal abilities for military purposes – a widespread delusion, as we know from the occult games played by the Wehrmacht – but in America, with disarming naïvety, pragmatism was always given free rein. Since the beginning of the Cold War the desire to always be one step ahead of the Soviets had been paramount, and the opportunity to put this into practice arose in 1972. Out of this came a research and development programme to investigate the possible application of anomalous information transmission for military purposes that was to last for 23 years. It is the story of psi espionage in the high-tech age, the story of 'remote viewing'.

# Chapter Two
# REMOTE VIEWING

## TRANSCONTINENTAL REMOTE VIEWING: ROME–DETROIT

It was a cold, windy day in November in Rome, and for the sixth time I was supposed to go to a place that had been selected at random. This time the note in the sealed envelope said 'Fiumicino Airport'. I had time to spare, and I knew from earlier excursions to an area that was rich in antique monuments that there were some hills near the airport from which I would have a good view of it. That was all I had to do. I had to be at the selected spot at the agreed time – 5 o'clock in the afternoon – and look around for a quarter of an hour. At the immediate spot where I was standing, I noticed some holes in the ground that had probably been dug by grave-robbers who had been looking for archaeological spoils near the Roman and Etruscan excavations. In the background lay the landing strips and the terminal.

At the same time my American colleague Marilyn Schlitz had made herself comfortable in her apartment. It was 11 o'clock in the morning, and she was 8000 kilometres away in Detroit. Marilyn relaxed and began to record her fragmentary impressions on tape: 'Flight path? Red lights. Strong depth of field. Elmar seems detached, cold. A hole in the ground. A candle-shaped thing. Flower – maybe not real. Possibly painted. Outdoors. See sky dark. Windy and cold. Something shooting upward.'

When she had finished, she wrote down a summary of her perceptions: 'The impressions that I had were outdoors and Elmar was at some type – I don't know if institution is the right word – but some place. Not a private house or anything like that – something – a public facility. He was standing away from the main structure, although he could see it. He might have been in a parking lot or field connected to the structure that identifies the place. I want to say an airport but that just seems too specific. There was activity and people but no one real close to Elmar.'

Remote viewing (RV) was the latest thing in parapsychology in those days. The experiments follow a simple routine: one person stays in the laboratory, while a second person goes to a place that had been chosen by lot. The person in the target site allows the impressions to sink in for about 15 minutes, while at the same time the person in the laboratory attempts to describe the place. After several experiments of this sort, evaluators with copies of the descriptions go to the designated place as well as to all the other possible locales not selected, without knowing which site is the target in which experiment. They compare the statements in the descriptions with the actual places and rank them according to how well they compare. In addition to this ranking, they also assess the degree of comparability and obviously must also evaluate cases in which there is no correspondence at all.

The case described above was one of several remote viewing experiments and was a 'direct hit'. Both Marilyn Schlitz and the evaluators unanimously ranked the airport as number one. Marilyn Schlitz had also described other target spots so accurately that a statistical analysis showed a probability of 1 to 200,000 against the results having come about by chance.[12]

Remote viewing was the US answer to the Soviet psi threat. The format of the experiment was developed by the SRI in 1972 with funds provided by the CIA and was painstakingly perfected in the following years. The central figure in this development was the New York artist and psychic Ingo Swann.

## INGO SWANN

Swann was born in Telluride, Colorado, in 1933, and as a child he had many paranormal experiences. He studied biology and art, but being unable to continue his studies, he joined the army. During his training at Fort Knox, Kentucky, he read Aldous Huxley's *The Doors of Perception*, and this was to have a strong influence on his subsequent life. Huxley's book was regarded as the 'bible' of the counter-culture, one of the triggers that set off the burgeoning preoccupation with drugs and mysticism. Swann spent most of his time in the army in Korea and the Far East, but in 1958 he decided to go to New York and take up art. For ten years he kept his head above water by taking a job with the United Nations, and during this period he because increasingly preoccupied with sociology. His interest had been awakened by something he had learned from Huxley – that the doors of perception in a person can be open or closed. They can either allow someone to enter into the fields of transpersonal experiences and achieve their artistic potential, or they can shut them out. Swann was interested in the application of the 'doors of perception' at the higher level of social structures. What are the social conditions that permit a creative society with 'open doors' and which conditions create a repressive society where the doors are closed?

Towards the end of the 1960s, through his acquaintance with the artist Buell Mullen, Swann was introduced into the higher echelons of New York society, where psychics and mediums were popular as a form of entertainment. Mullen came from a wealthy family in Chicago, and among other things had organized meetings with mediums for the Chinese leader Chiang Kai-shek, who had fled to Taiwan in 1949. At a dinner party, Swann learned from the wife of the dean of the technical faculty of Columbia University – she 'collected' English mediums – that the British secret services, MI5 and MI6, occasionally worked with psychics. Up to this time Swann had never considered that he was a psychic, someone with paranormal abilities. Although he had undergone strange experiences, he had not considered these, or himself, to be anything out of the ordinary. He had never imagined that the secret services could be interested in psi.

One of the men Swann met at these parties was John Wingate, a professor at New York University. Wingate was a member of the council of the American Society for Psychical Research (ASPR), which had been founded in 1885 and was the oldest parapsychological association and research institution in the United States. In 1971 Wingate introduced Swann to the ASPR and thereby became the indirect instigator of remote viewing research.

Another person who helped determine the direction of Swann's life was Cleve Backster, an expert on lie detectors (polygraphs). Backster gained world fame through experiments in which he demonstrated an alleged primary perception in plants. The 'Backster effect' postulated that plants that had been connected to a polygraph showed 'emotional' reactions to negative human thoughts or to the killing of shrimp that were thrown into boiling water. His theories were never accepted by the parapsychological community, even though they did receive extensive publicity.

Backster conducted several experiments with plants, as well as experiments in psychokinesis with Swann, who was meanwhile being recommended as a psychic by his patrons. Backster showed himself impressed by the results, which made the rounds, and Swann was eventually invited to take part in experiments by the well-known parapsychologist and member of the American Society for Psychical Research Gertrude Schmeidler, professor at City University in New York, and Karlis Osis, research director of the ASPR.

In an experiment conducted by Schmeidler, Swann was supposed to cause variations in temperature in sensitive measuring instruments.[13] Some of the temperature-measuring instruments stood about openly in the room while others were sealed inside Thermos flasks. The variations they registered were recorded continuously on dials. Swann was not permitted to move about during the experiment and was instructed to concentrate on a different instrument during each sequence of the test. In between, he was granted periods of 45 seconds in which to relax.

During one of these periods of relaxation a particularly remarkable change in temperature occurred. Swann was wondering exactly where the measuring instrument was positioned inside a specific Thermos flask. At this moment Larry Lewis, an assistant who had been monitoring the recordings on the dials in an adjoining room, came rushing in. He thought that one of the Thermos flasks had been opened because for 30 seconds the recording dial had constantly registered a change in temperature of almost 1°C. He found Schmeidler and Swann sitting comfortably in their chairs. None of the flasks had been touched. The dial that had recorded the remarkable reaction was the one connected to the measuring instrument in the flask Swann had been thinking about.

The experiment confirmed the observation that the psi effect frequently occurs during tests when the subject's concentration and will to achieve a positive result lapse and the subject relaxes. This effect is known as release of effort. Apparently, an over-intense mental effort prevents the free flow of psi.

These highly successful experiments led to an unexpected interest from the media, which were exploiting the fears that abounded at the time. If, it was said, Swann were able to influence an instrument for measuring temperature, could he not also set off an atomic bomb? Swann tried not to let himself be influenced by the sudden public interest in him. The strange effects he was able to produce had aroused his curiosity, and he continued his experiments with Cleve Backster. He next succeeded in influencing the cells in a drop of blood that had been taken from him. As soon as Swann began concentrating on the blood, the isolated blood cells frequently reacted by changing their potential. Backster, who was the acknowledged expert on lie detectors and was in touch with many leading members of the executive and the intelligence services, only remarked dryly: 'Well, you've just done something the Soviets have been working on for a long time. The potential of invading someone's body by mind alone.'[14]

# BEYOND THE BODY OR BEYOND THE SENSES?

At the American Society for Psychical Research Karlis Osis was working in the field of out-of-body experience (OBE), and Ingo Swann was called in to take part in these experiments. Swann, who had never had an OBE, was asked to try to bring about such an experience by an act of will. There was a rather nondescript room with a gallery high up under the ceiling, on which pictures, numbers and symbols had been placed. The subjects, who were connected to measuring instruments, would be able to see these hidden objects only if they were to rise up to the ceiling in an out-of-body experience.

The story of remote viewing began in this room. Swann had no idea at all of how he was to go about triggering an OBE, yet his very first attempt was a success, even without an OBE. In the course of time, however, his hits became less frequent. This frustrated him, because in his work with Backster he had discovered that paranormal effects tended to improve with the duration of the experiments. He began thinking things through and hit on the problem. In the experiments he was required to dictate his impressions of the target pictures on tape through a microphone, and in order to be able to do this, he had to stop 'seeing' and start thinking about how to articulate what he thought he 'saw'. The image impressions in the right hemisphere of his brain came into conflict with the analytical work being performed by his left hemisphere, the speech centre. In addition, the mostly senseless target pictures caused further confusion in the perceiving mind.

Swann suggested that he should not talk about his perceptions but simply sketch them. This change worked like a charm, and he began sketching things without knowing what they were supposed to mean. The degree of similarity with the meaningless target pictures was astonishingly high. Swann did not interpret this as either an OBE or a paranormal ability, but as an unknown biologically based form of perception. All he had to do was to perceive. In an experiment that took place on 24 November 1971, he was able quite accurately to reproduce several target objects, including a circle with something that he called TU or UT. If the UT had been connected by a short line, it would have looked like the numeral 5 lying on its side. In fact, there was a circle with a large 5 inside it on the gallery. Everybody at the ASPR was impressed. Only Swann was dissatisfied. He felt that he should have been able to perceive the 5. He believed that the system of extrasensory perception worked according to its own laws and logic, and that, above all, it worked below the level of conscious control, on a subliminal level. The objective was to discover how the cognitive conscious mind interacted with the hidden psi system of perception and how this interaction could be improved.

While he was waiting for the start of another experimental session, a further effect attributable to a slackening of concentration occurred. Swann's consciousness suddenly found itself in the street. He 'saw' a woman passing by in a ridiculous orange raincoat. He was so astonished by this impression that he wanted to confirm it immediately. He tore the electrodes for the electroencephalographic recordings from his head and rushed out into the street, together with assistant Janet Mitchell. They were just in time to see an orange raincoat turning the corner of Central Park West.

Swann, who still did not know if this had been an OBE or if he simply 'saw' things from a distance, developed his own experiment with Janet Mitchell. Someone was to prepare a series of sealed envelopes containing the names of major American cities. In addition, the telephone numbers of the local weather stations of the cities were to be noted. The object was to describe the weather conditions at the place in question, and Janet was then immediately to call the weather station and get a report on the actual weather.

On 8 December 1971, after a session of the OBE experiments, Swann heard Janet's voice over the intercom: 'Ingo, I've got the envelope. Let me know when you're ready.' She opened the envelope that she had been given by Vera Feldman, a colleague from the ASPR: 'The target is Tucson, Arizona.'

'Now something wondrous and magical occurred,' Swann recalls. 'Of course, I really had no idea how to "get" to Tucson from the rather ugly experimental room in New York. And when I first heard the mention of Tuscon, Arizona, a picture of hot desert flashed through my mind. But then I had the sense of moving, a sense that lasted but a fraction of a second. Some part of my head or brain or perception blacked out – and there I was – there. Zip, bang, pop – and there I was ... something I would refer to in years ahead as "immediate transfer of perceptions".'

Everything went so fast that Swann began to talk immediately: 'I am over a wet highway, it is cold. There is a strong wind blowing and it is raining heavily. This is a real rainstorm!'[15] Swann was spot on. Tuscon was experiencing rain and storm and the temperature was close to freezing point, something that was quite unusual.

In order to describe this phenomenon, Swann suggested the term 'remote sensing' to the scientists at the ASPR.

# TURMOIL AT THE ASPR

Subsequently several things occurred that spoiled Swann's work at the ASPR for him. In early 1972 he was visited at the institute by two strangers. No one ever found out who these people were, but a rumour soon went round that Swann was under surveillance by the CIA. This encounter was less unpleasant for Swann than the intrigues at the venerable ASPR, however. In his search for modern esoteric philosophies, Swann had, in 1967, come into contact with the Church of Scientology, which was, in the 1960s, a far less controversial organization than it is today. One of Scientology's basic precepts is that humans possess innate 'psi abilities', and the movement ran courses in which a technique was taught to improve people's hidden paranormal potential – one of the many methods, incidentally, that were then being offered in workshops and seminars within the context of the alternative culture's enthusiasm for the occult and psi. In those days many people came into contact with Scientology without knowing or caring anything about the ideological concepts of its founder. They were only interested in learning psycho-techniques, nothing more or less, and Ingo Swann was no different. He studied Scientology, just as he did Rosicrucianism and other occult societies, without ever becoming a member of the Church of Scientology.

In February 1972 the story began to circulate that Swann was a spy for L. Ron Hubbard, the founder of Scientology, and that he was going to be ejected from the ASPR. At least, that is what he was told by one of the board members. As was later revealed, his interest in Scientology had been known at the ASPR for a long time. The curious secrecy surrounding this fact appeared to serve no other purpose than to create a basis for spreading rumours in order to sabotage the OBE experiments.

The balloon went up when the results of the formal OBE experiments were ready for publication. The editorial committee of the *Journal of the American Society for Psychical Research*, a recognized scientific periodical, rejected the report. Not because the experiments could be challenged on the grounds of their methodology or because they had not been professionally conducted. The reason was that the committee found the results to be too good! There had to be something wrong with them. It was a scandal. Karlis Osis, the research director, was completely taken aback, and Janet Mitchell was so incensed that she arranged for the results to be published in the ASPR *Newsletter*. This publication could not compete with an official journal, where articles were the subject of evaluation and appraisal by scientific colleagues. The chairman of the editorial committee was John Gaither Pratt, and Swann suspected him of being behind the intrigue. It is alleged that Pratt was convinced that experiments in parapsychology could never be repeated, including those that Swann had successfully repeated with Backster, Schmeidler and Osis.[16]

Swann thought that his career as a psychic was coming to an end, but just at this difficult moment, Backster gave him an article to read that had been written by a physicist. The article was about an application for funds for the investigation of quantum-biological processes, including the anomalous exchange of information between mind and matter. The author was the laser expert Harold 'Hal' Puthoff of the Stanford Research Institute, and he was circulating his application among colleagues in the hope of generating interest for his planned experiments.

Swann was impressed. Since Puthoff was working on tachyons – particles that travel faster than light – he hoped to find an answer to his superfast psi contacts. Puthoff didn't have the answer; instead he invited Swann to the SRI.

## HAL PUTHOFF AND THE MAGNETOMETER

At the physics department at Stanford University there was a magnetometer that was completely insulated and that was being used in experiments for the detection of quarks. In those days it was the most advanced piece of equipment of its kind, and it was unique. The meter itself was contained in a concrete jacket beneath a cellar in which its reactions were recorded. Before Ingo Swann arrived in California, Hal Puthoff arranged for him to be given access to the meter. The meter was in perfect working condition. Under the watchful eyes of famous physicists from the university, including Arthur Hebbard and Marshal Lee, Swann succeeded in influencing the meter from a distance by an inexplicable, apparently psychokinetic effect. The uniform, mathematically exact sine curve the stylus was recording was interrupted by an inexplicable, strong deflection at the very moment Swann was preparing an accurate sketch of the complex internal workings of the meter, about which nothing had ever been published before.[17] Puthoff had this impressive result of the experiment copied and circulated among his colleagues. A few weeks later two men from the CIA knocked on Puthoff's door.

The CIA officers wanted to conduct some exploratory experiments with Ingo Swann and promised funds for research if these experiments were successful. They were successful, and Ken Kress from the CIA's Office of Technical Service (OTS) provided Puthoff with funds for an initial 8-month research programme.

In Hal Puthoff the CIA had found an impeccable scientist, and the money was well spent. Puthoff enjoyed a reputation for being a genius. When he was only 33 years old he had been granted a patent for an adjustable infrared laser he had invented, and he was the co-author of the standard physics textbook *Fundamentals of Quantum Electronics*. In the early 1960s he had done military service as a naval officer and subsequently served as a civilian employee of the National Security Agency (NSA). He had worked on Project Light for the army, when he investigated glass fibre optics, lasers and high-speed computers, and he held the necessary clearances for access to top secret information. As far as the CIA was concerned, he was the kind of colleague with whom its officers could talk openly. In short, he was the ideal scientist for a secret psi project. Puthoff's motivation for cooperating with the CIA sprang from his belief that almost all wars had been the result of poor intelligence. As far as he was concerned, the best weapon for ensuring peace appeared to lie in improved intelligence.

Unfortunately, the collaboration with the assistant Puthoff had selected proved to be difficult at times. Russell Targ, also a laser expert, was a beanpole of a man, with a deep, monotonous voice, his head framed by a wild mop of hair; he stared at the world with unnaturally enlarged eyes from behind unbelievably thick glasses. Targ was the animated cliché of the 'mad professor'. He was not, however, as far removed from mundane matters as he appeared to be.

At Swann's suggestion, the first few weeks at SRI were spent in continuing the experiments in remote sensing that had been begun at the ASPR in New York. At the end of February 1972 Swann had conducted an experiment in New York with a 'sender'. Vera Feldman had gone to an unknown place and moved to a different spot every five minutes. Swann, who was connected to an electroencephalograph (EEG) at the ASPR, had described each new spot. Vera Feldman had been inside the Museum of Natural History, and Swann's impressions had proved to be astonishingly correct.

At the SRI the protocol for such experiments was methodologically refined and they received a new name, remote viewing. People no longer spoke of a 'sender', as in earlier telepathy experiments, but of an 'outbound experimenter', because in each case this was a scientist who was involved in the design of the experiment and who went to the place that had been selected at random. People also no longer spoke of 'general extrasensory perception' because it was impossible to determine if the impressions that Swann recorded were telepathic – that is, they came from the mind of the outbound experimenter – or if they were based on clairvoyance and he was getting them directly from the place in question. The new term, 'remote viewing', was a reflection of the newly gained confidence. At the SRI nobody cared about the history of parapsychology, and earlier experiments and concepts were not under review. Puthoff and his team set out to re-invent parapsychology.

And in a sense they were successful. The term remote viewing became standard and replaced the traditional terms telepathy, clairvoyance and precognition.

# Chapter Three
# STANFORD RESEARCH INSTITUTE AND THE CIA

## COORDINATE REMOTE VIEWING

Remote viewing requiring an outbound experimenter was obviously impracticable for espionage purposes. In order to secure the approval of their paymasters for a longer period, the researchers had to find a way to achieve good results without having a person on the spot. But how was the psychic to focus his antenna on the target? This appeared to be relatively easy, psychologically speaking, with a person, who could act as a sort of beacon to which there was a direct connection. For espionage purposes, however, the 'psi radar' had to be precisely adjustable without any guiding beacon.

Swann discussed the problem with everybody he met, until Jacques Vallee, the well-known UFO expert, came up with a brilliant idea. He believed that it was necessary to find an 'address' in order to be able to adjust the anomalous perception channel with precision. One evening, in the swimming pool of the apartment complex in Mountain View, California, into which Swann had moved, Vallee had an inspiration: 'Try it with coordinates.'

Coordinates can, however, be defined so precisely that even a geographic super-brain would find it impossible to identify the correct spot for every latitude and longitude, let alone describe it in detail. When Swann proudly presented his idea to Puthoff and Targ at the SRI next morning, they were in complete agreement: it was the most ridiculous suggestion they had ever heard. Even if it took a while, they subsequently had to completely revise their opinion. The first hundred experiments with coordinates on which Swann had insisted were far from promising. But with time, the results appeared to get better and better.

## Stanford Research Institute, Menlo Park, California, 3 May 1973

Ingo Swann's breathing was slow and steady. He was ready. Hal Puthoff read out the coordinates: '2° south, 34° east.' Like a shot, Swann replied: 'First time sense of speeding over water landing on land. Lake to the west.'

The target was Lake Victoria, and thus over water and not on land. Puthoff and Targ therefore enter this result in their list of rankings of accuracy as a miss. Swann is dissatisfied, because his impression had been so vivid. He talks Puthoff into getting a more accurate map. Together they drive downtown and buy a *Times Atlas of the World*. Lo and behold, on the exact coordinates there is the island of Ukerewe in the south of the lake. Most of the water surface lies to the west. A direct hit and an astounding proof of how accurately remote viewing can work.

## Stanford Research Institute, Menlo Park, California, 29 May 1973

An official from the CIA, who was known as 'the East Coast challenger' and who later went under the name of Richard Kennett, sent coordinates to Puthoff. By now the CIA had decided that the idea of coordinates was worth pursuing, and the accuracy of the process was now to be tested. Swann gave a detailed description of a military installation with extensive underground facilities.

A few days later a Patrick 'Pat' Price called Puthoff. He had heard about the experiments at SRI and wanted to have his abilities tested. There were few jobs that Pat Price did not hold in the course of his life. For a short period during the 1950s he had been a police commissioner and deputy mayor of Burbank, a suburb of Los Angeles, and even then his intuition, so he told Puthoff, helped him to solve complicated cases.

Acting spontaneously, Puthoff read Kennett's coordinates out to him. To Puthoff's astonishment, three days later Price sent a five-page document containing extraordinarily detailed descriptions of a military installation. They tallied completely with Swann's descriptions. Puthoff found the protocol so remarkable that he immediately contacted Price and asked him to 'have a look' inside the subterranean facilities described, to inspect the desks and to 'read' nameplates or code words. Price appeared to be so talented that such an assignment might not be impossible.

Another few days passed, then Price submitted a list of names, which he claimed to have recognized on the backs of files by paranormal means, and headings on documents, which obviously contained code words.

Richard Kennett himself did not know what was on the coordinates, for he had received them from a friend, a CIA officer. This friend had a bitter disappointment in store for Kennett: the coordinates were those of his holiday cabin in the Blue Ridge Mountains in West Virginia!

A terrible disgrace for the psychics at SRI? Kennett was not satisfied. Why had Swann and Price described the same military installation? Kennett drove to his friend's cabin and looked around. He soon came to the end of a dirt road and found himself in front of a sign bearing the US eagle and warning unauthorized persons not to trespass. In the distance he recognized satellite antennae – beyond any doubt, a secret military installation! Clearly Swann's and Price's 'psi radar' had found this installation to be of far greater interest than the holiday cabin.

Kennett showed the statements by Swann and Price to a CIA officer who was, he assumed, familiar with the military base. The result was that Kennett, Puthoff and Targ suddenly found themselves in the middle of a very unpleasant security investigation. The intelligence service assumed that confidential information had been leaked. At the designated spot the US navy maintained a secret base with extensive underground facilities that were under the control of the National Security Agency (NSA). Part of their task included the supervision of US spy satellites.

At first glance, the results of this case appear to be very impressive. On closer examination, however, the assumption can naturally be made that during the three days before Price presented his report, he had had enough time to do a little research. The coordinates were known, and he could have looked at detailed maps and investigated the area shown. He could have called on his contacts. He could even have flown to West Virginia and had a careful look at the area before he wrote down his alleged impressions. He could have invented names and code words, because it could not be expected that the secret service would either confirm or deny the statements made.

I do not wish to suggest that this is what happened – indeed, from everything I know about Puthoff and Price it is highly improbable. All I want to do is point out that claims that are not subject to strict control are of no use for understanding the psi process. It is impossible to identify Price's sources beyond any doubt. For the SRI's clients, however, such results were sufficient to convince them of the importance of investigating remote viewing.

**Stanford Research Institute, Menlo Park, California, 21 July 1973**
The first official remote viewing experiment using coordinates was carried out for the CIA. All kinds of security measures were put in train. Immediately before the experiment, a CIA officer handed over a sealed envelope. Puthoff opened it and read out: '49° 20′ south, 70° 14′ east.'

Swann began a detailed description of an island, specifying buildings and an installation that seemed to him to be a meteorological station. Suddenly he described a sort of military installation and asked: 'Is this a former base for Nike missiles?'

But that did not satisfy him. The impressions were so clear that he wanted to make a drawing, and, as if in trance, his hand automatically moved across the paper. Puthoff had to keep holding out new sheets, because his hand moved over the edge of the paper. In the end, eight sheets of paper had to be pasted together in order to show the whole island. The drawing depicted a strongly indented coastline with many bays and peninsulas.

The anonymous CIA man who evaluated the experiment showed his astonishment. Swann's statements were correct in every detail. The island in question was the small island of Kerguelen in the southern part of the Indian Ocean, which is under French administration. Swann's drawing corresponded extraordinarily accurately with the actual coastline. On the island, the French and the Soviets jointly maintained a secret weather station – although why a weather station should be secret nobody was able to say. The Soviets and French learned about the experiment because it was not classified and some information about it became public, and they protested – unofficially, of course – to the US State Department about 'paranormal espionage' on their clandestine island.

# GREETINGS FROM JUPITER

Ingo Swann underlined his paranormal abilities with an interesting experiment. He suggested 'visiting' Jupiter by remote viewing before NASA's space probes *Pioneer 10* and *Pioneer 11* were scheduled to fly past the planet in 1973 and 1974 and send back pictures to Earth. He wanted to find out if remote viewing would work over enormous distances, if it would take longer than usual before mental images occurred and if these impressions would later be verified by the photos transmitted by the probes.

The experiment took place on 27 April 1973. *Pioneer 10* was already on the way to the distant planet but was still too far off to send pictures back to Earth. Swann recorded the impressions he received. Ten copies were sent to scientists noted for their integrity, including two astrophysicists at the famous Jet Propulsion Laboratories. They all accepted Swann's notes. Two further copies, one of which was sent to a well-known American astronomer and the other to a famous author of popular scientific books, were rejected and sent back. One of the recipients could not resist the temptation to include a letter denouncing the experiment as ridiculous.

Normally, critics accuse parapsychologists of not filing their data with sceptics before the data can be verified. Swann and the SRI researchers had thought of this. They contacted two well-known 'sceptics' – the self-chosen term of the defenders of reason and fighters against what they believe to be superstition – and asked them to keep copies of the raw data. Both refused to do so. Such conduct makes sense only if it is based on the fear that the data would actually prove to be inexplicable and that – against their own unshakeable prejudices – the 'sceptics' would later be called on to testify to the reality of paranormal phenomena.

Additional copies were deposited with various scientists at the SRI and in Silicon Valley, and one copy was clandestinely sent to a journalist in San Francisco who immediately published it.

What had Swann perceived? Experiment number 46 had begun at 6 o'clock in the evening local time. Four minutes later Swann began to speak: 'There is a big planet there with stripes. I hope it is Jupiter.' To his chagrin, he saw a ring around the planet, and he asked himself whether he had mistakenly undertaken a remote viewing of Saturn. The astronomers who had received Swann's drawings and notes were not impressed, and they scoffed at them – until 1979, when pictures from the space probes *Voyager 1* and *Voyager 2* were transmitted back to Earth. Six years after the experiment there was a sensation: the pictures sent back by the probes showed that there was indeed a ring around Jupiter that took established science completely by surprise. It should be noted that Puthoff and Targ had published Swann's statements in 1977, long before the discovery of the Jupiter ring.

The astrophysicists were so impressed that Beverly Humphrey, a research assistant and statistician at the SRI Radio Physics Laboratory, wrote an official report on the experiment entitled 'Swann's Remote Viewing Attempt of the Planet Jupiter'.[18] The information and its confirmation were so detailed that four pages of raw data resulted in a scientific report of 300 pages.

Swann's statements included the comment: 'I think the planet must have a very thick hydrogen mantle. If a space probe made contact with that, it would be maybe 80,000 to 120,000 miles out from the planet surface.'

In September 1973 an article about Jupiter in *Scientific American* said: 'Above the hypothetical core is a thick stratum in which hydrogen is by far the most abundant element ... The outer layer extends to about 70,000 kilometres and consists mainly of liquid hydrogen in its molecular form.'

Swann also said: 'Are we dealing with a thermal inversion here? I bet we are.'

In May 1975 *Science* reported: 'In particular, the appearance of the inversion at about 260° Kelvin is strikingly similar to the *Pioneer 10* entry profile.'

Commenting on the rings, Swann had said: 'Very high in the atmosphere there are crystals, they glitter, maybe the stripes are like bands of crystals, maybe like rings on Saturn, though not far out like that, very close within the atmosphere. I bet you they'll reflect radio probes. Is that possible if you had a cloud of crystals that were assaulted by different radio waves?'

On 19 March 1979 you could read in *Time*: 'Coming within 278,000 kilometres (172,400 miles) of the swirling Jovian cloud tops, the robot survived intense radiation, peered deeply into the planet's storm-tossed cloud cover, provided startling views of the larger Jovian moons and, most surprising of all – revealed the presence of a thin, flat ring around the great planet. Said University of Arizona astronomer Bradford Smith: "We're standing here with our mouths open, reluctant to tear ourselves away".'

A high-ranking NASA official insisted on receiving a copy of Swann's RV report on Jupiter, albeit unofficially and under the condition that he would deny it if his name were disclosed. The report was also offered to the Committee for the Scientific Investigation of the Claims of the Paranormal (CSICOP), the leading organization of 'sceptics' in the United States. CSICOP regards itself as the police force charged with maintaining law and order in science. For CSICOP 'law and order' equates to naïve and largely outdated concepts of what should and what should not be permitted. In connection with CSICOP there can be no talk of 'scientific investigation' but only of campaigns against anything that CSICOP has decided is superstition.

Psi researchers already have their hands full with combating the superstitious behaviour of gullible occultists. Their work has nothing in common with such ideas, however. It deals instead with the unprejudiced investigation of anomalous mental phenomena by means of the traditional methods of the empirical sciences. Nothing more, but nothing less.

Hal Puthoff and Ingo Swann were soon to learn how committed CSICOP was to 'scientific research'. Those in positions of authority at CSICOP simply refused to receive the official report on the remote viewing of Jupiter. The 'sceptics' continued to believe they had to turn a blind eye to any convincing proofs.

The CSICOP case, as well as those of the prominent astronomer and the supercilious author, demonstrates how little has changed since the days of Galileo Galilei (1564–1642), and this comparison is apt on two counts. Using a telescope developed in the Netherlands, Galileo discovered the phases of Venus, the first four of Jupiter's moons and the rings around Saturn. The scientists to whom he wanted to show his discoveries simply refused to look through his telescope. They wanted to close their eyes to new insights in order to safeguard their geocentric view of the universe. For much the same reason, the 'sceptics' refused to look through Swann's 'psi telescope'.

## SCANATE AND THE SEXY COORDINATES

After the completion of the initial pilot studies, things became serious. Project SCANATE (Scanning by Coordinate) – financed by the CIA – came into being and lasted from 1973 to 1975. The coordinates were selected by an NSA official and transmitted to the SRI via a CIA contact.

At the SRI they spoke of 'sexy' coordinates whenever targets were to be approached that were of importance for intelligence operations – in other words, when the 'remote viewers' at the SRI were to act as psi spies.

For some time the CIA had suspected that there was a secret installation for underground atomic tests at Semipalatinsk in the extreme northeast of Kazakhstan. Among the members of the secret service, the installation was known as URDF–3 (Unidentified Research and Development Facility, Number 3). The Air Force used another, more humorous term, PNUTS, which stood for Probable Nuclear Underground Test Site. There was no further information available.

In 1973 Puthoff was given the 'sexy' coordinates of the site in a sealed envelope. Pat Price immediately sketched industrial buildings, including a special crane several storeys high, which moved over tracks on wheels that were higher than a man. The CIA was astounded. Through 'conventional' spying, it knew more or less what the facility looked like. A drawing by a CIA artist showed a remarkable similarity to the sketch by Price.

In a subsequent phase of the experiment, Price specified his impressions. He saw a series of huge gas cylinders, and these were later confirmed by satellite photos. In the third phase, Price described technical details of the facility that gave a clear indication of a Soviet research and development laboratory – information that was not known to the CIA but that confirmed its fears.

Among other things, Price described a large hall in which people were engaged in assembling huge metal spheres about 18 metres in diameter. He assumed they were intended to absorb and store the energy from fissionable nuclear material. Price described the process as a new welding technology. Sometime during 1974 or 1975 a US spy satellite managed to take a picture of the steel spheres outside the buildings. Experts on photoanalysis estimated the diameter of the huge balls to be exactly 18 metres. Later on it was discovered that they had, in fact, been put together by means of a new welding technology. The steel spheres at Semipalatinsk made the US secret services increasingly uneasy. In 1977 a reporter from *Aviation Week* succeeded in obtaining some information, and in May of that year he published an article about nuclear weapons that had been under development at Semipalatinsk for the last ten years.

Price died in 1975 without having learned about his impressive success. It was only many years later that the SRI received the confirming information from its client. Russell Targ recalls his disappointment when the CIA stamped the report of this experiment with the words 'exempt from automatic declassification'. This meant that the results could not be made public even after 20 years. In May 1994, 21 years after this unusual experiment, Targ applied for the release of the material. When nothing had happened after a year, he engaged two lawyers in Washington and appealed to two Representatives and a Senator, with the result that he was given the documents on 11 August 1995. Targ wrote: 'Thus, I am finally able to thank the CIA for their generous support of this research without going to prison for referring to ESP and the CIA in the same sentence.'[19]

## ANOMALOUS INFORMATION TRANSMISSION

At the end of 1974 the CIA contract for SCANATE came to an end. For Puthoff and Targ the liaison with the intelligence services appeared to have been nothing more than a short episode in their careers. Richard

Bach, author of the best-selling novel *Jonathan Livingstone Seagull*, kept the work alive by a donation of $40,000. This was followed by a small contract from the Office of Naval Research (ONR), whose main objective was the identification of the positions of submarines and other military objects.

A secondary objective was telepathic transmission, which was supposed to manifest itself in electrical activity in the brain. In this experiment, a subject who had shown in preliminary tests that they were able to produce a uniform electric activity in the brain by intensive concentration, served as a telepathic percipient (receiver). The subject was able not only to make alpha waves[20] appear on an electroencephalograph – thereby indicating a condition of extreme relaxation – but also to produce very similar electric frequencies in both the left and right hemisphere of the brain. Normally, an alpha rhythm in the posterior region of the brain (the so-called occipital region) is interrupted when flashes of light are perceived. This is because the occipital region is the primary projection area for optical impressions, and as soon as an optical stimulus is received, the inward-directed condition of relaxation is interrupted and more rapid beta waves[21] occur in this region.

During the experiment the percipient sat in a darkened room and had to relax and attempt to produce as uniform an alpha rhythm as possible. At the same time, a second person – the telepathic sender – sat in another room. From time to time the sender was shown flashes of light. The subsequent study of the percipient's EEG showed inexplicable interruptions of alpha waves in the occipital region, even though they had not been shown flashes of light.[22] Although the effect was never as strong as the researchers had hoped, there was still a correlation between the flashes and the partial suppression of alpha waves, which could have been achieved only through an anomalous transfer of information.

The results from California and Puthoff's untiring presentation of the work in Washington finally led to results. During the second half of the 1970s funds began to flow from new government channels. The Defense Intelligence Agency (DIA), the air force and a number of other institutions commissioned the team to undertake further work. A key figure in this was Jack Vorona, a former nuclear physicist and head of the DIA's Technical Directorate. Vorona, himself a brilliant scientist, was enthusiastic about Puthoff's work, and it was because of his political acumen and influence in Washington that the research was able to continue. Puthoff could now count on an annual budget of almost $1 million. Ingo Swann was ordered back to California, where he made himself at home on the third floor of building number 44 at the SRI, announcing his presence with thick cigar smoke. Edwin May, a physicist, was added to the team, and it soon became apparent that this was an excellent choice. Jim Salyer lived on the site in a mobile home as the DIA's contract monitor. He sat at the secure telephones and faxes and passed on the 'operational' assignments to the remote viewing team – assignments that were no longer experiments but the gathering of information about the unknown installations of enemy nations, the content of which was then to become part of the normal espionage effort by agents. The game had become serious. Psi espionage was ready to begin.

# TRIUMPHS AND DEFEATS IN RESEARCH

The SRI team began to look for further paranormally gifted subjects, and its numbers were soon augmented by Hella Hammid, a photographer of German descent, Keith Harary, a psi researcher and psychic, and Gary Langford, a computer expert at the SRI. Together with Swann and Price, they studied the process of remote viewing in countless astonishing experiments.

Even after great operational successes, such as Semipalatinsk, the primary concern at the SRI was still research. Experiments of various kinds were conducted with volunteers and with the group of gifted subjects, and the quality of the results, particularly those of the gifted subjects, continued to astound Puthoff and Targ.

On one occasion the target for an RV experiment was a footbridge over a highway. The bridge had a unique appearance, winding over the flat landscape like a long, thin tube, the resemblance to a tube resulting from the closely meshed wiring that surrounded it over its whole length. Hella Hammid sketched a series of concentric squares that looked like a view into a tunnel – exactly the view you would have if you were standing on the bridge, looking ahead. She noted: 'Some kind of diagonal channel up in the air.'

Keith Harary made several drawings, all of which emphasized the grill. He wrote: 'Criss-crossing metal, similar to a bridge ... something people climb on ... footbridge.' On one sheet he drew a meshed fence and cars, on another he drew a mesh with the words: 'Metal cyclone fence?' On another page the tube with the grill can clearly be seen. His note read: 'Bridge ... beaten up metal.'

Working with psychics is not easy for scientists, and the same is true the other way round. There are prima donnas to be found in both camps, and their ideas about what is worth investigating are often very different. Normally, such decisions are left to the experts, the scientists, but in the field of anomalous mental phenomena, where there are so few hard facts, it has not been decided who qualifies as an expert – the scientist, who is best qualified to decide how a methodologically sound experiment must be designed in order to find the answer to a question, or the psychic, who has a natural entry to the world of the paranormal and is, therefore, in the unique position of being able to recognize the mechanisms that play the decisive role in the way psi functions? The problems this dichotomy created underlay all the research at the SRI and sometimes prevented even greater gains being made from the empirical data.

An example will serve to illustrate this. It was the intention that, during further research, the scientists would take a closer look into the brains of the remote viewers in order to achieve a better understanding of the secret of anomalous information-gathering. The small group of gifted subjects was taken to a research installation that enjoys an almost mythic status in military circles, the Los Alamos National Laboratory in New Mexico. Next to the Lawrence Livermore Laboratory in California, Los Alamos is considered to be America's foremost centre for research into, and the development of, nuclear weapons. At Los Alamos, it was believed, there was exactly the right instrument for the sort of research the team from the SRI wanted to do. The instrument in question was a high-tech EEG of most superior quality, a so-called magnetoencephalograph (MEG). An MEG is capable of revealing the changes in brain activity with a far greater degree of accuracy than an EEG because the magnetic field penetrates the skin, the skull and the meninges without being dispersed.

Keith Harary has unpleasant memories of the series of expensive experiments conducted at Los Alamos. 'One of many opportunities was missed there,' he told me. Ed May and his assistants had designed the experiment, which was very similar to Puthoff's experiment with the tele-pathic transmission of light flashes that May had already successfully repeated with Targ and Puthoff.[23] Before the actual remote viewing began, alpha waves were to be produced in the brain. Harary – like anyone who has undergone biofeedback alpha training – is able to do this. Harary explained to me: 'Who can say for sure that an alpha condition is what you need to look for in remote viewing? If you make this assumption, the results are already being forced in a certain direction. The opposite approach, to look for the brain waves that occur with psi, would have been better.'

The experiment called for a computer installed at one end of a large room to register flashes of light. The remote viewers were to establish an anomalous remote contact to the computer and the experimenter stationed in front of it. The hope was that the patterns of the light flashes would be recorded in their EEGs. The computer was not programmed with any target images to be reproduced. According to Harary, this made it impossible to determine whether contact to the computer had been established at all. At the end of this elaborate experiment May discovered that the data had been incorrectly recorded.

In defence of Ed May, a truly creative and intelligent scientist, it should be noted that Harary's criticism can be explained by his disappointment that the results of such an elaborate experiment, requiring lengthy preparation and excellent equipment, were not more rewarding. That, however, is the fate of any research that attempts to track down elusive phenomena. The creation of an alpha rhythm in the brain was the decisive factor, because flashes of light block the alpha rhythm. The absence of alpha waves during those periods when the flashes of light appeared in another room could have been seen as proof of an anomalous transfer of information. The correct reproduction of a target image at the 'contact point' would not have been important in such an experiment. The issue was not the conscious reproduction of psi impressions but a physiologically recordable unconscious anomalous reception of information.

In fact, the MEG experiments at Los Alamos were technically excellent.[24] Unfortunately, however, the initially good results could not be successfully replicated, and despite the approval of the experiment by a high-grade scientific supervisory board, which included two Nobel laureates, a minor mistake was discovered in the format of the experiment, and this made the data useless.

What Harary was wondering was why they were investigating the possible subconscious reception of information when the real issue was to track down the mechanisms of RV – and remote viewing is always the ability to record psi impressions consciously.

Such examples show how great was the gulf between what the psychics thought was actually worth investigating and what the scientists wanted to study. As far as May was concerned, the issue was to investigate a fundamental process, the clarification of which might also have been important for our understanding of other forms of anomalous cognition. For remote viewer Harary, anything but the investigation of psi functions in 'real-life settings' was a waste of time.

Despite this, the fact that highly successful research was being conducted at the SRI is documented by a report summarizing the work done between 1973 and 1988. During this period, a total of 154 experiments on anomalous cognition were carried out, consisting of more than 26,000 individual runs using 227 subjects. Of these, almost 20,000 runs were made according to the forced-choice method, in which the subject knows a given set of target symbols and has to 'guess' their random order. More than 1000 runs used the free-response method – that is, a free description of an unknown target. These were all remote viewing experiments, during which the six most talented remote viewers participated in 196 sessions.

The statistical results were so overwhelming that it was impossible to attribute them to chance. If chance had been involved, such a result would only have occurred once in $10^{18}$ (one trillion) cases!

# Chapter Four
# THE PSYCHIC SPIES AT FORT MEADE

## CODE NAME GONDOLA WISH

With financial backing secured, research began to pick up momentum at the Stanford Research Institute during the second half of the 1970s, and it was soon being mentioned in military circles that ways had been found to make psi practicable for gathering secret information. Lieutenant Frederick Holmes 'Skip' Atwater of the army's Systems Exploitation Detachment (SED) at Fort Meade, Maryland,[25] was the first to show an intense interest in the project. He asked himself why such work should be left exclusively to the scientists. What would be wrong with employing this new means of spying directly within a department of the army?

Atwater recommended setting up a small experimental group of paranormal talents. It was to be established on the east coast as a military group for operational assignments in parallel to the civilian group at the SRI on the west coast. The idea was approved by Major General Edmund Thompson, assistant chief of staff for intelligence, and the project was launched under the code name Gondola Wish.

Atwater and Lieutenant Colonel Murray 'Scotty' Watt, a surly, hard-bitten fellow who had been put in over Atwater's head as commander of the unit, went to see Puthoff and Targ at the SRI. They wanted to find out how to filter out potential candidates for RV from within their own ranks. The scientists advised them to test as many people as possible in simple RV experiments and then to continue working with those who did best. This suggestion was unwelcome to the military – after all, Gondola Wish was to be kept secret. Instead, a way had to be found to select candidates without the entire army quickly hearing about the project. This made the whole thing suddenly appear to be much more difficult than anticipated.

Until then, the SRI scientists had not paid much attention to medical and psychological variables that might help identify potentially superior subjects. The results of psychical research regarding this were somewhat contradictory – or at least not conclusive – and they therefore recommended concentrating on people who were regarded as being creative and who had an artistic talent and a highly developed ability to visualize three-dimensionally. The ability to record psi impressions appeared to be quite similar to the ability to describe in detail pictures seen only fleetingly. People who had these qualifications should be employable for remote viewing. And naturally, the most important qualification was that anybody who had already had paranormal experiences was bound to be a good candidate.

Atwater and Watt began collecting their recruits by asking the department heads at Intelligence and Security Command (INSCOM) at Fort Meade and at headquarters in Arlington Hall, Virginia, about members of their units who fitted this description. They also sent the SRI profiles to the chiefs of the National Photographic Interpretation Center (NPIC). They assumed there would be people with the necessary visual abilities among the photograph interpreters, and they were correct in this assumption. Among the applicants who were asked to come to Fort Meade – they were told only that this was for a study on psi among the military ordered by INSCOM – was Mel Riley, an expert in photograph interpretation with a 'paranormal history'. It was regularly noted in his assignments that he possessed an outstanding intuition about where reconnaissance aircraft should be sent and cameras aimed. As a photo interpreter he could detect things on pictures no one else could see. In one case he was able to recognize part of a Russian gun on a reconnaissance photograph of an East German factory site even though the intelligence service had not suspected any military installations. The astonishing thing about this was not Riley's extraordinary observational ability. The weapon in question was covered by a tarpaulin and impossible to identify from the photograph. Riley sketched his 'perceptions' and these were ultimately confirmed by a photograph taken by a spy satellite. It was obvious that Riley was already subconsciously applying psi in his everyday military work.

Gondola Wish started off with a small group of promising soldiers and civilians working for the army. The operation not only had to subsist on a very tight budget, but also was beset by problems. After only a few trial sessions had been conducted, the top brass ordered an investigation into the project. Those responsible had developed cold feet, because it was not clear to them exactly what was being done with the subjects. Remote viewing was classified as 'human use experimentation', and the United States had a disreputable record to live down in this field. Since the mid-1970s hearings in Congress had been making unfavourable headlines. About 200 secret research programmes came to light that the CIA had conducted in the 1950s and 1960s under the code name MKULTRA. Many public figures saw MKULTRA as a confirmation of their worst fears – the CIA was experimenting with people by manipulating minds and practising brain-washing. It became known that there had been experiments with LSD and various 'truth serums', which soldiers had been given without their knowledge. One group of people had been administered LSD for 77 consecutive days in order to find out if they could then be brain-washed. It was alleged that Soviet double agents had died from taking experimental drugs. One of MKULTRA's sub-projects, number 136, had involved the possible application of psi, although nothing about the details of this project became known. When Hal Puthoff first received funds from the CIA in 1972, Sidney Gottlieb was still head of the CIA's Technical Services Division (TSD), and Gottlieb was regarded as one of the key figures in the MKULTRA scandal.

The intelligence services had to be careful. Any project suspected of being concerned with 'brain-washing' or 'mind control' was subjected to meticulously detailed examination. Nobody who wanted to continue with a military career could afford a scandal. Critical projects either had to be discontinued or their secrecy classification upgraded.

The study of the telepathic transmission of light flashes that the SRI was conducting for the Office of Naval Research carried the apparently harmless title, the Sensing of Remote EM [electromagnetic] Sources (Physiological Correlates). This title caused Sam Koslov, a scientific assistant with the navy, to end the project in 1976 because he suspected that the investigations had to do with electromagnetic mind-control, and he began to analyse the documented data. When he discovered that the experiments were of a parapsychological nature, his astonishment must have been even greater. He had the project closed down for good.[26]

The remote viewers at Gondola Wish and the SRI had to sign piles of informed consent. Physicians, all the way up to the Surgeon General of the Army, had to give the programme their approval. The whole procedure took several months. After all that, the first RV team at Ford Meade was established. It included six remote viewers, Mel Riley, Joe McMoneagle, Ken Bell, Fernand 'Fern' Gauvin, Nancy Stern (pseudonym) and Hartleigh Trent. These promising recruits were sent to the SRI for tests, and for several weeks they had to perform numerous classic RV experiments, with and without 'senders' at the target spots. After sufficient data had been collected, Targ and Puthoff sent the military people back to Maryland with a note to their superiors saying that they had made an excellent choice. All six were qualified for operational assignments as psychic spies.

## SPYING ON YOUR OWN COUNTRY

The driving force behind the psi effort at Fort Meade was unquestionably Major General Ed Thompson. Together with the commander of INSCOM, he succeeded in having Gondola Wish transferred to a more favourable site in 1978. The programme was given a new code name by the Pentagon, Grill Flame, under which title the scientific experiments at the SRI and the operational assignments at Fort Meade were united. Government funds also began to flow, and these made it possible to employ three full-time psi spies at Fort Meade, Mel Riley, Joe McMoneagle and Ken Bell. At first, the 'operational unit' at Fort Meade received most of its assignments from the Pentagon, but subsequently it undertook work for the various intelligence services. The unit was normally involved when conventional intelligence methods had failed to produce any results.

The military clairvoyants were housed in two simple, unsightly wooden buildings at 2560 and 2561 Llewellyn Street, near the Kimbrough Army Community Hospital, but separated from the other installations at Fort Meade. In this relative seclusion, the 'operational unit' was able to conduct its work with great enthusiasm and with the necessary peace and quiet.

The first assignment for the remote viewers at Fort Meade was to spy not on enemy installations but on America's own secret installations. Spying on your own country? At Fort Meade there was a department called Operations Security Group (OPSEC), whose job was to protect secret US installations against foreign spies. One of OPSEC's major tasks was to spy on these installations in order to uncover possible security leaks. These assignments were ideal for testing the efficacy of psi espionage, because all the information obtained by RV could be immediately checked against reality. And if it was successful, the superiors would have had an immediate impression of what to expect if the Soviets really did have psi spies at work.

One day Skip Atwater received a photograph of an aircraft hangar. The remote viewers were supposed to find out what was inside.[27] The clients tried to mislead them. Inside, they had hidden the new XM–1 tank, which was still under development. Joe McMoneagle began to describe an instrument that looked like a keyboard and was connected to a computer. He saw an optical system and large explosive shells. Finally, he recognized a structure that he could not precisely interpret but that he was able to sketch. This turned out to be a quite accurate drawing of a tank, complete with ammunition storage and feeder, the turret lock-downs, the main gun assembly mounting, various high-tech weapons and a diagram of the laser-targeting system. When they saw the drawing, the people responsible for the security of the XM–1 development programme turned pale. If McMoneagle had been a Soviet psi agent, they would have had to appear before their generals in an even greater state of mortification.

Mel Riley pulled off a similar coup during an OPSEC assignment. Atwater had received a photo that was so blurred that it was virtually impossible to determine what it was supposed to show. It could have been almost anything. Riley received impressions of a strange object with wings, like those of a bat, and a cupola-like cockpit, similar to that of a jumbo jet. It appeared to him as if the aircraft were steered by wires. When he tried to look at these more closely, all he saw was light. Riley had the impression that it was a toy, the weirdest thing he had ever seen.

As soon as the air force officers received Atwater's report they became frantic, demanding that the blurred photo be returned immediately and issuing orders that the object was not to be targeted again by remote viewing. Now all they could do was pray that the enemy did not have similar talents available. Naturally, neither Atwater nor Riley was told what the grey spot on the photograph had been, and the solution came to light only several years later when the closely guarded secret weapon, the B–2 stealth bomber, was unveiled. Its appearance tallied exactly with Riley's description. Among other things, the engineers had used fibre-optic control wires instead of electromechanical or hydraulic lines in order to make the aircraft less easily detectable on radar.

We should not be seduced into thinking that such achievements were everyday occurrences at Menlo Park and Fort Meade. Quite the opposite was true. Thousands of sessions were held, and only a few of these resulted in such close agreement with the target. Nevertheless, there were good reasons to believe that the results could be improved upon. The best remote viewers had already been filtered out, and their preferences were known. The conditions under which they could achieve better results were also known. At the SRI a method had been developed by which the signal could be more accurately tapped, the so-called consensus technique, which consisted of comparing the results achieved on the identical object by several remote viewers. They were told the features on which they were in agreement, and on the basis of this edited information, they again zeroed in on the target.

Despite the obvious successes of the operational unit, the results must be interpreted with caution. The remote viewers were members of the army. Most of them had been recruited from sectors of the intelligence services, and some had very high security clearances. They were in a position to be informed about secret projects, and they knew about many secret operations and had even taken part in many of them themselves. It would be pointless to pretend that suddenly all this information had been erased from their memories and that they had turned into the perfect subjects – innocent, unknowing mental machines for the gathering of information.

Realistically, we should assume that the people at Fort Meade, as opposed to the group at the SRI, knew about the current acute problems of the intelligence services because they were familiar with them from their day-to-day work. After all, 2560 Llewellyn Street was not exactly an isolation ward. Their natural environment was a military command centre, the offices of an intelligence service, and it was not difficult for the people involved in Grill Flame to make educated guesses about an OPSEC task that came from the air force, even when it was in the form of a blurred photograph. They certainly knew about the development of the new wonder weapon, the stealth bomber. Information about details was unnecessary – the possible target could be described on the basis of rumours and stories from insiders.

Nevertheless, despite this caveat, there were some excellent results which could not have been based on rumour or found out by conventional means.

## EIGHT MARTINI RESULTS

An amusing incident occurred during ABC's *Nightline* programme on 28 November 1995, when the whole nation was being informed about the CIA's psi activities. It demonstrates the quality of the work performed. During his interview, an anonymous member of the CIA removed all doubts with an insider joke: 'If you want to hear about eight martini results, I'm not going to say a word.'

What on earth are 'eight martini results'? This was the jocular term used within the intelligence services for remote viewing results that were so good that they caused the view of reality held by those who experienced them to fall apart. All that was left to them was to go to the nearest bar and down eight martinis in order to regain their senses. Pat Price at the SRI and Joe McMoneagle at Fort Meade in particular were responsible for several eight martini results.

In 1974 the police had made use of Pat Price's services in connection with the kidnapping of Patty Hearst, the daughter of newspaper tycoon Randolph Hearst. Price immediately gained the impression that the abduction was to do not with money but with political objectives. He pulled three photographs out of the usual pile of mug shots, and the Spanish word *lobo* flashed through Price's mind in connection with one of these. *Lobo* means wolf. Two days later the police received their first communication from the Symbionese Liberation Army, as the terrorists called themselves. They were not asking for money, but for food for the poor. All three of the suspects whom Price had selected were members of the group. One of them was a drop-out from Berkeley. His name was William Wolfe, and he was known as 'Willie the Wolf' – he was 'lobo'.

One of the first espionage assignments involving an enemy nation given to the three remote viewers at Fort Meade came from the intelligence service of the air force. When Riley had relaxed by means of a special series of exercises, Atwater, who was acting as the interviewer, laconically told his remote viewer: 'The target is an object. Describe your impressions to me.'

The first impressions to appear before Mel Riley's inner eye were of metal, wires, electronics, then a small steel egg with a 'yolk' made out of tritium. Finally, he had the impression of a baseball with two wide funnels sticking out at opposite ends, and an hourglass on the side. McMoneagle also perceived something in the centre of the object that looked like an hourglass, and Ken Bell also described this curious detail. The clients from the air force were visibly impressed, but they refused to give Atwater any information about this component of the object, because his security clearance did not cover critical details on the construction of atomic weapons. He was permitted to know only that the object was an atomic bomb developed by the Chinese and that up to that point the Americans had been convinced that the Chinese were not capable of integrating this technical detail, which resembled an hourglass, into their device.

The air force then wanted the remote viewers to supply details about an event connected with the object, and Atwater gave his psi spies the coordinates of the place where the event had taken place. Pictures of a desert appeared before Riley's inner eye, and he saw concentric circles around a central tower. He saw an aircraft that had obviously dropped a bomb. But then nothing happened. Joe McMoneagle, however, experienced a gigantic detonation, but in his opinion the bomb drop had been a failure. There was no nuclear explosion.

The remote viewers had been brought in because at the time reconnaissance aircraft had not been able to detect a nuclear explosion at the Chinese testing ground near Lake Lop Nur. It was discovered later that the psi spies had been correct in their statements. The parachute on the bomb had failed to open, and the bomb had bored itself into the ground. The detonator had not functioned properly, and although there had been a loud bang, there had been no nuclear explosion.

## JOE McMONEAGLE

It soon became apparent at Fort Meade that Joe McMoneagle – like Pat Price at the SRI – possessed a singular talent as a remote viewer. McMoneagle was also the only remote viewer who remained with the programme from the inception of the INSCOM project Grill Flame until the end of the psi operation in 1995. At Fort Meade, where everything was given code words and functioned in accordance with strict military discipline, McMoneagle was only a number in the files. His assigned numbers were 001 for the army project and 372 while he worked at the SRI.

Joseph McMoneagle was born in Miami, Florida, in 1946. He had volunteered for the army and been selected for secret service operations by the army's intelligence agency. In 1978 he was sent to INSCOM at Arlington, Virginia. The high point in his career had been his appointment as a Special Projects Intelligence Officer in the 902nd Intelligence Unit, with assignments ranging from the Bahamas to Cambodia and Vietnam. One of his duties had been to identify the source of enemy intelligence transmissions.

In 1970 he was stationed with the army in southern Germany, and while he was visiting a restaurant in Austria, he suddenly suffered an attack of vertigo. He went outside to get some fresh air, but collapsed and swallowed his tongue. He was on the verge of suffocating, and friends put him into a car and took him across the border to a hospital in Germany. By the time he arrived, his heart had stopped beating. McMoneagle then underwent an OBE, during which he could see everything from an elevated position. First, he saw people working on his body in the emergency ward. Then, he had the impression of falling into a tunnel backwards. In front of a non-physical entity, from which pure love seemed to emanate, his life passed before his inner eye like a high-speed film. He felt heat on the back of his neck and turned around to discover its source, finding himself enveloped in a radiant white light, which he identified as God. The light ordered him to return to his body, even though he did not want to. Joe McMoneagle explained this experience to me: 'I was then told that I could not stay, that I had unfinished business and had to go back. I tried to argue, but to no avail. From the moment I woke up in the hospital, I've had what one would call spontaneous out-of-body experiences, and what I call spontaneous "knowings" – where you seem to just know something before it happens.'

He had hardly recovered from the coma when he began telling everybody about the wonderful white light. His superiors attributed McMoneagle's stories about God and the white light to brain damage and put him into a clinic in Munich for observation. But McMoneagle had not suffered any brain damage. He realized that it would be wiser not to talk about God and white lights any more, but his former concept of reality had broken down once and for all. When he returned to the United States in 1978, he came across an article on remote viewing by Puthoff and Targ.[28] He contacted Puthoff and was assigned to the initial psi team at Fort Meade.

McMoneagle's exceptional talent is demonstrated by an assignment he was given in September 1979. He was to spy paranormally on a huge building in the northern Soviet Union.[29] A satellite photograph had indicated some suspicious construction, but the US security services had no idea what was going on in the installation. On the basis only of the co-ordinates, McMoneagle described large buildings and chimneys close to the sea. The clients were convinced that McMoneagle was correct, so they showed him the satellite photo and asked him to 'look' inside the building. McMoneagle described and sketched a new type of huge submarine, which was obviously still under construction. It was much larger than any known type of Soviet submarine. In his drawing, he showed a craft with a long flat aft deck, a conning tower and missile tubes standing at curious angles. He put cruise missiles on it, as well as the correct number (18 or 20) of inter-continental ballistic missiles. McMoneagle even described its new drive and power mechanisms, its construction and the welding techniques being used.

The US security authorities were convinced that McMoneagle was wrong. There could not be any such atypical and enormous submarine that the intelligence services knew nothing about, and in any case, it would certainly not be being built in a building hundreds of metres away from any water. Joe McMoneagle told me about this operational task: 'Of course everyone disagreed with us. So I and another viewer from the unit produced a prediction that it would be launched on a specific date 112 days in the future. I believe we missed the date by three or four days. But, because of the prediction, they were able to watch the actual launch, which of course was an enormously successful operation.' In January 1980 the Russians blasted a channel to the sea. A spy satellite was able to take pictures of the largest submarine ever built, a Typhoon, which was sliding to the sea through an artificial channel. The long, flat aft deck and firing tubes for 20 ballistic missiles were clearly visible on the photograph. McMoneagle adds: 'We probably saved more money in that one day than we spent in the entire 18 years of the project.'

## SOVIET AGENTS WITHIN THE SRI

In the meantime a great deal of data on remote viewing had been collected at the SRI in California, and Ingo Swann had begun to work on a system that would permit achieving better results. Security, however, was not maintained to the same degree as with the military in Maryland. While secret assignments were not leaked to the public, the reason Puthoff and his team were being financed by the government was common knowledge.

When I visited Russell Targ at his home in Palo Alto in the mid-1970s, it was already obvious that the 'secret' psi programme at the SRI was one of the worst-kept secrets around. Even then, a lot of information was being circulated among colleagues, and there was no reason the Soviet intelligence services should not have been at least as well informed. At the SRI people quite rightly began to worry that the Soviets would recruit paranormally talented agents so that they could infiltrate the SRI programme. If they did this, they could kill two birds with one stone. They would be kept abreast of US progress at first hand, and they could 'psi checkmate' them on their own home ground.

The Soviets, however, did not appear to be dealing over-subtly with the American psi threat. Not long after the initial publications by Puthoff and Targ in two leading scientific journals,[30] the basic information about the remote viewing experiments had become internationally available. There was a curious incident when an article in the *Proceedings of the Institute of Electrical and Electronics Engineers*, the most important American engineering periodical, was to be translated for a Russian edition. The Russians refused to print the article without additional information, and it was obvious that they had been ordered to inveigle the American scientists into revealing as much as possible. Puthoff and Targ refused, and it took an unusually long time before the petulant Russians finally published the article.

Almost immediately a further attempt to penetrate to the heart of the SRI laboratory was initiated by the Soviet consulate in San Francisco. Vice-consul Oleg Sidorenko announced that he and cosmonaut Vitali Sevastyanov would visit the SRI. His cover story was that he wanted to discuss paranormal experiences in space with the SRI researchers. The third member of the party was Lev Lupichev, head of the Institute of Control Problems of the USSR Academy of Sciences, one of the state-controlled research institutions for 'psychotronics', as the Russians called parapsychology.

The scientists, forewarned of their guests' interest, received the small delegation in the SRI dining room. The laboratories remained closed to the visitors. Nevertheless, they tried to glean as much information as possible, particularly about if it was possible to protect targets against remote viewing, how to set about finding good remote viewers and the accuracy of the information gained by anomalous means. It is probable that the Soviet visitors were impressed by what they learned. Many pilot experiments were not classified, and Puthoff and Targ, and later Targ and Harary, published them in widely read books,[31] including such impressive experiments as the correct deciphering of microdots. In the everyday business of spying, microdots are a common means of transmitting information, and photographs of buildings, documents and so forth are reduced in size until they are as small as a dot, which is then inserted into an innocuous letter as a full stop at the end of a sentence. The microdot can subsequently be made readable by enlargement. Remote viewers do not need complicated equipment to do this – RV itself is sufficient to decipher the contents of a microdot. In experiments over long distances and in attempts to perceive events taking place in the future, the researchers demonstrated that the reception of anomalous information is not subject to the limitations of sensory stimulus transfer, neither as far as the constraints of distance and time nor as far as the resolution of the pattern are concerned.

# Chapter Five
# SWANN'S RV SYSTEM

## MENTAL NOISE AND ANALYTICAL OVERLAY

The possible options for intensifying 'psi signals' were limited, particularly since it was difficult even to identify them, and there were no criteria to enable the remote viewer to differentiate between pure fantasy and real paranormal impressions. Ingo Swann approached the problem from the other end, therefore. Psi could be defined as a very weak and easily disruptable signal that was embedded in many sources of interference. If the signal could not be intensified, perhaps the sources of interference could be identified and reduced. The central question was to find a way to render the signal-to-noise ratio more favourable for extracting accurate target-related information (signal) from information unrelated to the target (noise). This was certainly not an easy task, but Swann was determined to solve the problem.

Psi is embedded in a sea of 'mental noise', just like a weak radio signal that can barely be heard against the acoustic background static. Swann labelled one of the components of the noise that superimposes itself on the signal 'analytical overlay'. All analytical operations by the mind must be regarded as attempts to classify the noise according to known patterns and then to analyse it. This makes sense, because it is the way our normal system of recognition works. New impressions are compared with known patterns that are stored in the memory and then classified. If an impression is unclear – if, for example, we perceive a blurred silhouette through a thick fog – the system has many possible ways of associating the few signals, containing only the barest information, with a known image. It could be a cow in a pasture, a hut, a car or a rock; it could be a smaller or a larger object, because distance is also difficult to estimate. Part of our brain is fully occupied with analysing the object in terms of its possible configuration.

Let us consider an alternative example. For an impression to surface in our consciousness, it has to be of a certain intensity and duration. At the same time, we must bring a certain degree of attention to bear. Sensory stimuli are often intensive enough, but we are usually occupied with entirely different matters and shut these stimuli out from our perception. In other cases, we cannot consciously recognize stimuli even when we concentrate intensely because they do not reach the critical level of intensity and duration. Many such stimuli, however, are recorded subconsciously, and these are known as 'subliminal' stimuli. Images shown for less than 3 milliseconds, and therefore not consciously perceivable, are regarded as subliminal visual stimuli. Sometimes fragments of such subliminal impressions can be brought up to the level of consciousness because we remember certain parts of them, such as shapes, colours or feelings. Sometimes it is even possible to draw unclear sketches without knowing what the subject is.

Swann regarded the paranormal perception system as very similar. In many respects, the work of a remote viewer equates to the attempt to lift a subliminally received impression to the level of consciousness. The remote viewer constantly has to detect extremely weak signals in a thick fog. The automatic analytical activity of the brain prevents us from clearly recognizing the structural particularities of the object perceived. If the signal cannot be clearly recognized, perhaps the interfering factors can be more accurately identified. Swann therefore turned his attention to the analytical activity. As soon as we become aware that a possible target picture is being analysed, this has to be noted. By doing this, the analytical noise in the mind can be eliminated and we can continue to concentrate on the actual objective.

Swann's precise observations during countless RV sessions enabled him to define the role played by analytical overlay in more detail. If it occurred early in a session, it indicated an overly active mind attempting to give meaning to a pattern of noise. If it occurred very late, however, at a time when many details of the possible target had already been detected, it could well be an analytically correct conclusion. The issue was to find a method by which the psi information perceived by the viewer as a weak signal in a sea of mental noise could be filtered out, without falling prey to analytical overlay too early on.

It is one of the luckiest breaks in the modern history of psychical research that, through the funds provided by the intelligence services, a man like Ingo Swann was given the opportunity to concentrate fully on the solution to this problem, and, if we are to believe Ingo Swann, he solved it. The breakthrough came in 1983. He developed a precise model of how the subconscious transmits target information to the conscious mind, and his model included detailed instructions. If these were followed, anybody could train and employ their remote viewing abilities to some extent, abilities that, in his opinion, were biologically available in everyone.

Swann claims to have discovered that the process of anomalous information gathering is based on a natural structure. If this structure is followed, we move along a 'signal line', which will lead us to the correct identification of the target. For a long time in the field of para-psychology the myth existed that psychics needed time in which they could 'collect' their extrasensory information. This belief dated from the days of séances, during which the medium often made statements very slowly and after long lapses of time. Swann discovered that it was all a matter of concentration. As soon as he had zeroed in on his target, the impressions were there – immediately. This fact fascinated him. How this instant appearance of anomalous information was possible was the question that had brought him to Puthoff and the SRI in the first place. Now he no longer asked 'why', but tried to make use of this singularity of the process. Swann had discovered that the pre-conscious psi information could initially best be grasped kinaesthetically. It mani-fested itself in involuntary movements of the body. Sometimes he could start sketching immediately, even before a visual impression had occurred.

## THE STAGES OF COORDINATE REMOTE VIEWING

At first Swann believed that remote viewing had to be done according to the method of using coordinates that he had discovered. This approved procedure was labelled coordinate remote viewing (CRV),[32] and to depart from it was to commit sacrilege.

Swann distinguished four stages in the remote viewing process. Stage one occurs directly after the coordinates have been disclosed. The viewer should immediately give his hand a free reign and start sketching. Often, only a few lines are drawn automatically without conscious control. This may be the reason mediums preferred automatic writing and drawing. With his penchant for neologisms, Ingo Swann called these pictures 'ideograms', and as far as he was concerned, the automatic sketches done at the start of a session were the most important condition for successful remote viewing. The sketch determined the 'signal line', which was to be followed by other techniques.

During stage two, sensory impressions occur. These would include things such as 'cool', 'blue', 'white', silent', 'smells like wood', but as soon as too concrete a term appeared – 'sawmill', for example – Swann would break off and would have 'sawmill' noted on a piece of paper as an AOL (analytical overlay). Such interruptions demonstrate the importance of a trained interviewer in remote viewing. It is the interviewer's job to direct the viewer in such a way that, at any stage of the process, he will always produce relevant information and not lose himself in memories or fantasies.

An example may help to clarify this. During his training at the SRI, Joe McMoneagle was supposed to describe a target near San Francisco. It was a playground with swings in the shapes of dinosaurs made out of pipes, and McMoneagle drew line sketches of dinosaurs and said: 'Hey, this is like the old game in which you have to connect points by drawing lines. This is more fun than a barrel of monkeys.' The interviewer told McMoneagle to note down this sentence. It was later revealed that at the centre of the playground was a collection of iron bars resembling monkeys with their arms intertwined in the shape of a barrel!

This shows how important it is to pay attention to secondary impressions, even spontaneous remarks, and to be aware of all the possible means by which the subconscious is attempting to lift psi information to the level of consciousness.

Swann discovered that at this stage of the work emotionally charged impressions frequently appeared. They might have some connection with the target object, but were often overlays of the mind's normal conscious activity. These impressions also had to be noted down, with the identifying initials EI (emotional impact).

Stage three normally announced itself by impressions of dimensions such as 'gigantic', 'minute', 'heavy', 'light as a feather' and so on. By this stage the viewer could give in to the urge to make detailed drawings. In some cases one sheet of paper after another was filled with drawings, and many analytical overlays of what the drawings might signify had to be noted down.

It took more than a year of hard work before Swann was able to develop his own technique for gathering further details, and with this, stage four was accomplished. It consisted of a checklist containing material from the first three stages. Individual statements, impressions, information on dimensions, ALOs and EIs were listed on separate sheets of paper and divided into the categories of 'tangible' – wood, metal and skin, for example – and 'intangible' – useful, private and so on. The remote viewer put a mark against those elements on the lists that appeared to him to bear some relationship to the target object. This could be a lengthy process, and some elements were marked more than once, which frequently caused additional information to flash through the mind. The whole procedure often had to be repeated several times. In the end, the fragments of information could be put together into a final drawing and a statement, giving a quite accurate description of the target.

Later on Swann's system became even more elaborate, and it eventually had seven stages. During the last stage, the attempt was made to reproduce the exact name of the target by means of phonetic impressions. Still later, however, Swann rejected this development.

## THE REMOTE VIEWERS INSURGENCE

Swann's system might seem hard to credit. It has pedantic elements, and its extremely inflexible methodology stands in remarkable contrast to the variety of ways in which paranormal impressions are experienced by different people.

For the organizations that were paying for operation Grill Flame, however, Swann's complex technique, garnished as it was with neologisms reminiscent of high-tech terminology, was exactly what they wanted: a didactic tool with which RV could be taught. Their enthusiasm was not shared by all, and successful remote viewers like Hella Hammid, Gary Langford and Keith Harary were not impressed. They did not think much of the idea of making a dogma out of the coordinate technique. Quite the opposite, in fact, for in their opinion this procedure gave remote viewing a bad name and was a continuing source of analytical overlay. Given the coordinates, anybody with a reasonably good knowledge of geography could roughly identify the position of the target and would then quickly get bogged down in fantasies – African veld, mountain landscape in the Andes, Australian outback, Antarctic Ocean and so on – about the possible target area, which made the recognition of psi signals all the more difficult.

Moreover, because of Swann's position as a teacher, a strange situation had arisen. In order to be accepted on the programme, Langford and the others had had to undergo numerous training sessions, which had been the method by which people with a talent for remote viewing had been selected. Then they had to undergo additional training with Swann, and it was found that they were able to produce good results. Many of them thought that this was a waste of time because the results could not in any way be attributed to Swann's unique methods. The remote viewers had demonstrated that they were successful at RV during the initial training sessions. Later on, Hammid, Langford and Harary were asked to evaluate Swann's training methods, and they concluded that the techniques could be helpful to some people but that they were not absolutely necessary. They appeared to be too rigid and too limited. Swann regarded this as tantamount to treason, and from then on he was completely at odds with the other remote viewers at the SRI.

At the same time, a totally unrelated problem bedevilled the development of remote viewing. It gradually became apparent that there were precedents for many of the features that were being pursued and practised with great enthusiasm as if they were novelties. Both researchers and subjects approached the problems without sufficient knowledge of the history of parapsychology. This can be an advantage or a disadvantage – possibly both. An advantage, because if old problems are approached without any historic preconceptions, new solutions become possible. A disadvantage, because results are lauded as providing new insights, although they have, in fact, been known for a long time.

## 'THE SUN OF WATERLOO'

The French chemist René Warcollier had been conducting intriguing experiments in telepathy and clairvoyance since 1909, initially in private and later as president of the Institut Métapsychique in Paris.[33] In the experiments Warcollier normally acted as a sender – that is, he concentrated on an image, which he tried to transmit telepathically to one or several percipients. On one occasion he was looking at an Indian or Tibetan mandala with a candle in its centre. A series of small bells and minute volute shapes emanated from the flame towards the red background, and Warcollier primarily concentrated on these. One of the percipients said: 'Red material, worked with silver, glittering, something silken, very pliable, like a black snail, with a wavery motion. A feeling of gentleness. A fakir or an Indian holding a snake. A scene in

India, possibly musicians or Indian dancers with small bells around their ankles.'

At this early stage Warcollier had discovered that percipients approached the image in stages in accordance with a particular system. He found that the information was received in fragments and that kinaesthetic elements were often the first to become available. Such dynamic aspects appear more quickly than static images. Furthermore, he came to the conclusion that sketching was more helpful than verbal descriptions, because extrasensory impressions are assimilated on the pre-verbal level.

Later, in remote viewing, the outbound person at the target site was dispensed with in order to avoid telepathy. Nevertheless, a phenomenon that Ingo Swann called telepathic overlay was still frequently observed – that is, elements were received that did not necessarily belong to the target picture but came from the thoughts and feelings of the sender.

On one occasion Warcollier was looking at a picture of a Native American totem pole. He wrongly thought that the totem pole was the work of Black Africans. Interestingly enough, one of the percipients made the statement: 'Negro drums.'

On another occasion Warcollier was looking at a group picture of soldiers from the First World War. He himself was in the group. While he was looking at the soldiers with fixed bayonets during his attempt at telepathic transmission, he thought about the trenches, the barbed wire and the desolate, chalky landscape of the Champagne area of northern France where the picture had been taken. None of this was visible in the picture. All it showed was an arranged photograph of the unit. Several female percipients were taking part in the experiment, and one of them noted the following impressions: 'Clashing arms, a feeling of strength, of battle, of sharp objects which tear and render, in the background much rectangular wire mesh.' Another stated: 'The sun of Waterloo, a battlefield, swords, guns, dead horses, a feeling of death. Hills covered with snow, a landscape, white in white with black dots (people?).' This description equated exactly to what the sender Warcollier was thinking about the Champagne. Both cases demonstrate what was, in Swann's terminology, a telepathic overlay.

At the SRI something else was rediscovered – that extrasensory content is often misperceived. The correct basic shapes are assimilated and can be reproduced in sketches, but they are interpreted incorrectly. In Ingo Swann's words, 'they are analytically overlaid'.

This peculiarity of extrasensory perception was demonstrated most noticeably during the telepathic experiments the American author Upton Sinclair (1878–1968) conducted with his wife Mary Craig during the 1920s.[34] As the telepathic sender, Sinclair drew a simple sketch. His wife, who was quite some distance removed, had to try to reproduce it. On one occasion the diagrammatic picture of a hoe was precisely reproduced by the percipient but interpreted as a part of a pair of glasses or scissors. From a target picture of a reindeer, Mary Craig Sinclair clearly perceived the shape of the antlers, but believed this to be a sprig of holly.

In modern terminology we would say that the misinterpretation during this experiment was due to an analytical overlay by mental noise based on the percipient's memories from early childhood. Mary Craig Sinclair had often spent Christmas in surroundings in which holly was used for decorations and where there were tame reindeer that left a lasting impression. Apparently the psi information merged with emotionally charged experiences at deeper levels of the psyche and penetrated into consciousness in a compressed, dreamlike form.

A further example of the misinterpretation of psi information comes from Warcollier's experiments. The target picture was a postcard showing an intensely blue lake with a small island and four boats with triangular sails. The percipient received: 'A very blue lake. A feeling of peace, infinity, a flat surface, a gaping hole in the centre, snow, a field of snow.' The island was interpreted as being a hole, the clouds as snow.

It had long been recognized that anomalous cognition is a very complex process, during which association (patterns according to which things have been learned and filed in the memory), emotions (how a person feels) and so on interfere with the psi signal. In their analyses of the telepathic communication process, both Warcollier and well-known American psychologist Gardner Murphy emphasized the phenomena of fragmentation, repetition and assembling. They discovered that within the fragmented material received, some meaningful elements are often repeated, as if the intention were to give these particular emphasis. The conscious mind attempts to assemble these details and more or less intelligently pieces them together to form an image.

When we look at this description, we are inevitably reminded of the stages of Swann's remote viewing process, all the way up to his stage four.

In fact, the use of coordinates did not seem to be important for the quality of remote viewing. When Puthoff converted the coordinates into an indecipherable code by means of a cryptographic algorithm, which was then read out to the viewer, the results produced by the remote viewers at the SRI did not deteriorate. One of the dissidents, Keith Harary, even suggested that no information at all should be given. The target picture should be placed in a sealed envelope and safely filed. Puthoff came into the experimental room and simply said, 'Target'. Harary's statements were still accurate. The paranormal process of perception is apparently goal-directed and does not have to be aimed at its target by means of a 'cosmic address'.

In the early 1980s the theoretical controversies at the SRI came to a head, and the research threatened to degenerate into a series of cults around individuals, each of whom was attempting to protect his own methods. Within the group of experts on psi research that had grown up at the SRI, the pretensions of the various protagonists began to interfere with the continuation of worthwhile and innovative work. Ingo Swann saw himself as a 'guru' and wanted to become leader of the group; Ed May wanted to pursue his own research projects; Russell Targ wanted to be famous.

And Hal Puthoff, the scientist who had started it all and whose integrity had never been questioned, found himself caught between these conflicting interests. When he returned from a trip to China, during which Targ had had to prepare a report about a series of experiments, he found a catastrophe waiting for him on his desk. The Defense Intelligence Agency had accused Targ of having presented a sloppy research report and decided to take him off the Grill Flame payroll.

I can still recall the way that Targ appeared at the psi conventions, claiming that he had quit the project for ethical reasons. Psi research at the SRI was to be used for military purposes, he claimed, a development he refused to support, while Puthoff was made to appear as the bad boy, who continued to fraternize with the military in a questionable manner. Of course it was true that psi research was to be used for military purposes, but it was certainly not unethical to unravel the mysteries of remote viewing. It became evident only much later that quite a few people who had been involved in the project as researchers or subjects overestimated their own part in the venture. After all, the real issue was to put the fear of God into the nation's enemies all over the world. Scientific work was pushed into the background, and personal image-building became the name of the game.

Hella Hammid and Keith Harary drew their own conclusions and left the laboratory. For a time, Harary worked with Targ. They travelled throughout the Soviet Union, wrote a popular book and made the dream of every commodity dealer come true: with the help of an elaborate remote viewing technique they predicted the movements of prices on the silver market – correctly as it turned out. The end of this misalliance came about far sooner than expected, and included court injunctions and legal proceedings. Fame and fortune appear not to have agreed particularly well with either of them.

# Chapter Six
# PSYCHIC SPYING IN ACTION

## FRONT LOADING

In time the unit at Fort Meade developed its own procedures, applying one of two methods: coordinate remote viewing (CRV), developed at the SRI by Ingo Swann, and a method based on techniques of relaxation and meditation, known as extended remote viewing (ERV). But the team felt it had complete freedom in the way it conducted its sessions. The scientists at the SRI would probably have raised objections to this. Even though their research was, ultimately, intended to serve the ends of espionage, they had always been careful to subordinate practical considerations to scientific requirements. In psi research one of these requirements is a rigorous control of any gaps in the design of an experiment that could enable the participants to gain information by conventional sensory channels.

Skip Atwater's military psi group approached this problem with far fewer inhibitions. They were neither particularly well trained in parapsychology nor were they familiar with the stringent methodological requirements of this field of research. Indeed, when all is said and done, even the parapsychologists knew very little about how psi functions. When Atwater had the feeling that one of his remote viewers had located the target but was unable to provide specific details, he would provide support by disclosing additional information. Within the unit this was known as front loading by the interviewer.

For example, if the target was an industrial complex in Novosibirsk, and the remote viewer reported impressions of paths in the jungle, Atwater did not insist any longer for the attempt had obviously failed. There were many such sessions where the results were useless. On the other hand, if an industrial complex was described, together with workers conversing in a Slavic language, then it could happen that Atwater intervened and showed a satellite photograph of the target. 'This is the factory, go inside and describe the rooms,' or, 'Somewhere inside this factory there is a man whose name is Anatoli Duroshkin. Try to describe his surroundings at the present time.' Astonishingly enough, this rather naïve procedure, which was based on the idea of being able to direct the 'psi radar' by means of an 'anchor' – a picture, a person, a detail of the target – was often successful. At times it appeared as if the additional information was able to create an anomalous connection to the target. Detailed image impressions appeared immediately.

# A TELEPATHIC INTERVIEW

At times, however, the system of front loading was taken to questionable extremes, especially if the interviewer was after a certain result or wanted to have his pet theory confirmed. During the latter stages of the operational unit at Fort Meade, this was one of the reasons for the rapid decline in the quality of the work being carried out there.

The psi unit also developed a weird pseudo-telepathic method of interrogating people who were acting as targets in a psi espionage project. In view of the files recorded during such sessions, even people who were inclined to feel goodwill for the team were forced to begin asking themselves if it had not long gone over the top and if the remote viewers had not become suitable cases for the psychiatrist.

Just imagine the situation. A remote viewer 'contacts' an enemy agent and strikes up a telepathic conversation with them, during which the remote viewer attempts to discover the agent's assignments and secrets! It is hard to believe that Puthoff and Targ, who had been able to observe and document so many extraordinary psi results, would have regarded such a method as practicable, let alone promising. The people at Fort Meade were of a different mind, and their paymasters did not care how the information was obtained. They regarded the psi espionage team from a pragmatic point of view and believed that if these people actually did have these strange abilities, they should be exploited as long as the source continued to flow.

One of the craziest cases of this kind found its way into the top secret files in 1980. Norm Everheart (pseudonym), a specialist for CIA technical operations, arrived at Fort Meade with the photograph of a foreign-looking man. The assumption was that he had been infiltrated into Scandinavia by the KGB (the Soviet espionage and counter-espionage agency) and was currently in South Africa on a Scandinavian passport. Agents from the CIA were on his trail. The South Africans were alerted to his presence but were asked to let the man act freely so that his assignment could be discovered. Unfortunately, they rushed out and arrested the man, apparently through fear that some of their own state secrets might be revealed. The interrogations in a prison in Cape Town were fruitless. The man simply refused to talk.

There was one question that the CIA really wanted answered. It was known that the KGB spy probably received his instructions in code via short-wave radio. How did he decode these messages? It was decided to let the psi spies at Fort Meade have a go.

The specialist for people in the team was Ken Bell. He was the man called on whenever they needed to learn something about the thoughts and intentions of missing people or people in danger. Bell looked at the photograph and then, according to a long-practised technique, he relaxed until he was in a trance-like condition. He described a man on the second floor of a building in a city by the sea. The man was dressed in a strange garment, something like grey pyjamas. Prison dress. He was being questioned by two men in a language he could not understand. Bell had the feeling that the man was talking to himself in his mind, and he was convinced that he would never reveal the information he had.

At this point Skip Atwater calmly suggested that Ken Bell should talk to the KGB agent telepathically and elicit the information from him. This was nothing new for Bell. He tried everything he knew. The man remained obdurate.

Anyone who had thought that the hard-boiled CIA agent Norm Everheart would be amused or deterred by this strange attempt to establish a telepathic contact with a KGB agent would have been mistaken. It was true that he was disappointed, because after the accurate description of the man's interrogation in prison he had indeed expected much more – he had expected the solution of a minor conundrum that would develop into the solution of an immense problem, namely, how to get information from enemy agents without ever seeing them face to face – telepathic tapping! The consequences of this would be completely mind-boggling. There would be thousands of unemployed agents and secret remote viewing units everywhere, busy recording the intentions of the political and military leaders of hostile nations.

Everheart realized that things would not be all that easy, despite the enthusiasm generated by successful operations. Nevertheless, he did not give up. After a brief phone call on a secure line, he ordered a further session with Ken Bell. He front loaded Bell with valuable information on which he could direct himself mentally – the names of the KGB man's son and daughter – and then the apparent (or alleged) telepathic communication became even more remarkable, probably one of the weirdest interrogations in the annals of espionage. Bell sent the telepathic message: 'Your son Sergei misses you and your daughter Svetlana wants to know when you will be coming home.'

The steely Russian agent immediately became as soft as butter. Just as if it were a third-rate spy thriller, he melted into a pitiful heap in Ken Bell's mind. The James Bond with tears in his eyes murmured sadly: 'Sergei wants me to take him skiing. I promised him I would.' And Bell reinforced this: 'Yes, you promised. You have to go home quickly.'

'This was supposed to be my last assignment,' was the answer that appeared somewhere in the mind of Ken Bell, the quietly reclining remote viewer, who carefully moved forward and discovered that the KGB man had a pocket calculator with him.

When, in a second attempt at the same man, Mel Riley also came up with a pocket calculator, Everheart was sure he had discovered an instrument for the decoding of information. It was known that KGB agents frequently used pocket calculators to code and decode messages, and some of these were even equipped with special cryptographic chips. Enquiries in South Africa revealed that one of the officers who had interrogated the unknown man had actually found a pocket calculator on him and had taken it home. Even though the use of the calculator for the purpose of decoding was never confirmed, Everheart was convinced that that was what it had been used for.

The preferences of the remote viewers at Fort Meade had been established early on. Ken Bell was the specialist for 'personal matters'. Mel Riley's artistic talent helped him to reproduce his impressions in precise drawings. Hartleigh Trent was able precisely to zero in on targets, while Joe McMoneagle could make astonishingly accurate sketches of technical objects. McMoneagle had also developed the ability to recognize nuclear or fissionable material by a green haze. If he saw an orange flame, it was normally some form of radio-frequency radiation. All the remote viewers had problems with numbers. An exception was Pat Price, but Pat was an exception in many ways. The problem of accurately grasping numbers by extrasensory means was assumed to be related to the way the brain processed psi data.

# THE PSI ANTI-TERROR UNIT

On 27 July 1943 Hitler gave the order to rescue Mussolini. Operation Alarich was set in motion, but the intelligence service was unable to provide any information about Mussolini's actual location. Walter Schellenberg, head of the foreign intelligence service and one of the key people on Heinrich Himmler's staff, wrote in his memoirs: 'In this situation Himmler again turned to one of his occult idiosyncrasies – and this time even with a modicum of success. He had several "representatives of the occult sciences", who had all been arrested after Rudolf Hess's flight to England, brought together in a villa on the Wannsee. These were clairvoyants, astrologers and pendulum adepts, who were supposed to magically discover the Duce's whereabouts. These séances cost us a lot of money, because the needs of the "scientists" for good food, drinks, and tobacco were quite enormous. But lo and behold, after some time a "master of the siderian pendulum" discovered that Mussolini was being held on an island west of Naples. And in fact The Duce had initially been taken to one of the small Ponza Islands he had designated.'[35]

When things got serious, the military had always employed any means available to them to discover a person's whereabouts, and it was no different at Fort Meade. It was quickly discovered, however, that moving targets are very difficult to locate by means of remote viewing. The search for missing persons or objects proved to be a major challenge for the team. For many viewers it appeared to be much easier to aim at fixed targets, which could then be explored once a 'contact' had been established. When they were searching for objects at unknown places or for moving targets, the agents of project Grill Flame frequently got lost in their own mental noise.

An additional problem was created by the military, which had no knowledge of how psi worked. For reasons of security, they often kept the remote viewers in the dark about whether their statements were correct or false. Parapsychological research, on the other hand, had discovered that feedback was a decisive component of good and stable psi performance. At Fort Meade the remote viewers were not only under pressure to deliver good results all the time but also had to endure the poker faces of their patrons, who walked out without any pat on the shoulder, even when the psi spies had scored a bull's eye. A sad fate, but one that apparently did not discourage McMoneagle and his colleagues.

An example illustrates the discrepancies between the demands of the rather ignorant military and the results they expected. After the fundamentalists had seized power in Iran and the Shah had fled, in November 1979 a group of Iranian students stormed the US Embassy in Teheran and took the occupants as hostages. They demanded the return of the Shah in exchange for their release. President Jimmy Carter had Iranian assets in American banks frozen and stopped imports of Iranian oil. The United Nations Security Council condemned the act of terrorism by Iran. Neither this nor an appeal to the International Court of Justice had any effect on the precarious situation. Compared with the hostage crisis, all other burning international problems, including the Soviet invasion of Afghanistan, appeared to be of secondary importance. Carter had to act quickly, because the nation felt personally humiliated by the taking of the hostages.

From late 1979 until early 1980 the psi team at Fort Meade had only a single assignment covering hundreds of sessions – to discover the whereabouts of the hostages, to describe the buildings in which they were being held, to provide information about their physical and mental condition and to characterize their captors. The clients were the Ministry of Defense and the National Security Council. Day after day the team had to perform the same tasks. There were constant reports on television, and these slowly began to merge with the impressions gained by the remote viewers.

Jake Stewart of the National Security Council even called in Keith Harary at the SRI in California. Like Ken Bell, Harary was particularly adept at 'aiming' at people, and Stewart wanted him to provide information about the hostage Richard Queen, who was suffering from the early stages of multiple sclerosis. Nobody at the SRI knew who the target person was. Puthoff was told only that there was a 'target person'. Harary described a thin, bearded man in cold, spartan surroundings. He had health problems causing nausea and a serious nervous ailment, so that one side of his body was practically paralysed. Harary saw people around the man and had the impression that he would start off on a trip in an aeroplane within one or two days.

Puthoff and Harary thought the person in question was a head of state, particularly because Jake Stewart had said that the assignment was very urgent. Undoubtedly, Harary had hit the target. But what was all this about an aeroplane? Two days later all was revealed. Fearing that Richard Queen might die, his captors put him on an aeroplane to the United

States. A team of doctors confirmed the statements about the former hostage's health. When Richard Queen later read the minutes of the RV sessions with Keith Harary without being told where the information had come from, he became very angry. He was convinced that one of his captors must have been an American agent who had passed on to the US authorities such detailed information about his condition to the US authorities.

Harary's success was no doubt partly due to the fact that he had to aim at only one target connected with the hostages and that he really did not know what it was all about. Things were quite different for the team at Fort Meade. The unit were already exhausted by the numerous repeated attempts they were asked to make when Scotty Watt suddenly ordered them to pack their bags. They were taken a short distance from Fort Meade and quartered in a motel in Laurel, Delaware. Each member of the team had their own room, and there was a suite for joint meetings. Why had this strange accommodation been arranged? With a solemn face Watt explained that a covert operation to free the hostages was in the offing and that the remote viewers were to 'accompany' the action. They had been moved to the motel so that they did not endanger the project and to shield them from further information on television. The small, formerly enthusiastic unit was charged with the uninterrupted observation of the Iranian operation via psi. Such a crazy idea could have been thought up only on the basis of grotesque misconceptions about the applicability of such abilities.

Except for psychically completely overtaxing the remote viewers, this assignment came to naught, just like the rescue operation in April 1980, which ended in a fiasco when two aircraft collided, causing the deaths of eight servicemen and injuries to many others. The 'Iran convent' of the Grill Flame team led to serious nervous breakdowns. Nancy Stern and Fern Gauvin threw in the towel, and from that time the words remote viewing no longer appeared in their vocabularies. For the remaining participants, the horror trip was far from over. As a result of the abortive rescue attempt, the hostages were separated and their trails completely lost. There was a new job for the remote viewers. Once again on orders from above, their techniques were employed totally mistakenly, and at 2560 Llewellyn Street everyone knew these would be vain attempts to achieve the impossible. In the end President Carter got cold feet about making the same mistake twice, and the planned second operation was cancelled.

# PLAYING 'FIND THE LADY' WITH MISSILES

One of the great moments of operational remote viewing occurred in May 1978. A Soviet Tupolev–22 bomber had crashed somewhere in Zaire (now the Democratic Republic of Congo), and the race to find the wreck began. If the Americans could get there before the Russians, they would be able to take an invaluable look at the state of Soviet communications technology. The Pentagon charged Puthoff with the psi search, and Gary Langford seemed to be the one who produced the most interesting impressions. He saw a river in the jungle with the tail of the aircraft sticking out, and he went on to describe the area, the topography and the roads.

The information was passed to Kinshasa via the CIA's European office. As is often the case with operational assignments, the source of the information had to be kept secret in order not to overtax the local command with a reference to psi. When it came to military targets, a further serious problem was created by the chain of command. The communication network between the units on the spot, who wanted to work in peace, and the desk agents somewhere in the United States, who transmitted their mysterious information, was clearly the perfect environment for fostering egos. The unit leader in Zaire asked for more precise information and set off into the bush with his search team.

Dale Graff, a physicist with the air force, who had shown considerable interest in the work of Puthoff's team, occasionally worked with a woman, Frances Bryan, who was a good remote viewer. He had her look for the wreck as well, and she produced a fairly accurate sketch of the area Langford had already described. The drawing was so detailed that the terrain could be located on a map. When the coordinates arrived in Zaire, the team had already set out. It found the Tupolev–22, because in its search it came across Zaireans who were busy hiding pieces they had taken from the wreck. The machine was located within barely 5 kilometres of the spot Langford and Bryan had described. The photograph, which was later shown around at the SRI, amazed both the scientists and the remote viewers. Langford's sketch agreed with the picture so completely that he might have copied it.

In 1979 Dale Graff, who went on to become one of the key DIA contacts to the RV project, gave Puthoff an assignment of great importance for national security. The air force had developed the new MX intercontinental ballistic missile and was looking for places to station the rockets where it would be difficult for the Soviets to destroy them in a first strike. In the Utah and Nevada deserts each MX rocket was to be given a railway track, almost 50 kilometres long, with 23 'garages' along its length. A special covered railway car was to be in constant motion along the track in order to shuttle the warheads between 'garages'. Spy satellites would not be able to detect which missile silo actually contained an MX. According to the logic of nuclear war, which assumed two first strikes for each US intercontinental ballistic missile, this meant 46 missiles for every rail track – in other words, 46 enemy hits in order to destroy a single American MX. But nobody had thought about what might happen if there were some way in which the Soviets could find out where exactly where each rocket actually was. Could they possibly even outwit the unbelievably expensive precautions by means of remote viewing? The SRI team was told to find out.

Charles Tart, professor of psychology at the University of California at Davis and one of the most productive parapsychologists, had just completed an experiment to filter out the best psi talents from among 2000 subjects. With the ten who came out top he conducted the actual experiment, which in a way copied the military's 'garage game'.[36] In fact, it went back to the old game by which the gullible are often separated from their money. A marble is placed under one of the three shells, which are then moved about, and the gambler tries to pick the shell under which the marble is hidden.

In Charles Tart's case, there were ten shells and they existed virtually on a computer screen. The shells could not be distinguished from each other. After each round, the computer re-arranged the shells, which were identified by a number that was unknown to the player, and kept track of which shell was which. The marble was under one of the ten virtual shells. The idea behind this game was that, by means of clairvoyance, the shell under which the marble was hidden could be selected more often than the others to a statistically significant degree. The experiment was therefore based on an error-correcting protocol. It was not the individual hit that was being sought, but a higher percentage of correctly identified targets, which together was then counted as a hit.

On the basis of chance, the correct shell would be chosen in 10 per cent of the cases. But the selected gifted subjects came up with far better results. One woman reached an average hit rate of 25 per cent. This allowed Tart correctly to identify the shell with the marble in 20 consecutive games.

Let us imagine Soviet remote viewers of the calibre of Tart's best subjects, who are playing 'find the lady' with the MX missiles. With little effort they would be able to identify the correct position of an intercontinental ballistic missile in 80 per cent of the cases. Naturally, we do not know if the hit rate could be kept at such a level during repeated attempts or if it would be as accurate in an operational situation, which imposes far greater demands on psychological stability than a innocent experiment in a laboratory.

The results of Tart's experiment must have impressed the powers in the Pentagon. President Carter's successor, Ronald Reagan, decided against playing 'find the lady' with missiles. This decision was based not only on budget constraints but also on the fear of the 'psi units' in the Red Army. When I recently corresponded with Charles Tart about this experiment he confessed that he was glad that this work had become known. He regards it as one of the greatest achievements of his life that his work contributed to the cancellation of this unbelievably expensive and destructive missile system. He was never permitted to talk for reasons of security, however.

## 'GENERAL SPOONBENDER'

When Major General Thompson took up a new posting in 1981, the team at Fort Meade feared that the sun was about to set on remote viewing. His successor, Major General William Odom, had no interest in the unit and shunted it off to Intelligence and Security Command (INSCOM). There it received unexpected support from INSCOM's new chief, Major General Albert Stubblebine. Stubblebine, whose incredible resemblance to the actor Lee Marvin made him seem the epitome of the hard-boiled militarist, was, in reality, ready to believe anything and everything about psi. Together with INSCOM Colonel John Alexander, Stubblebine gave so-called 'spoon-bending parties'. At these get-togethers, which took place in a relaxed atmosphere, the participants were supposed to achieve what the Israeli psychic star Uri Geller was demonstrating everywhere on television, the alleged paranormal deformation of cutlery.[37] Because of his unusual faith in psi, Stubblebine was nicknamed General Spoonbender.

As far as the unit at Fort Meade was concerned, Stubblebine's appointment was just in time. He had great plans. With missionary fervour he intended to advance psi research for military purposes in all possible fields. Stubblebine was particularly interested in psychokinesis (PK), and at his 'spoon-bending parties' he was searching for useful PK talents. He urged Hal Puthoff and Ed May at the SRI to conduct experiments in psychokinesis, too, and he brought his political connections into play so that the psi programme might flourish.

It made sense to conduct extensive research on psychokinesis, particularly since nobody could be sure whether experiments on remote influencing of people were based on a telepathic or a psychokinetic effect. At the American Society for Psychical Research (ASPR) in New York, Ingo Swann had already demonstrated that he had psychokinetic abilities, and ultimately no one knew whether remote viewing did not also contain a physical – in other words psychokinetic – aspect. Swann's experiment with the magnetometer at Stanford University tends to favour this interpretation. In a report that has been recently released by the intelligence services, Puthoff and Targ describe a further experiment intended to discover whether the remote viewing channel had a bilateral component – that is, if energy from an individual could be transmitted to a remote object.[38] The target selected for this experiment was also a magnetometer. The device was situated in an adjoining laboratory. In ten attempts, each lasting for 50 seconds, the viewer simply tried to grasp the target object by remote viewing. During these attempts the magnetometer showed reactions that were statistically significant, and the researchers quite rightly considered this result to be important. Perturbations in a piece of sensitive equipment during remote viewing indicate that anomalous cognition and psychokinesis are based on the same process.

Stubblebine regarded the continuation of such research as of the highest priority, and several members of Congress, including Democrats Charlie Rose and Clairborne Pell, agreed to support him. Pell even hired a full-time assistant, C.B. Scott Jones, whose only job it was to keep him abreast of developments in parapsychological research. He was in contact with a large circle of psychics and self-appointed clairvoyants, who took on operational assignments for members of the intelligence community from time to time. The original centres – at Menlo Park mostly for research and at Fort Meade for practical operations – were slowly but surely being added to by freelance psychics. The massive interest displayed in psi by the highest authorities inspired people everywhere to forswear their opposition and let down their guard to all sorts of occult connections.

With the enhanced backing, Stubblebine set out to recruit psi talents from all quarters. The Texan Leonard 'Lyn' Buchanan, who had had a paranormal experience at the age of 12, for example, joined INSCOM as a linguist. While he was stationed at Augsburg in Germany a strange phenomenon had apparently occurred – he was said to have 'frozen' a computer through the power of his mind. He was clearly the ideal man for General Spoonbender. Other new members were Paul Smith, who was commissioned as a military intelligence officer and who turned out to be a talented remote viewer, and Tom Nance, who eventually become Swann's favourite disciple. There were also some who wanted to be transferred into the unit at any price, including Edward Dames, who had spent time in the Far East supporting National Security Agency missions and had later been sent to Germany to intercept and jam Soviet and Czech communications. In 1981 his unit had been assigned to identify the components of a Soviet biological weapon. Because it had been impossible to obtain any information, he had been considering whether he should try to enlist the help of a psychic when he discovered that the army was already working with psychics. Dames tried everything he could think of to be taken into the RV programme. His perseverance was rewarded.

## 'THE NEW MENTAL BATTLEFIELD'

In 1981 the remote viewers at the SRI and Fort Meade were instructed to find the highly dangerous terrorist Carlos, who, it was feared, had travelled to the United States. During one of the numerous sessions, Gary Langford described a blue van with unusual white markings on the sides, which, he said, was being driven by terrorists who looked Latin. In the bus was their hostage, who was a high-ranking US official. Langford had the impression that the incident was inevitable and would occur very soon. Puthoff found these statements to be strange, because they were unlike anything else that Langford had produced in previous RV sessions about Carlos.

A few days later the Italian Red Brigades kidnapped NATO General James Dozier in Verona – they used a blue van with white markings on the sides. The intelligence services initiated a tremendous effort to free the general. There was to be no second disaster such as had occurred a few years earlier when Aldo Moro, leader of the Italian Christian Democrats, had been found shot to death in the boot of a Red Brigades car after a similar abduction. Langford was ordered to the Pentagon, where he impressed high-ranking officials with further psi information on the case, but the problems associated with locating a moving target again surfaced. The information was too inaccurate to be able to locate General Dozier.

The intelligence services were stumbling about in the dark and interfering with the work of the trained psi agents by indiscriminately hiring
'clairvoyants' of all sorts, and they almost brought about the very disaster
they had wanted to avoid at all cost. One of them was even flown to
Vicenza to provide guidelines for the search on the spot. He had nothing
better in mind, however, than had the former pendulum adepts used
during Operation Alarich – he demanded special treatment in food and
lodgings. He finally gave some vague information, but his description of
a farmhouse in the vicinity would have fitted any of a thousand buildings.
Nevertheless, the Carabinieri stormed the house the self-appointed clair-
voyant had indicated. Instead of terrorists with a NATO general, all they
found was an Italian family almost frightened to death.[39]

Meanwhile, at Fort Meade, Joe McMoneagle described an apartment
on the second floor of a house in Padua. He drew a radiator on the wall
and the eye-catching front of a shop below. The street map he drew was
almost an exact overlay of the map being used by the Italian police. By this
time the leaders of the operation in Italy were not interested in hearing
any more about psi. They had succeeded in catching several terrorists who
had revealed the location of the 'people's prison' where Dozier was being
held. When the right flat was stormed and Dozier had been freed, it was
found that he had been held in a second-floor apartment, which
McMoneagle had apparently described correctly – there was the radiator
on the wall and the shop with its distinctive front.

Stubblebine did not let himself be deterred by such outcomes. Instead,
he initiated numerous projects on psi, on altered states of consciousness,
on techniques for visualization and so on, which his assistant John
Alexander coordinated with great enthusiasm. In 1980, before joining
INSCOM, Alexander had published an article in *Military Review* under the
title 'The New Mental Battlefield', in which he had discussed the possibilities of influencing the brain's electrical activity by telepathy.[40]
Alexander claimed that the Soviets had a 'psi weapon', the lethal effectiveness of which had been proved. Its greatest danger lay in the fact that
it was difficult to locate because it required only a single human as its
source of energy. In 1983 Alexander initiated the Jedi Project (named after
the Jedi in the movie *Star Wars*). The objective of the project was to seek
and achieve maximum physical, psychological and paranormal excellence
by unconventional means.

In their multifarious activities Stubblebine and Alexander were doubt-
less skating on thin ice. The borderline between the attempt to utilize psi

within an appropriate defined framework and the concept of training psi as an extraordinary ability in man of the future had been erased. The new ideas of the chiefs at INSCOM came suspiciously close to concepts such as those formulated by Friedrich Nietzsche in his notes to *Thus Spoke Zarathustra*: 'Our nature is to create a higher being than we ourselves are. To create beyond ourselves!'[41] The enthusiasm we observe here did not attempt to hide its roots – the New Age swamp of unreflected occultism together with the self-deluding hope of belonging to the generation that would achieve the leap to the next stage of evolution.[42]

In a book written in cooperation with two co-authors, John Alexander noted: 'The purpose of the book is to unlock the door to the extraordinary human potentials inherent in each of us. To do this, we, like governments around the world, must take a fresh look at non-traditional methods of affecting reality. We must raise human consciousness of the potential power of the individual body/mind system – the power to manipulate reality. We must be willing to retake control of our past, present, and ultimately, our future.'[43]

Stubblebine and Alexander were clearly prepared to increase the 'potential power of the individual body/mind system'. An entire series of ambitious projects was to be undertaken by the remote viewing unit at Fort Meade. Stubblebine converted it into an official sub-department of INSCOM (called Detachment G), gave it the code name Center Lane and put it under his own direct command.

The new recruits were sent to Ingo Swann at the SRI for training; later, after Swann had moved his training school to his native city, they were sent to New York. Stubblebine had great plans for his psi spies. They were therefore also sent to an institute founded by someone for whom Stubblebine had great expectations in the achievement of his programme for the realization of the hidden human potentials – the Monroe Institute, where training on OBEs and various states of altered consciousness was being conducted.

## BRAIN WAVES AND OUT-OF-BODY EXPERIENCES

When small electrodes are attached to the outer surface of the skull, they make it possible to record fluctuating electric potentials that are caused by the electric reactions of billions of brain cells. In the course of decades of constantly improved methods of detection and analysis, it has been demonstrated that the electrical activity recorded from the scalp, the so-called electroencephalogram (EEG), could be associated with various states of consciousness.

Within the waking state, several degrees of alertness can be distinguished. They are accompanied by the irregular pattern of an amplitude of between 10 and 20 mV (millivolts) and a frequency of between 10 and 40 Hz.[44] A condition of relaxed alertness is accompanied by the so-called alpha rhythm. Alpha waves show a fairly regular rhythm and a frequency of 8–13 Hz. A deteriorating alpha rhythm and the appearance of slower waves (theta waves, 4–8 Hz) normally accompany a state of sleepiness. A person is asleep as soon as the so-called sleep spindles appear. Sleep spindles are short bursts of waves at a frequency of about 14 Hz, which begin with a low amplitude and rise to 30–40 mV within only a few cycles, only to decline again. During sleep further stages occur, especially the various phases of dreaming. During deep, dreamless sleep there is an increase of extremely slow delta waves (1 Hz or below) with high amplitude (100 mV or more).

In 1965 psychologist and parapsychologist Charles Tart had the opportunity to make EEG recordings with a man who claimed that he could deliberately induce OBEs. This subject was Robert Monroe,[45] a successful producer of radio programmes. Monroe reported on OBEs experienced during a state of quasi-sleep, and during his attempts to create OBEs, Tart detected a high variability in the EEG wave patterns. Not only were there alpha waves over the whole spectrum from 8 to 13 Hz, but these had a wide amplitude, ranging from 40 to 100 mV. The theta waves during sleep were also anomalous in their intensity. Never before had Tart seen theta activity exceeding 50 mV. Monroe showed bursts of from three to eight theta waves, which had amplitudes of 150 and 200 mV. On the other hand, Tart was unable to detect any delta waves during sleep.

Apparently Monroe was able to maintain himself in a condition of half-sleeping, half-waking for a longer period. Another of Tart's subjects who reported spontaneous OBEs during sleep appears also to have had these experiences while in this intermediary state. In fact, people who frequently experience OBEs all complain about sleeping badly. They often find themselves in a transitional state between waking and sleeping, during which so-called hypnagogic hallucinations occur. These are very vivid, dreamlike images accompanied by the conviction of being awake. This is a condition we are normally unable to control. We are sleepy and perceive the appearance of a series of pictures. Shortly thereafter we fall asleep. Techniques consciously to control this intermediary stage have been under discussion in the occult literature for a long time, because traditionally this has been regarded as the borderline condition containing the richest potential for paranormal experiences.

In the following years Monroe wrote several books about his experiences and devoted all his time to the study of out-of-body experiences (OBEs).[46] In 1974 he founded the Monroe Institute, which moved to Faber, Virginia, in the beautiful countryside in the foothills of the Blue Ridge Mountains a few years ago. Monroe headed the institute until his death in 1995.

# INTO OTHER REALITIES WITH HEMI-SYNC

From the beginning the Monroe Institute maintained close contacts with government authorities and the Pentagon, and Stubblebine, who had attended many courses there, chose the institute to conduct secret research for INSCOM. The project was to discover whether the Hemi-Sync technique developed by Monroe could increase the concentration and abilities of soldiers.[47]

Hemi-Sync is an auditory guidance system working with binaural audio beats. Signals of two different frequencies are presented through headphones, one to each ear. The brain detects phase differences between these signals, and through a process of perceptual integration, the two signals are perceived as a third 'beat' frequency – the binaural beat. It is believed that the brain waves will adjust themselves to this frequency. According to a study carried out by the National Research Council, the method leads to an increase in the ability to learn.[48]

The remote viewers from Fort Meade also received training at the Monroe Institute, because Stubblebine was not satisfied with Swann's method. He wanted his psi spies to develop additional paranormal abilities, so they were sent to learn how to produce controlled OBEs. The Hemi-Sync tapes were later used during the 'cooling-down phase' before an RV session to help them more easily achieve a state of relaxation.[49]

Joe McMoneagle alone spent 14 months at the Monroe Institute, where he learned partially to control his OBEs by the use of the Hemi-Sync tapes. Then an unexpected phenomenon occurred. The more he was able to control his OBEs, the worse his abilities as a remote viewer became. As Swann and Harary had already assumed, OBE and RV are independent phenomena. McMoneagle felt that remote viewing was the more important and decided to give up the training of OBEs.

Even while he was at the Monroe Institute, McMoneagle had not been inactive and had carried out remote viewing assignments. One day he was locked into a windowless room so that he could not see who would come to bring the target pictures. It was a member of NASA. He brought several envelopes containing coordinates. At the start of the session the co-ordinates were read out to McMoneagle. The first impression McMoneagle had was of a pyramid. He assumed the target area to be in Egypt, but was confused because he described corridors and rooms he knew did not exist in Egyptian pyramids. In this fashion he described all the target areas. The first six were correct, but when he got to the seventh he was tired and had no success. Everybody believed these were archaeo-logical structures. After the experiment, McMoneagle was asked what impressions he had received about the culture that had built these monu-ments. McMoneagle stated they came from beings who were far bigger than man, and a culture that was far older than our own.

The man from NASA had seemed to be very impressed, because McMoneagle had been able to make such exact statements about the first six targets. Only he knew where these targets were and he kept this infor-mation to himself.

Five months later the team at Monroe received a call from NASA. They were informed that the next mission to Mars would target the coordi-nates McMoneagle had described. Unfortunately, the mission was a fail-ure. Later on the pictures of the so-called Martian pyramids caused a sensation. McMoneagle is convinced these are not natural formations but served as an intermediary station for an unknown civilization. McMoneagle refuses to commit himself, however, because he knows far too well that in remote viewing it is practically impossible to distinguish between the real and the imaginary. He rarely experiences completely convincing impressions and mostly only when he has worked on a target for a long time. Suddenly something appears in his mind and he knows all there is to know about the target. 'It's like an orgasm,' McMoneagle recently said in an interview. In these extremely rare cases he can clearly distinguish between reality and a concept of reality.

# Chapter Seven
# DECLINE OF THE RV UNIT

## WITCHES, CHANNELLING AND ALIENS

When the army's funds for the remote viewing unit ran out in 1985, the Defense Intelligence Agency (DIA) took over, apparently on the advice of Jack Vorona. After many weeks of polishing doorknobs with Hal Puthoff – from the White House through the FBI all the way to the Customs Office and the Coast Guard – Vorona was finally able to secure the research programme at the SRI for a further five years. One of the key departments at the Pentagon, which has remained anonymous until the present, contributed $10 million.

The primary beneficiary of these funds was Ed May. Puthoff had long begun to move in a different direction. He was on the track of a mystery increasingly discussed among physicists in recent years – zero-point energy, energy out of nothing. This technology of the future, which is still very much pie in the sky, was the ideal field for Puthoff and one to which he wanted to devote his intellectual abilities. As soon as he had secured the research funds for the SRI, he left the laboratory he had made famous. The torch was taken up by Ed May, and under his leadership research was intensified. Since the funds arrived as Puthoff was leaving, the lion's share of more than 70 per cent came to Ed May. Indeed, May's research accounted for about 85 per cent of all the data compiled during the 23 years the secret programmes lasted.

Nevertheless, May was restricted in the projects he was able to select. After Dale Graff had been promoted to department head and project manager of the operational unit at Fort Meade he was closely involved during the 1990s in allocating the assignments to May's research team. Both Graff and May had to cope with constant insurmountable bureaucratic barriers and political influences, which determined the direction the research was to take. They were a far cry from what May would have preferred to work on as well as from the concepts of the applications-orientated 'task force' at Fort Meade.

In the summer of 1986 Mel Riley returned to the 'operational unit'. What he found was no longer the small, dedicated group governed by the vision of working to develop a mental technology and applying it gloriously for Uncle Sam. He found chaos, a zoo, a caricature of the team he had once belonged to. Protégés of Stubblebine had been infiltrated into the team. They had neither undergone training with Swann nor were they interested in doing so. Among them were three women known as 'the witches'. One of these practised palmistry; another went into trances during her sessions just like in a spiritualist séance; the third used tarot cards and 'channelled' information she received as 'inspirations from outer beings'.

Even after the power structure had shifted yet again, nothing changed in this fairground atmosphere. When the son of a general reacted to the Hemi-Sync tapes by falling into a state of mental confusion that required psychiatric attention and when Stubblebine himself reported strange visionary experiences after a course at the Monroe Institute, control of the RV group was taken away from him in 1984. The small unit was now put under the direct control of the DIA. Obviously, this called for yet another new code name, and Center Lane was replaced by Sun Streak. The only people remaining from the old team were Skip Atwater and Fern Gauvin. Ed Dames, the manipulator who had wanted to become a remote viewer himself, was only permitted to act as an interviewer.

One year later Atwater left the unit and became Director of Research at the Monroe Institute. The morale of the group was visibly falling apart. Jealousies were rampant and chaos reigned supreme. 'Outer beings' announced their presence via the new member, Angela Dellafiora, as soon as she fell into a trance – 'Maurice', for example, or 'George' and even 'Dr Einstein'. These spirits manifested themselves through automatic writing. To give this kind of anomalous gaining of information a spurious air of being scientific, it was treated as a hybrid form of remote viewing and designated by the term written remote viewing (WRV). First-hand sources reported that results were less than meagre and fell far below those of the techniques developed at the SRI.

Nevertheless, Angela Dellafiora sometimes achieved remarkable hits in her trances. In January 1989 the Pentagon wanted to know how Libya would react to the American claim that chemical weapons were being produced in Rabat. In answer, Dellafiora wrote automatically that a ship named 'Patua' or 'Potua' would arrive at Tripoli in order to transport chemicals to a port in eastern Libya. A ship named *Batato* then actually did make fast in Tripoli, was loaded with freight the nature of which remained unknown, and which was then taken to a port in eastern Libya.

Nevertheless, there were considerable controversies with the other remote viewers, particularly with Ed Dames. The high-tech RV system propounded by Ingo Swann was dominated by men, and it found itself opposed by the occult procedures of mediumistic séances, which, it was believed, had been superseded long ago. The magico-mythical archaic swamp had come back to the citadel of the knights of the spiritual renewal of mankind with a vengeance.

In February 1988 the DIA wanted to know where Lieutenant Colonel William Higgins, a senior US Marine officer, was being held in Lebanon. The remote viewers trained by Swann described a specific building in a village in southern Lebanon. Dellafiora, however, wrote automatically that he was being hidden beneath an open field. Shortly thereafter, the remote viewers began receiving the impression that Colonel Higgins was dead. Dellafiora, on the other hand, saw him as still being alive and wrote automatically that he would soon be set free. Higgins was not released. A short time later his tortured body was found. A hostage who had been returned confirmed that at the probable time, Higgins had been held in the building the viewers had described.

Dames, Smith and the other remote viewing recruits had undergone Swann's rigorous training and had received their final polish at the Monroe Institute. They had had enough of the 'witches', who 'channelled' spirits in rattling voices, wrote 'automatically', read palms and gave readings for members of Congress and high-ranking officers. The trained remote viewers were especially annoyed by one of the 'witches'. But no matter how good or bad their allegedly paranormal abilities were, they had to cope with the situation, since persons in rather influential political positions supported the untrained psychics who had established themselves at the unit.

Dames, who was only permitted to be an interviewer, was constantly attempting to gain more influence and, in his turn, contributed to the rapid decline of Sun Streak. The really interesting assignments were few and far between. Always uneasy about diligently doing his duty as a psi spy, Dames filled his leisure time with targets he had chosen himself. Most of them were not on Earth, and he pursued his extraterrestrial interests without any inhibitions. He also had the viewers look into the future and the past, to become witnesses to great historic events like the Crucifixion or the battle of Waterloo. They were also allowed to be present at the appearance of the Virgin Mary at Fatima or to uncover the secret of the Loch Ness monster by paranormal means. During their trips into the world of myths and legends, the remote viewers confirmed what Ed Dames had known all the time: Atlantis lay in Peru – at the bottom of Lake Titicaca. There is no doubt that Ed Dames threw open the door to speculation far wider than the 'witches' had ever done, and the remote viewers willingly walked through completely different 'doors of perception' than Ingo Swann had ever had in mind. This type of data could not be checked in any way. Nevertheless, Ed Dames maintained that 'his' troop was more often right than not, because it confirmed what he himself dreamed up about his mysterious targets. He forgot, however, that he was supplying the viewers with massive doses of front loading in order to achieve the desired results.

## 'PSYCHIC WARRIOR'

The military psi department, which had started off with great ambitions and interesting results, experienced a downfall of Mephistophelian dimensions – a descent into a 'sea of madness'. Nobody epitomized this better than David Morehouse. Captain Morehouse, a member of the Sun Streak team for two years, from 1988 to 1990, was a remote viewer of indifferent success. To compensate for this, he intended to sell his story as a remote viewer all the better. He joined up with Dames, who had left the army and founded the remote viewing consulting firm PsiTech in 1989. Together they wanted to write a best-seller and thereby at least gain the recognition they believed was their due. They hired a professional writer and sold the rights for an advance of $100,000. Morehouse had not hesitated for a second before writing a book about a military project that was top secret, even though he was still in the army. INSCOM learned about the plan and Morehouse was within an inch of receiving a less than honourable discharge. To make matters worse, the wife of a comrade reported him to a superior for sexual harassment. The result was an internal investigation.

Morehouse was clever enough to check into Walter Reed Army Medical Center in Washington, D.C., for psychiatric treatment. He played the part of a depressive and a potential suicide, who was being tortured by visions of angels. It was all the fault of remote viewing, he claimed. It had thrown him completely off balance and he was now in danger of going mad.

Meanwhile, his literary agent was spreading the story that she and Morehouse were being harassed and intimidated by intelligence agents. He was hardly out of hospital before his lawyers were demanding access to information on the secret programme in order to learn about the dangerous methods that had destabilized their client.

This was checkmate for the army. It could not risk a court case that would endanger the secret operations. An out-of-court settlement was reached by which David Morehouse resigned under 'other than honourable' circumstances. Although Morehouse had lost his entitlement to a pension, he now devoted himself all the more unrestrainedly to the glorification of his own person. The original publisher had developed cold feet and pulled out, but in 1996 another publisher issued Morehouse's book under the sensational title *Psychic Warrior*.[50] David Morehouse sold the film rights to Hollywood for $300,000 and no wonder, because in the story the artful author, who had never even heard of psi before he arrived at Fort Meade, appeared as the paranormal super-hero, a Rambo on the mental battlefield. He tells his astonished readers that he was hit on his helmet by a bullet while on a military training exercise in Jordan in 1987. Since then he constantly has visions and OBEs. He is suspended from the services because he refuses to employ psi as a weapon. He is, he alleges, ordered by the Pentagon to send 'malignant brain waves' against the enemies of the state, including Saddam Hussein. These 'brain waves' are intended to cause confusion and disorientation in the target persons and even to kill them. Remote viewing had sunk to such a level of nonsense.

## STAR GATE AND THE END OF THE PSYCHIC SPIES

In 1991 Ed May moved the SRI laboratory a few blocks down the street to a new site, the Cognitive Sciences Laboratory (CSL) of Science Applications International Corporation (SAIC), a major research institute that was also receiving many assignments from the Pentagon.[51]

Ever since Puthoff had left, the psi researchers at the SRI – and later at SAIC – had again been mainly engaged in research. As intended, the research was attempting to support the operational work at Fort Meade to the best of its ability and its newest results were presented directly to the clients. These, however, appeared to show very little interest. Either they were relaxing in highly paid jobs, or their egos had become so inflated that they wanted to impose their own concepts of psi espionage. Where this led is exemplified in the unfortunate written remote viewing with its return to the dawn of occult warfare or in strange excesses, such as the extraordinary story of David Morehouse.

By now the unloved project was being kicked about like a stray dog. In 1994 the DIA again changed the programme's scope and the code name, and relaunched it as Star Gate. But the governmentally supported remote viewing adventure only had one more year to live. The story came full circle in 1995, when the DIA tried to shunt it off to the organization that had started it all almost a quarter of a century before – the CIA. The secret service washed its hands in all innocence and claimed never to have had anything to do with remote viewing.

Congress had requested that the CIA should take over responsibility for the secret project, but before the CIA would accept the obligation, it insisted on having the project evaluated by the American Institutes for Research (AIR) in Washington, D.C. The report was negative. The CIA then publicly disclosed the existence of the programme as well as its intention to give it up. In fact, the project was officially terminated at the end of 1995, but the CIA went so far as to state that from time to time it would work with private contractors. The selection is large, because many of the former remote viewers now have their own companies and offer remote viewing to clients who are prepared to pay.

How did it come about that AIR came to a negative conclusion, despite the obvious successes achieved and the progress made in the development of the methods applied? The answer is simple but appalling. One of the evaluators was Ray Hyman of the University of Oregon at Eugene. He is regarded as being one of the pre-eminent psychologists in the US, but he has been a declared and bitter opponent of parapsychology for many years.[52] The material put at his disposal stemmed exclusively from the final two years of Sun Streak and Star Gate – that is, from the days of the 'witches', RV excursions to Mars and the search for the Ark of the Covenant.

During the long period of funding and application of psi by the intelligence services, innumerable documents piled up in filing cabinets. In order to be able to come to an impartial conclusion, AIR would have had to have studied thousands of pages of data and interview numerous people. AIR was satisfied with short interviews with the three remaining remote viewers and the evaluation of three projects carried out within one year towards the end of Star Gate. The results of one year – and the year of total decline at that – were weighed against uncounted assignments undertaken over a period of 20 years.

AIR conducted a more than questionable test with the three remote viewers. Two of them used 'automatic writing' – the controversial WRV method – and one of the 'witches' consulted her tarot cards like a clairvoyant at a country fair. The third had become so frustrated with his superiors that all he was prepared to say about the programme consisted of cynical remarks. The data made available from the files on intelligence assignments showed how far RV at Fort Meade had fallen. It was clear that extensive 'front loading' had become normal practice.

On the basis of this totally inadequate investigation of the project, AIR came to the untenable conclusion that remote viewing had never been of any real use for intelligence purposes. If AIR had taken the trouble to read all the documents carefully, it would have found reports in the files by clients from former years – the intelligence services, the NSA, various military groupings, even the CIA – which described the usefulness of remote viewing for the gathering of intelligence, sometimes even in glowing terms.

Naturally, not all of the opinions were positive. But the successes far outnumbered the failures, and this is the only explanation why the method was so popular for so long with many services.

It is quite legitimate to speculate whether the AIR report was intended to mislead the public. Was it a clever gambit by the intelligence services? Was the chapter on remote viewing to be declared closed as far as the public was concerned, so that the application of RV could continue in secret?

For several months, a Mr X drew attention to himself on the Internet with a summary of the remote viewing project and the AIR report.[53] Behind the pseudonym – in view of the issue at stake the French term *nom de guerre* would be more appropriate – was Paul Smith, a member of the Fort Meade RV team from 1983 to 1990. He was one of the few chosen ones who had been trained in coordinate remote viewing (CRV) at the SRI by Ingo Swann personally in 1984. Smith was also the primary author of the government RV programme's CRV training manual, and he served as theory instructor for new CRV trainee personnel as well as recruiting officer and unit security officer. He is credited with over a thousand training and operational remote viewing sessions during his time with the unit at Fort Meade.

In his statements Smith made it clear that the AIR report was not a manoeuvre by the intelligence services. The programme had died, and nobody in the services was interested in it any longer. The evaluators had found results that did not justify any further support for the programme. When the material had been given to the AIR, it had included 19 packages containing reports, recommendations and a collection of methods, which had been compiled at the SRI and SAIC and given to the managers of the 'operational programme' between 1988 and 1994. The packages were never opened! How much could be learned from the enormous mass of data from Fort Meade is still – at least for the time being – a secret. In the files there are thousands of carefully documented RV sessions, conducted both for training purposes and during actual operations.

The second evaluator named by AIR was the respected statistician from the University of California at Davis, Jessica Utts. Utts was originally regarded as a sceptic, but became so convinced by the quality and results of the research that she is now one of the most important methodological supporters of parapsychology. In her work, Utts concentrated on the analysis of the scientific work performed at SRI and SAIC, and she came to extremely positive conclusions.[54]

Utts compiled the following catalogue of conclusions about the remote viewing experiments:

1. Remote viewing, the free description of unknown targets, was much more successful than 'guessing' at a limited number of known target symbols.
2. A group of six individuals far exceeded the achievements of unselected subjects.
3. Mass screening showed that about 1 per cent of the volunteers were consistently successful in the tests. Remote viewing is an ability that is unequally distributed among people, in the same way as athletic ability or musical talent.
4. Neither practice nor a variety of training methods led to a continuous improvement of RV achievements.
5. It is unclear if feedback – the disclosure of success or failure – is necessary, but it appears to provide psychological support.
6. The distance between the target and the subject has no effect on the result.
7. Electromagnetic shielding does not inhibit performance.
8. There is overwhelming evidence that precognitive remote viewing, in which the target is selected only after the test person has given the description, is also successful.
9. There is no evidence to support the existence of anomalous perturbation (psychokinesis) – that is, a physical interaction with the environment by psychic means.[55]

In view of the research results, even Ray Hyman, the outspoken critic of parapsychology, had to make an admission in the end that, coming from him, is not far from sensational: 'The statistical departures from chance appear to be too large and consistent to be attributable to statistical flukes of any sort ... I tend to agree with Professor Utts that real effects are occurring in these experiments. Something other than chance departure from the null hypothesis has occurred in these experiments.'[56]

# RETURN OF THE REMOTE VIEWERS

The diehards among the remote viewers climbed out of the ruins towards new adventures. After terminating their military careers, some of them set off to polish the myth of RV as well as their own.

Fortunately, the best remote viewer of all, Joe McMoneagle, has stayed with research. He still works with Ed May in his Cognitive Sciences Laboratory and has just finished his second book, *The Ultimate Time Machine*. In addition, he puts his paranormal talent at the disposal of Dean Radin for his studies at the University of Nevada in Las Vegas. Here he plays an important role in the development of a technology for the future.

When he left the military, McMoneagle's extraordinary achievements as a remote viewer were officially recognized, although, naturally, in rather roundabout terms. Even in view of the well-known plaudits normally offered to departing officers of long service, the words uttered in connection with his being decorated with the Legion of Merit for outstanding intelligence work are rather noteworthy. In the award document McMoneagle is recognized for having been 'one of the original planners and movers of a unique intelligence project that is revolutionizing the intelligence community'. The document goes on to say that he had demonstrated his talents and abilities during more than 200 missions conducted at the behest of the highest intelligence authorities. In the end he had held the position of Special Projects Intelligence Officer. In this capacity, he had used his abilities and specialized knowledge 'addressing essential elements of information ... producing crucial and vital intelligence unavailable from any other source'.[57]

Today McMoneagle offers his services as a remote viewer through his company Intuitive Intelligence Applications. The others from the former team are not far behind. Lyn Buchanan left the service in 1992 and formed a company in Mechanicsville, Maryland, for the training and data analysis of controlled remote viewing (CRV) under the name of P>S>I (Problems>Solutions>Innovations). Paul Smith works as a remote viewer and RV consultant in his own firm, Remote Viewing Instructional Services, Inc.

Ed Dames founded PsiTech in Albuquerque, New Mexico, and then moved to Beverly Hills. His disciple, Courtney Brown, a professor of political sciences at Emory University in Atlanta, went independent in 1995 with his Farsight Institute which, believe it or not, now offers scientific remote viewing (SRV).[58]

Most of these people exaggerate the possibilities of the trainability and practical application of psi. If you listen to Ed Dames, for example, you might come to the conclusion that the psi researchers can close down their laboratories. The controlled application of extrasensory perception has become a reality. Dames claims PsiTech practises remote viewing with a success rate of 100 per cent. In his company brochure, he promises his commercial clients that by using technical remote viewing (TRV) they will realize 'a previously never achieved success rate of 100 per cent'.

In reading such an assertion, about the only thing that can be guaranteed to 100 per cent is the nonsense of the statement. But Ed Dames wants to sell something, after all, and it is not exactly cheap either. A training course lasting one week costs $4500. Meanwhile, dubious training courses are being offered in other countries as well. Such claims and promises only serve to discredit remote viewing and psi research.

Nevertheless, it is important to ask why PsiTech has not yet achieved any of the high-sounding objectives Dames promises – the discovery of the origins of the AIDS virus, for example. The 100 per cent success rate achieved by his team, which applies RV in Ed Dames's words 'with military precision', is restricted to self-announced triumphs that are all – who would have guessed? – top secret and for which we can therefore expect neither confirmation nor denial.

Dames is also dealing in the business of fear and has predicted that terrible catastrophes would occur in 1998. But nobody needs to become unduly worried. Only a few years ago he predicted that there would be public contact with aliens in Chaco Canyon in August 1993. It is quite obvious that PsiTech has neither a reputation to uphold nor the alleged important clients to lose. Ron Pandolphi, a scientist with the CIA who evaluated new and exotic techniques during the days of Sun Streak and Star Gate, only laughs when Dames's company is mentioned. The only paying client PsiTech ever had was a rich man from Baltimore, Dan Smith, who paid $3000 to remote view a crop circle being made!

If somebody pays a lot of money for a course at PsiTech, it will be their own fault. The – according to Dames – highly complex training in TRV can be obtained in a sort of mail-order course from his disciple Courtney Brown under the abbreviation SRV. He entered his manual for scientific remote viewing in the Internet home page of the Farsight Institute.[59] The promises the apprentice makes his readers sound no less astonishing than those made by his master. SRV enables anybody 'to extract accurate and detailed information from distant locations and across time ... with tremendous precision'.

Brown's textbook is primarily based on Ingo Swann's system. He differentiates five phases:

1. Ideograms and recognition of the primitive descriptive characteristics of the target.
2. Involvement of all the senses, the initial perception of magnitudes that are related to the targets dimensions.
3. The preparation of an initial sketch of the target.
4. 'Intimate target contact': the 'subspace mind is allowed total control in solving the remote viewing problem by permitting it to direct the flow of information to the conscious mind'.
5. Guided exploration of the target, including six specialized procedures with which to achieve a dramatic increase in the amount of information gained.

During phase four a complex matrix is prepared, with nine columns for each 'data type', from sensory data (S) to emotional data (E). Now we begin to hold our breath. Brown tells us that we never get anything unless we ask for it. Remote viewing is no exception. Asking consists of moving a pencil to the column for which we wish to receive data paranormally. Since this is a delicate process, we should only touch the paper lightly with the point of the pencil and hold the contact for about one second. The impressions appear as soon as contact with the paper has been made. If the contact is too brief, a sufficiently deep perception cannot occur; if it is too long, the conscious mind interferes.

The point of a pencil on the virginal diagram as a mental on-switch for psi information! It is quite clear what remote viewing, in itself a highly interesting process, has become. The regulations have become far more rigid and 'crazy' than they ever were in the Wehrmacht, despite the vaunted German 'thoroughness'.

# Part 2

## CONTEMPORARY PSI RESEARCH

### Towards a New Understanding of Reality

'Sit down before fact like a little child, be prepared
to give up every preconceived notion, follow humbly
to wherever, and to whatever abysses nature leads or
you shall learn nothing.'

*Thomas Huxley*

'I believe in science, and I am confident that a science
that can boldly contemplate the origin of the universe, the
nature of physical reality $10^{-33}$ seconds after the Big Bang,
anthropic principles, quantum nonlocality, and parallel
universes, can come to terms with the implications of
parapsychological findings – whatever they may turn
out to be. There is no danger for science in honestly
confronting these issues; it can only be enriched
by doing so.'

*Charles Honorton*

# Chapter One
# PARAPSYCHOLOGY IN RUSSIA
## LEGEND AND FACT

### THE STRANGE CASE OF ROBERT TOTH

Since Mikhail Gorbachev's policy of *glasnost*, and even more since the collapse of the Soviet Union and the Warsaw Pact, western researchers in the pay of the CIA have increasingly sought to make contact with their colleagues 'on the other side'. Together with parapsychologist Larissa Vilenskaya, who had emigrated to the United States several years previously, Ed May went to Russia and the Ukraine to obtain a detailed picture of the state of official and unofficial psi research. May met Russian colleagues who had conducted research for the Soviet intelligence service that was very similar to his own. At present May and the still unnamed Russian scientists are in the process of exchanging their experiences.

Were American efforts in parapsychology to re-establish the balance of power of the superpowers only an ongoing attempt to chase after a chimera? As we have already seen, the threat to which the remote viewing programme reacted appears never to have existed. Was it nothing but hot air on both sides? It is quite possible that parapsychologists on both sides have more reason to thank the journalist who spread the story about the USS *Nautilus* than they realize. Before this event, the few research institutes that existed operated on a shoestring. In the Soviet Union the news undoubtedly caused some confusion, and the reaction led to the establishment of broadly designed research programmes that were generously supported by the government. Yet these were basically nothing more than some initial steps in a field that strenuously resisted opening itself to scientific exploration and were nothing the political leaders in the Soviet Union needed to lose any sleep over. But, as we know, it is precisely those things about which we know least that we worry about most. It was more than enough for the Soviets to learn that the United States had put together a research and applications programme, funded by public money and in amounts that the parapsychological institutes could only dream about.

At first, the secret research that had begun in the Soviet Union was, as in the US, as insubstantial as a bubble. But soon incontestable results began to emerge and had to be taken seriously by the other side. The scientists had created the very conditions they had been called upon to counter.

During the First International Symposium on Psychotronic Research, which was held in Prague in the 1970s,[1] Puthoff and Swann appraised the advances in research in the Eastern Bloc, and shortly thereafter a report by the Defense Intelligence Agency (DIA) portraying the dangers of Soviet and Czech parapsychological research was being circulated in intelligence service circles.[2] Had the Russians meanwhile actually achieved their objective and so far developed the anomalous distant influence of humans that they were ready for operational use?

An event that occurred on 11 June 1977 throws some light on the situation. On that day, Robert Toth, a correspondent for the *Los Angeles Times*, was arrested in Moscow and accused of having received illegal papers that disclosed a 'state secret'. The documents had been given to him by the Russian biophysicist Valery Petukhov, and in them Petukhov expounded a complicated theory claiming that living cells emit certain particles when they divide and that these particles could transport information. This process could serve as an explanation for telepathy and related phenomena. Petukhov was the head of the biophysics laboratory of the state-controlled Institute of Medical and Biological Research.

Toth was questioned and told the papers contained top secret material about parapsychological research at a scientific institute of the Soviet state. Shortly thereafter Toth was permitted to leave the country. His story made the rounds in the US press but was then forgotten. The US intelligence services, however, were convinced that Toth had had a glimpse of the tip of the iceberg of secret Soviet psi research.

We must ask ourselves if the bungled hand-over of the documents had been engineered by the KGB. What appears to be suspicious is the fact that the KGB confirmed that 'top secret psi research' with important biological results was being conducted in the Soviet Union. Why make all that fuss if the Russians were bent on keeping this kind of research secret? The feeling remains that the Soviets were attempting to impart deliberate disinformation in their power game with the Americans, who for several years had been successfully conducting psi research at the SRI at the government's behest. Did they intend to create the impression that they were far more advanced in this field than the Americans believed? Ultimately, of course, no one really knew 'if both sides were just playing with each other or if there really was something being developed in the field of extrasensory perception'.[3]

The Soviets were obviously quite willing for the West to learn that psi research was being conducted, and the research was not entirely kept under wraps and carried out away from the public gaze. Increasingly, opinions were allowed to be published in periodicals which were widely circulated and in which the limitations imposed by the state ideology were elegantly turned against themselves to make parapsychology publicly acceptable. One of those who was adept at using this dialectic trick to the advantage of parapsychology was the science writer Leonid Fillipov. In the atheist periodical *Nauka i religia* ('Science and Religion') he criticized the unshakeable hostility to psi of mathematician Alexander Kitaygorodsky with the words: 'What if telepathic phenomena conform to some new, as yet undiscovered laws that do not contradict already known rules governing electrons? Rejecting *a priori* the possibilities of telepathy and other processes still unfamiliar to science amounts to rejecting Lenin's idea that, on any given level of scientific development, our knowledge of the work remains incomplete.'[4]

## DISTANT INFLUENCE: MOSCOW'S ANSWER TO REMOTE VIEWING

In addition to the research that was being carried out behind locked doors, therefore, an official parapsychology was permitted to exist in public, although it did not enjoy the privileges and funds granted to the state-controlled research institutions. In Moscow the military application of psi was being investigated in a well-guarded research institute, the Institute of Problems of Information Transmission. This, however, was only a side show. The real research was being done far away in western Siberia, in the shadows of the Altai Mountains. There, in the centre of the city of Novosibirsk, the Communists realized their concept of a central-ized research facility and called it Akademgorodok, 'Science City'.

In one of the almost 40 scientific centres in Science City, the Institute for Automation and Electrometry, was the mysterious Special

Department 8, which could be visited only by holders of a special code. In Special Department 8 about 60 scientists from all over the Soviet Union were investigating telepathy and distant influence under the heading of 'biocommunication'. One of these, August Stern, who emigrated to France in 1977, revealed details of some horrible experiments that were conducted at Special Department 8 in which kittens were subjected to electric shocks, while their mothers were being monitored for telepathic signals by means of electrode implants in their brains. Another experiment conceived there involved taking baby rabbits under water in a submarine. They were killed far beneath the surface while the brain waves and heart frequencies of their mothers were being recorded on land.

Stern also reported on numerous experiments with biophotons. Photons are the smallest physical units of light on wavelengths of high coherence – that is, light that has been very tightly focused as in a laser beam and is able to transmit information on a low energy level. Biophotons are light units of this sort that radiate from living cells.

The research was into the importance of biophotons in the transmission of information on a cellular level. In one experiment bacteria in a culture were separated by a sheet of glass in order to discover whether a mortal illness could be transmitted to other cells via photons. One group of researchers allegedly succeeded in demonstrating the anomalous transfer of an infection into a sealed cell culture.[5] A change of leadership in the Kremlin led to Special Department 8 being closed down in 1969.

At about this time the KGB and the GRU (the military intelligence service) assumed control of parapsychological research. A nationwide search for paranormally gifted subjects began, and, if we believe the rumours, the Soviets found their own Ingo Swann and Pat Price somewhere in the villages of Siberia and among the academic élite. It is said that Mongolian masters in the martial arts, Tibetan monks and shamans from central Asia were flown to the laboratories to test their abilities in distant influence. These possibilities suggested themselves almost automatically because Novosibirsk lies in a region populated by tribes with shamanic traditions.

In those days V.P. Leutin, a scientist from Leningrad, was conducting experiments in which the EEG patterns of people were recorded while another person in a remote room was receiving 'electrical stimulation' through his fingers for periods of 10 seconds. The 'stimulation' was provided by electric current of varying degrees of intensity, depending on the subject's pain threshold. Leutin found a 'significant correlation' between the electric shocks administered to the sender and the EEG pattern of the percipient, although it was never reported what this significant correlation was.

The only 'significant' aspect of this for the impartial observer is that electric shocks on the borderline of the medium's pain threshold were used to investigate an anomalous transfer of information. We have already seen that at the SRI flashes of light were used, and there are many physiologically relevant stimuli available that are far less cruel. These few examples show that Soviet research was far from squeamish. The researchers no doubt were seeking to obtain the strongest anomalous reactions possible and therefore chose intensive physiological stimuli. Moreover, the institutes that were controlled by the secret services had no need to fear that public disquiet would lead to investigations like those conducted in the United States during the MKULTRA scandal. 'Freedom of research' during the era of the USSR gave psychotronics a hideous face. Distant influence of any sort whatever – that was the declared objective of psi research in the Soviet Union.

In their defence the Soviet scientists claimed that negative emotions were more readily transmittable telepathically and would produce more dramatic results. In one instance an experiment had to be discontinued because the doctors who were observing the EEG of actor Karl Nikolayev recorded such drastic changes that they feared for the health of the percipient. What had happened was that Nikolayev's friend Yuri Kamensky had decided not to transmit pictures telepathically as in previous experiments but rather to transmit emotions. He vividly imagined that he was strangling Nikolayev, who allegedly had to struggle for breath.

A favourite experiment with top psychics in the former USSR appears to have been to make the heart of a frog stop beating. An isolated frog's heart in a physiological solution will usually continue to beat for 30 to 40 minutes and sometimes even longer. Normally the heart can be reactivated by electrical stimulation. The well-known psychokinetic medium Nina Kulagina is said to have caused a frog's heart to stop beating after 40 seconds from a distance of 1 metre under the watchful eye of Gennady Sergeyev. Electro-stimulation was unable to reactivate it. A pathological examination showed that the heart had, literally, been torn apart.

Sergeyev and his colleagues also discovered in their experiments that people with heart problems are well suited to be percipients and that the heartbeats of such people telepathically adjust to the heartbeat of the sender. Sergeyev also had Nina Kulagina influence the vital functions of mice. Under her hand they became immobilized, just as if they were dead. As soon as she took her hand away, they again moved normally.

# PARANORMAL TROJAN HORSES

In the 1970s the KGB required the Popov Institute to install 'bio-electronic' – that is, parapsychological – research laboratories all over the country, in Leningrad, Kiev, Alma Ata, Kishinev, Taganrog, Minsk and Tallinn. As Martin Ebon – probably the foremost expert on the relationship between psi and the KGB in the former Soviet Union – points out, the control of psi research by the KGB need not necessarily be regarded as the workings of a sinister power.[6] The KGB was an integral part of everyday life in the Soviet Union. Its commitment to psi research indicates only that the KGB developed an increased interest in the possibilities of exploiting this paranormal potential. In 1983 Martin Ebon listed no fewer than 29 institutes under the control of the KGB that were conducting psi research.

One of the fears being seriously discussed in the United States reminds us of ancient ideas about magic. It was believed that the Soviets were impregnating presents for western diplomats and politicians with 'negative psi energy' (whatever that was supposed to be). These energies would emanate from the gifts over time and, it was alleged, lead to neurological damage. These fantastic fears had arisen when the West heard news of the psychotronic generators the Czech engineer Robert Pavlita claimed to have invented in the 1960s. These tiny, fantastically designed machines, sometimes reminiscent of Constructivist sculptures, appear not to have served any real purpose, but their inventor claimed that they could store, enhance and radiate psychotronic energy. The scientists in the East applied the term psychotronic (or bioplasmatic) energy to a form of energy that is available to all humans and that is supposed to cause psi phenomena. In the United States there was no instrument that could measure 'psi energy' in any way, let alone accumulate and increase it. For the American intelligence services, with their faith in technology, the rumours about Pavlita's toys were more than reason enough to fear that the Soviets were again in the lead and were possibly planning to do terrible things with invisible and undetectable beams. Meanwhile, psi research in the West was not worried about the 'psychotronic generators'. If psi had been available for technical exploitation by these means, such generators would have been built long ago.

The remote viewers at Fort Meade, however, assumed that if the presents were not contaminated by psychotronic energy that would cause illness, they could possibly be intended to act as 'Trojan horses'. The idea was that Soviet remote viewers had 'memorized' the presents before they had been given to western visitors to the Soviet Union. As with a directional beam, they could then identify the location of the gift mentally and take an uninhibited look around via psi.

Skip Atwater, who, in light of the results achieved by his small team, was prepared to believe almost anything, in all seriousness wrote a report in which he recommended that politicians should not keep presents from Communist countries on the TV set at home but should, instead, keep them in the cellar or in some other place where they would not constantly be confronted by them. A samovar from Brezhnev on the sideboard in the Oval Office in the White House? What a disaster that would be!

Atwater went even further in his recommendations, and it is clear that he took his OPSEC work very seriously. It was obviously impossible to provide protection against remote viewing. No project, no matter how secret it was, could remain hidden from the inner eye of the psi spies. It was necessary, therefore, to develop ways of confusing the enemy remote viewers. Atwater suggested placing absurd objects in sensitive installations – gigantic Mickey Mouse balloons in the silos of intercontinental ballistic missiles, for example. If a Soviet remote viewer were to locate the target and report on a cartoon figure with huge ears, the controllers would conclude that the remote viewer's 'psi radar' had been off target. The US military, however, was not prepared to follow this logic.

Such fears and speculations in the West about the technical uses and strengthening of psi gradually led to the idea that the Soviets had a 'psi weapon'. This certainly sounded extremely dangerous, but no one really knew what this psi weapon was supposed to do. Martin Ebon was able to prove that although Soviet psi research was real and applications-orientated, it was far behind what was being done in the West, and there could be no talk of a 'psi weapon'.[7] Nevertheless, as we have seen, the US government allowed itself to be convinced by the 'psi wars' lobby, thus creating the paradoxical situation that the United States continued to support psi research programmes that were based (as we now know) on a fallacious understanding of Soviet successes in this field.

What the 'psi weapon' was actually all about can be determined with some degree of certainty today. The issue was the influencing of humans by electromagnetic waves – microwaves and extremely low-frequency

(ELF) waves. These can, in fact, have terrible effects on humans, and they do, therefore, constitute a real danger. But they have nothing in common with psi, except for some unsubstantiated rumours.

## SHADES OF THE PAST: RUSSIA'S NEW PSI RESEARCH

The doyen of Russian parapsychology is Alexander Dubrov of the Library of Natural Sciences of the Russian Academy of Sciences in Moscow. He is regarded as the spokesman for the modern attitude to psi, and he is more of a theoretician than an empiricist. As such, he has taken over the formula repeatedly expounded in the West during the last two decades: the natural sciences are undergoing a fundamental change, in the course of which parapsychology will receive its place in the developing new structure. Dubrov regards psi phenomena and the physics of consciousness as a quantum-mechanical process and man as a 'quantum subject', thereby leading straight to the controversy that lies at the heart of the discussion about modern consciousness research. He suggests that science should investigate the physical side of psi and the psychophysics of altered states of consciousness in order to come to a better understanding of paranormal phenomena.[8]

But something that sounds reasonable, 'modern', almost 'western', is still a long way from becoming a programme. It is still a wish, a recommendation, perhaps. Russian psi research still has to free itself from the accretions of the past before it can present itself afresh, unencumbered by ideological restrictions and political directives. Simply adopting a new terminology and forming new associations is just not sufficient. Many of the new programmes are still focused on the old theory of distant influence and the study of human energy fields, although in this context in Russia the term now used is 'energo-informational fields'. In Russia old-fashioned extrasensory perception, which in the West has now mutated into anomalous cognition, does not deny its biological-physical origins. There, the anomalous transfer of information is called an exchange via 'energo-informational channels', and one of the new associations supporting research in this field is consequently known as the Committee for the Study of the Natural Energo-Informational Processes. Anomalous mental phenomena are regarded as a new scientific trend in research on the phenomenon of 'healing', which is called 'bioenergetics'.[9] Official medical organizations now employ gifted healers, and an association of Russian healers has been formed. At many symposia we see how strong the interest in this topic has become, but we also observe the alarming degree to which the quality of the work performed in this field varies. In this sector, as in so many others, Russia is certainly undergoing a period of transition.

The hope remains that a change towards positively directed research will yet come about. Because of its long tradition in the area of distant influence, Russian science can contribute a wealth of experience that may prove of great value in the solution of pressing problems on the question of healing. A brief summary of the best and most important current research programmes offers some insight into a Russian psi research that is caught between the old and the new paradigm.

At the A.S. Popov Association for Radio-electronics and Communication in Moscow Anatoli Arlashin recently conducted an experiment in which trained psychics attempted to interfere with the mental processes of another person from a distance.[10] The volunteer students who took part in the experiment were not told what it was about. Their task was only to solve mathematical problems with their eyes closed and without the aid of paper and pencil. The mental 'interference' was to be provided by a group of psychics who had been trained in special methods of imaging. The students were first led into the room where the psychics were assembled, allegedly to answer some questions but, in fact, with the sole purpose of allowing the psychics to meet their target group personally in order to establish a contact. In the experiment, the psychics attempted mentally to bombard the subjects with a stream of numbers. At the same time, they tried to send feelings of panic, insecurity and lack of self-confidence. During the experiment the students and the psychics were in different rooms. The students were assigned to different groups at random. In one group the mental interference took place during the solution of the first three problems, in another it took place during the solution of the last three, and in a third it was during the solution of the second, fourth and sixth problems. A fourth group served as control group and was not subjected to mental interference.

The first group, which had to solve the first three problems under the influence of mental interference, needed a significantly longer time than those not being anomalously distracted. It took them 42 per cent longer to solve the problems by mental arithmetic. It was notable that two of the psychics, Ludmilla Korabelnikova and Karl Nikolayev, whom we previously came across in the experiment with the mental stranglehold, were able to create particularly strong effects. Under their mental influence, the time required for the solution of the problems rose by 71.6 per cent.

When mental interference was applied during the solution of the last three problems, the time required for solution still rose markedly, but only by 21 per cent. Interestingly, this effect is comparable to 'normal' interference during the mental solution of problems. When we prepare for the solution of a problem requiring concentration, any distraction will affect the process and therefore the time required to solve the problem. If we are already further along in the process before the distraction occurs, we tend to react to the distraction by concentrating more.[11]

Such experiments remind us of reports alleging that during summit meetings, Soviet psychics interfered with the thought processes of western diplomats and high-ranking politicians.

Andrei Lee, director of the Moscow Leonid L. Vasiliev Trust for Parapsychology, is one of the busiest researchers in modern Russian parapsychology. He studies altered states of consciousness under the influence of magnetic, electromagnetic and acoustic fields, by which the effectiveness of anomalous transfer of information is supposedly increased.

Juri Dolin, who is among the most conscientious researchers in modern Russian parapsychology, is also currently studying mental influencing. In one of his experiments, subjects were telepathically to put a person in another room into alternating conditions of activity and relaxation.[12] The subject was in a dark room, which had been acoustically and electrically shielded, and his EEG was continually recorded. He did not know whether a given phase of the experiment was a control phase or an experimental phase. Dolin wanted to find out if the mental command to become active would result in a suppression of alpha waves and if the mental intention to relax would cause an increase of alpha waves. During the phase of activation, the alpha waves in both the left and the right hemispheres diminished significantly. During the phase of relaxation, an increase of alpha frequency could be observed in both hemispheres.

What is remarkable about current research in extrasensory perception in the independent states of the former Soviet Union is the strong preference for the influence model. The researchers show a clear tendency towards wanting to reduce almost everything paranormal to psychokinesis. We can deduce this from the fact that in telepathy experiments Russians concentrate more on the sender than on the percipient. Consequently, they call the sender an 'inductor' – that it, someone who actively causes an effect. In western parapsychology, on the other hand, the focus is on the percipient. This is clearly demonstrated in the evolution of the remote viewing process, which initially began as a classic experiment in telepathy with an outbound experimenter acting as a sender. In the course of time, the sender was dispensed with and the process of anomalous cognition came to be regarded primarily from the point of view of information reception and not information transmission.

# LIVING SYSTEMS AS TARGETS

Psychokinetic distant influence of living systems has its roots in 'classic' Russian tradition. In this context we may also speak of bio-PK (psychokinesis on biological systems). The orientation of research is not towards exploring the possibilities of paranomal healing but towards basic research, and the key question being examined is how different living systems react to mental influence. Far more emphasis than in the West is being placed on the search for psi detectors within organisms, on the assumption that psi is primarily a biological mechanism that 'reflects' much more strongly in living systems than in other material systems.

Georgi Gurtovoy, head of the Laboratory on Applying Isotopes in Ophthalmology in Moscow, and physicist Alexander Parkhomov have devoted themselves to the distant influence of physical systems that produce random fluctuations. Their instruments have been able to register micro-PK effects, even between Moscow and Novosibirsk, a distance of about 3000 kilometres. But the two scientists also worked with living systems as targets for anomalous distant influence, such as with *Gnathonemus petersii*, a species of fish. These fish direct themselves by means of electric signals, which they send in pulses. Apparently, psychics were able to slow down the rate of the pulses.

Biologists Tatjana Krendeleva and Sergei Pogosyan of the Division of Biophysics of Moscow State University conducted some interesting experiments for the mental influencing of living systems. In a complex experiment, the psychic and healer Igor Verbitsky succeeded in increasing the ability of certain cells to react to a compound (latex) that stimulates cell activity. The effect was achieved by an increase in the production of active forms of oxygen.

Sergei Speransky, a toxicologist at the Institute of Hygiene in Novosibirsk, is responsible for a series of interesting psi experiments with animals. In one experiment a population of mice that had grown up together in the same cage was separated. While one group was fed as usual, the other group was starved. The mice that were being fed normally suddenly and inexplicably began to eat much more than before and gained weight significantly. Speransky believes that the experiment reproduces a natural situation in which one part of an animal population 'feels' that another part is starving, leading to a psi-based compensatory behaviour in which it eats more. On the basis of such experiments, Speransky came to the conclusion that telepathy is a basic biological function for the maintenance of primary life-conserving needs – thus, the starving mice automatically send a signal meaning 'food is scarce', which leads those mice that can find food to eat in excess of their needs in order to lay in a store of nutrition.

Sir Alister Hardy, the famous British biologist at Oxford University, had already proposed the theory that telepathic communication between animals can affect evolution and adaptation. According to him, animal habits can spread by a 'quasi-telepathic' process, and a 'paranormal pool of existence' among the members of a species can function by a method that could be compared to telepathy. The newest controversial theories advanced by the English biologist Rupert Sheldrake are based on such considerations. Sheldrake postulates the existence of 'morphogenetic fields', within which non-local effects – undiscovered forms of communication over space and time – occur within a species by means of a mysterious 'morphic resonance'.[13]

Together with the electrical engineer Leonid Porvin, Sergei Speransky recently conducted a further study, in which the eating habits of mice were to be influenced over a distance of almost 3000 kilometres. Five experimental and five control groups of mice were in Novosibirsk, while Porvin himself was in Moscow. Porvin was given photographs of the groups of mice. The animals were left without nourishment for 18 hours but were then given generous amounts of food and water. Porvin chose one of the photographs and, following a protocol of random selection, concentrated on whether 'his' mice were to gain or to lose weight. In a series of 70 individual attempts, the results showed statistically significant correlations to Porvin's intentions.

At the Division of Animal and Human Physiology of the Simferopol State University, Natalia Yanova conducted a series of experiments with animals as targets.[14] Yanova's field of interest is the complex pattern of social interaction of rats and whether this can be influenced by the intentions of a psychic. In a group of six rats one animal normally dominates, two or three are subdominant, and the rest are passive. If individual animals are taken out of the group after the social pattern has been established and are kept in social isolation for a time, they will subsequently fight to regain their territories. This leads to an effect with which biologists are familiar – that is, the dominant animals remain dominant, the subdominant animals remain subdominant, but their specific role behaviour has become more marked because they have been in isolation.

Under these control conditions, Yanova ran three different tests to identify the influence of magnetic fields, the influence from the intentions of an observer and the influence of a magnetic field together with an observer. The observer was to attempt to produce a stimulating effect with positive emotions from a distance of about 4 metres. Under the influence of the magnetic field, the subdominant animals became dominant and the degree of aggression of all the animals rose markedly. Under the mental influence of the observer, the hierarchic structure in the social pattern disappeared. Dominant and subdominant animals could no longer be distinguished from each other. Under the joint influence of the magnetic field and the observer, the animals behaved as they had under the influence of the observer alone; in other words, social differences disappeared.

This experiment may be interpreted as the attempt to find a way to counteract the possibly harmful or destructive influences of electromagnetic fields with the help of a focused mental effect. And in a sense, it was successful, as was shown by a biochemical examination of the animals. Increased amounts of noradrenaline and dopamine appeared in the brains of the animals exposed to magnetic fields; these are neurotransmitters that govern behaviour in both animals and humans, and an increase of these two substances results in increased aggression. Interestingly, the dominant animals that were subjected to the mental influence of the psychic still showed a fairly high level of noradrenaline, but they no longer behaved like dominant animals. Under the influence of both magnetic field and observer, the amounts of noradrenaline and dopamine were of the same order of magnitude as under the magnetic field alone, but there was no increased aggression. .

The scientists assume that the psychic exerts an influence similar to the regulatory function that is performed by the human cerebral cortex. A person with a generally heightened level of noradrenaline does not exhibit aggressive behaviour. It would appear that an anomalous, purely mental, regulating and controlling influence on animal behaviour is possible. The question of how far the behaviour of the group is influenced by a telepathic exchange of information among the animals after social isolation was not considered in this study, and it would be worth extending this innovative work in contemporary Russian psi research by further experiments to explore this question.

Such experiments have been conducted in France in recent years. The imaginative experimenter is the French biologist René Peoc'h from Saint Jean de Boireau. Peoc'h chose rabbits for one of his experiments because these animals are very prone to fear, and stress can clearly be identified by physiological measurements. Even when they are in a state of relaxation, rabbits show spontaneous fear reactions. From a single litter, Peoc'h raised the female rabbits in pairs in complete isolation for a period of eight months. He recorded the animals' peripheral circulation by means of photoplethysmography. During the experiment, the animals were separated and put into sound-proof isolation cages for periods of 16 minutes. In such cages the animals behave in a much more relaxed manner than when they are in the open. After an animal had been removed from its normal environment, a distinct change in circulation, lasting for at least 6 seconds, was defined as a spontaneous attack of fear. It was discovered that the attacks of fear in animals that had been raised together frequently occurred close together in time (within no more than 10 seconds). In animals that had not been raised together, a correlation in the time span in which attacks occurred was observed far less frequently. They occurred within a pattern of random distribution. This statistically significant effect indicates an anomalous exchange of information between the animals that had been raised together.[15]

Psi research with living systems naturally also includes plants. At the international symposium of the Parapsychological Association in Toronto in 1993 a research team led by Juri Dolin reported on results that might reopen the debate on the Backster effect (see Part I, Chapter 2).[16] Dolin prepared electrophysiological recordings of 7- to 15-day-old cucumber plants. The plants and the measuring equipment were placed in a grounded metal chamber. The subjects, who were in another room, were told to increase or inhibit the plants' physiological reaction to an external stimulus. The external stimulus consisted of a change in the light conditions. For periods lasting 3 minutes, the plants were exposed to darkness. Before each attempt, the subject stated whether he would concentrate on inhibiting or increasing the plant's reaction. The results were compared with control measurements at which no subject was present. The difference between stimulation and inhibition was constantly in agreement with the subject's intentions, and a statistically significant effect was observed, which clearly indicated a mental interaction with the electrophysiological reaction of the plant.

A further experiment in this series, in which only one of two plants standing 40 centimetres apart was to be influenced, was particularly convincing. It was shown that the mental interaction can be directed and would lead to the desired effect only in the target plant.

An experiment with Yevgeny Bondarenko, an experienced dowser,[17] confirmed the selective precision of bio-PK effects. In the early 1990s Bondarenko was involved with the navy in St Petersburg in locating enemy ships and submarines by paranormal means. The Russian army even organized special courses in the use of divining rods and pendulums for its soldiers. When he was with the navy in St Petersburg, Bondarenko was also put at the disposal of biologist Yuri Tyagotin, who was carrying out experiments. It is alleged that Bondarenko was able to distant influence a single cell culture chosen at random from of rows of between 24 and 96 cell cultures. The adjacent cultures, which were only 2 centimetres away from the target culture, were not affected.

## THE AWAKENING OF THE SOUL

Parapsychology in the independent states of the former Soviet Union has many different aspects. We have seen that its historical roots were grounded in a materialistic view of the world. The scientists were investigating physical and physiological effects without taking the psyche or any spiritual connections into account. Research was regarded as purely operational, with the aim of finding how anomalous human functions could be exploited in practice. The ideal, to which the most daring hopes, wildest speculations and darkest wishes clung, was distant influence of any sort whatsoever.

A second, powerful tradition attempted to make itself heard in the related field of parapsychology. Since the collapse of state-prescribed communism, an inherent source, long closed off, has resurfaced. Spirituality and religion, the pre-eminent features of the Russian soul, which were forced underground for so many decades, are again raising their claims to be the guiding principles in the understanding of man and his position in the world. In the field of anomalous mental phenomena, this tradition appears in the connection between psi and transpersonal psychology. Suddenly the fear of a spiritualization of science has disappeared. The scientists in those regions formerly protected by the Iron Curtain from the curiosity and the decadent way of life of the West have recognized and emphasized the connection between transpersonal psychology and paranormal experiences far more strongly than their colleagues in the West.

The so-called 'transpersonal' point of view includes any field of interest seriously studying an expanded reality[18] – a reality that transcends the personal, the experience of reality tied to the small personal ego. Any transpersonal orientation has to do with the dimension of religion, therefore, but with a religion or spirituality that is non-denominational and expresses the urge to expand mentally in the depth of one's own soul. This is one reason why transpersonal psychology employs eastern spiritual practices, such as meditation, to create the framework in which man's spiritual being can shake off its inhibitions on the road to expansion.

This new point of departure appears to have come in the nick of time in the independent states of the former Soviet Union. Had the enormous country not encompassed many different cultures, ideologies and religions? Today, in a return to tradition, they are being rediscovered and examined in the search for answers to the unfathomable phenomena of existence.[19] Modern psi research in Russia is primarily looking to Asian religious concepts to provide a framework for extrasensory and psychokinetic effects, in order to find new, untried approaches to research. In addition, transpersonal psychology is being welcomed with enthusiasm as a link in this chain, because it appears to offer an encompassing picture in which mystic experiences and 'experiences of enlightenment' can just as readily be accommodated as experiences of rebirth, near-death experiences or extrasensory communication with other people and beings.

This was demonstrated in April 1997 at the international conference in Moscow on Special States of Human Consciousness, Experimental and Theoretical Parapsychological Research. Of the 55 papers read, 12 were on the subject of transpersonal psychology. Many speakers referred to spiritual content, meditation and psi healing. While the quality of the contributions varied to a surprisingly wide degree, the conference showed how vigorously questions of parapsychology are being discussed in Russia and how urgently research is searching for a new paradigm to guide this field of science. The new generation is quite obviously prepared to throw off the fetters of the materialistic and biologically orientated tradition that led to the dubious programmes of distant influence. At the same time, by adopting the transpersonal point of view, it will be able to regain the central religious dimension that is so important in Russian tradition and that was buried for such a long time.

It is interesting to note in this context that in the West the traditional school of parapsychology defined its work as a battle against materialism. The great pioneers J.B. Rhine and Hans Bender repeated this conviction time and again. If it was possible to prove the reality of the paranormal, man's mental, spiritual dimension would be saved. While it may sound paradoxical, Rhine and Bender rejected the mixing of psi and religion. Bender used to repeat an instructive anecdote. In the early 1970s, when Uri Geller caused a virtual 'epidemic of spoon-bending', Bender's Institute for Border Areas of Psychology and Mental Hygiene in Freiburg examined numerous people who claimed they could bend spoons para-normally, just like Geller. The tests were disappointing, and none of the people was able to demonstrate this alleged ability.[20] One elderly woman had reported that during one of Geller's appearances on television she had been holding a large ladle in her hand and it had bent without her having done anything. On closer questioning the lady admitted that she had bent the ladle by force, 'so that Geller would be right, because there is something religious in this!'.

Bender used this story to illustrate the illusion to which, he believed, many people succumb in connection with psi phenomena – that is, an inadmissible connection between psi and the sphere of religion. But the connection is possibly closer than the old élite of parapsychologists were ready to admit. The new Russian parapsychologists apparently believe that the connection is quite plausible.

Parapsychologist Erlendur Haraldsson from Iceland recently presented some arguments in support of this point of view. Haraldsson discovered that very religious people and those who believe in life after death did much better in psi tests than those who described themselves as being barely religious.[21]

In Russian psi research we can detect a change that may lead to a new orientation through the return of the spiritual dimension. The sphere of spirituality in which parapsychology is being placed has also given west-ern researchers pause. One of the great challenges facing future research will be the examination of the connection between mystic experiences, religious convictions and the experience of psi.

It would appear that scientists from another country may be able to contribute fundamental insights in this context. This country was an unmarked page in the history of parapsychology but could, because of its position *vis-à-vis* the great powers, be seen as an ideal candidate for secret military psi research, a country that almost completely robbed itself of its heritage in a cultural revolution without precedent. I am obviously speaking about the People's Republic of China, but there too, a return to traditions is responsible for east Asia today experiencing a previously unknown interest in anomalous phenomena.

# Chapter Two

# PSYCHIC REVOLUTION IN THE MIDDLE KINGDOM

## EXCEPTIONAL FUNCTIONS OF THE HUMAN BODY

It is rumoured that, after the collapse of the Soviet Union in 1989, a time when the transfer of such information on the black market was seen as a business opportunity, the Russians sold their psi files to the Japanese as a package. According to insider information, the clever Russians also sold a copy of the files to the Chinese.[22]

Whether such stories are pure fantasies – an explanation I tend to believe – or whether the American intelligence services regarded China as a serious threat in the psi race remains a secret for the time being. In any case, since the Communists came to power in China, the tender shoot of 'parapsychology' was regarded as having been weeded out. Was there, then, really anything to fear?

Long before the Soviet psi files were alleged to have fallen into Chinese hands, an occult storm broke out in China, the like of which had never been seen before. On 11 March 1979 the Chinese newspaper *Sechuan Daily* published a report about a 12-year-old boy, Tang Yu,[23] who was alleged to be able to read texts held to his ear. Two months later, children appeared all over China who were able to perform this feat equally well. The clair-voyant children triggered a boom, just as Uri Geller's 'spoon-bending' had done in the West. Was it a trick or a paranormal phenomenon?

In October 1981 parapsychologist Stanley Krippner of the Saybrook Institute in San Francisco organized an expedition to China with some of his colleagues. One of those who went along was Hal Puthoff. The para-psychologists were shown the clairvoyant children and the results of experiments during which inexplicable physical effects had occurred. Chinese characters on a piece of rice paper in a light-proof box were laid on a highly sensitive film. Inside the box were electro-optical detectors, which registered the occurrence of photons. As soon as a child attempted to ascertain – in Hal Puthoff's terminology to remote view – the charac-ters, the optical detectors recorded light impulses on the infrared as well as on the visible band. The light impulses were allegedly sufficient to expose the film, on which the characters then appeared. This was true, however, only for those characters that had been correctly identified.[24] It was this observation that led to Puthoff's investigations into whether the RV process was also accompanied by psychokinetic effects.

In the West other scientific circles took notice when, at the conference of the Parapsychological Association in Cambridge in 1982, scientists Chen Hsin and Mei Lei from Beijing gave a presentation on the subject of the unbelievable achievements of the Chinese children.[25] Apparently, the children were able to reproduce numbers, symbols and sketches with astonishing exactitude, even though they had been hidden from their eyes on a piece of paper that had been folded, simply by holding the paper to a part of their body. The Chinese scientists did not call this clairvoyance but classified the ability under the heading of exceptional functions of the human body (EFHB). Since then, this has been the official label under which psi research is conducted in China.[26] The term is also a programme – there are rare, extraordinary phenomena in connection with abilities of the human body and the mechanisms of the central nervous system. Their investigation is no more than an extension of the known sciences of medicine, physiology and biology.

Shortly after the conference in Cambridge, we were visited at the Institute for Border Areas of Psychology and Mental Hygiene in Freiburg by Dr Wei Nengrun, Vice-president of the Chinese Parapsychological Association and faculty member of Wuhan University. He reported some almost unbelievable achievements. Under strictly controlled scientific conditions, some children were allegedly able, in over 80 per cent of the cases, correctly to identify drawings, numbers and letters held to their ears. Such a high success rate contradicts the data from parapsychologi-cal research. It is safe to assume that in these experiments, the conditions might not always have been 'airtight', making normal sensory perceptions possible.

The German physician Stefan Buchmann had taken part in some of these demonstrations under the supervision of Wei Nengrun. The psychics were two girls, Xiong Jie and Li Hong-wu, and they astounded the investigators by obviously being able clairvoyantly to perceive not only sketches, numbers and Chinese characters, but also Latin letters, which were unknown to them. The pieces of paper were folded so that the drawings could not be seen and then placed in their armpits or in the hollow of their knees. After a short time, the young Chinese girls drew what they had perceived. The degree of accuracy was astonishing and often contradicted the observation – also rediscovered during remote viewing – that anomalous information is normally perceived in fragments.

The girls were able to reproduce not only characters, but also the sketch of a house exactly in perspective, or the symbol $\pi$, and the Latin letters 'EKG' were reproduced as 'EAG'. On one occasion Stefan Buchmann wrote the number 28 on a piece of paper, carefully folded it so that Xiong Jie could not read it and placed it in the hollow of her knee. About five minutes later she first drew a 2, then a Q. Stefan Buchmann stated later: 'Even though this did not correctly reproduce the number I had written, I must admit that some form of perception had taken place.'

While the precautions taken during such exploratory experiments were not ideal, it soon became apparent that China must have a fantastic arsenal of paranormally gifted subjects. This is hardly astonishing. The mass screening at the SRI had shown that approximately 1 per cent of the population has extraordinary psi talents, and although 1 per cent does not sound like very much, in a population of over 1 billion people as in China, we are talking about a potential of 10 million extraordinary psychics.

The wave of enthusiasm for exceptional functions of the human body resulted in the formation of groups for the study of the phenomenon at all the universities and even in schools. More than 500 scientists took up the challenge. From the very beginning one of the most important Chinese scientific periodicals, *Ziran Zazhi* ('Nature Magazine'), published numerous articles in which experiments in this field were described. The topic was extended to include psychokinesis after it was discovered that some of the children were able to influence small physical objects. For example, they were able to bend matches or move the hands on a clock. Such reports deserve to be treated with some degree of scepticism. After all, a standard parlour trick involves moving the hands of a wristwatch so adeptly and quickly that the wearer of the watch does not notice anything. Yet scepticism quickly changes to astonishment when we read reports about such experiments, including, for example, those by biologist Zhu YiYi from Shanghai, who took part in many experiments and later became the publisher of a scientific periodical for this type of research. 'The subjects faced the back of the clock, and the monitors faced its front. The monitors could see the movement of the clock hands clearly. I was fortunately able to observe these tests in the laboratory of the University of Yun Nan several times. You can understand my surprise when I saw the clock hands turn around very quickly without any physical manipulation.'[27]

This was not the only surprise awaiting the biologist. Once she examined a 13-year-old girl who claimed that she could unlock doors by mental force alone. Zhu YiYi brought a padlock along that she had bought in Shanghai specially for this test. With it she locked a door, took out the key and put it in the pocket of her jacket where she held it firmly in her hand through the duration of the test. After 14 minutes of intense concentration the girl declared that the lock was open. And in fact, it was open![28]

Because they had been isolated from the rest of the world for so long, the Chinese scientists were the 'wild boys' of parapsychology, acting just like Kaspar Hauser. They set out to discover paranormal phenomena as if from scratch. Because they had no inkling of the results of a century of intensive psi research in the West, they were able to adopt a completely new approach. They used a range of instruments as possible detectors and were able to record modulated infrared emissions and gamma photons, while physical, chemical and biological detectors recorded other inexplicable emissions. The researchers soon discovered how weak the phenomena of exceptional functions of the human body are and how extremely difficult and complex psi research can turn out to be.

## QIAN XUESEN AND THE PSI BOOM

During this period of enthusiasm for the new field of research the presence of one man sealed the subsequent fate of the burgeoning science. This man was no less a person than Qian Xuesen, China's 'father of space technology'. During the 1930s Qian had studied at the Massachusetts Institute of Technology (MIT) in Boston, and later on at the Jet Propulsion Laboratory of the California Institute of Technology, where

he advanced to become Goddard Professor of Jet Propulsion and a leading pioneer of rocket development. In 1955 Qian applied for permission
to return home. Unwillingly, the US government decided to let the great
scientist go in exchange for 11 American pilots from the Korean War. The
American government allegedly later regretted this decision. It was
believed that without Qian Xuesen, China would not have been capable of
joining the circle of nuclear and space travel powers so quickly.[29]

Qian Xuesen pointed out that extrasensory and psychokinetic phenomena were only the secondary effects of an underlying means of information
transfer, namely the life energy *qi*, and he told the publishers of *Ziran Zazhi*
in a private conversation in 1980: 'Nobody has ever undertaken to discover
the ultimate capabilities of the human body. Henceforth, we should use
science and technology to study human potential. Thus we should study
Chinese traditional medical theories, qigong, exceptional functions of the
human body, and so on. In the end, all this will result in developing the
exceptional functions you have been studying.'[30]

After this quite optimistic initial public statement, a bitter controversy
developed between Qian and the dogmatic social scientist Yu Guangyuan,
whose numerous posts included that of Director of the Institute for
Marxism, Leninism and the Thoughts of Mao Zedong. Yu claimed that
paranormal phenomena contradicted Marxism, Leninism, dialectic
materialism and the known laws of contemporary science and that they
could not, therefore, be true. Furthermore, he refused to take part in any
EFHB experiments. The debate escalated. Qian, who meanwhile called the
new science 'somatic science', predicted a breakthrough that would lead
to a new revolution in science and technology and completely alter the
future of mankind. This change would be far more fundamental than the
scientific revolutions at the beginning of the twentieth century, which
had been set off by the development of relativity and quantum theory.[31]

In a centrally controlled state such controversies are decided not on
the intellectual plane but by political judgement. Since nobody wanted to
be on the side of the loser, both sides appealed to the Party to pronounce
a verdict. On 13 May 1982 the Secretary General of the Communist Party
of the People's Republic of China, Hu Yaobang, decided in favour of Yu,
but Qian's great fame led to a diplomatic decision. Psi research was
classed as a 'not officially accepted field of research', but a small circle of
scientists was given permission to continue to investigate these phenomena.
Any mention of the phenomena in the media was prohibited, and the
scientists were allowed to report their results only in papers circulated

within the group. From then on no further articles on psi could be read in *Ziran Zazhi* and the topic disappeared from newspapers, radio and television. Among the population as a whole the matter was soon forgotten or people wrongly believed that psi phenomena had been exposed as fraudulent and that the Party had banned their investigation.

For four years the innumerable passionate and chaotic investigations that had thrown the country into turmoil were replaced with quiet research projects that were carried out behind the closed doors of a few selected institutes. The most important projects took place in a militarily controlled institute in Beijing. The sudden disappearance of psi from the public stage combined with the fact that the military was continuing research in secret made the Americans assume that China had now also jumped on the bandwagon of the psi arms race.

## BREAKING THROUGH THE BARRIER OF MATTER

The Institute of Space Medico-Engineering (ISME) in a Beijing suburb is a huge scientific complex. In its three departments, space medicine, the man–machine–environment system and the science of the human body are being studied. But ISME is a military institution, and the scientists wear uniforms. The institute had originally been founded in the 1960s to provide medical support for Chinese astronauts. When manned space flight was postponed indefinitely, the excellent laboratories and experienced scientists were left with nothing to investigate. Together with Zhang Zhenhuan, a high-ranking political and military functionary, Qian Xuesen succeeded in having psi research installed under Chen Hsin, the head of ISME. Thus the investigation of exceptional functions of the human body found a home in the third department of the ISME.

On the campus of ISME you would frequently run into a friendly young man who was always accessible and ready to have some fun. The man was neither a student nor a scientist. His name was Zhang Baosheng, and he was an ordinary worker from the province of Jiangsu. But that appeared to be about all that was 'ordinary' about him. Almost everybody knew him, but many of those on the site looked at him askance. Zhang lived in a roomy house on the campus of the institute, with a television set, a video recorder, a video camera and much else besides. His own cook took care of his physical well-being, and when he wanted to have a bit of fun, he made the streets in Beijing unsafe in his American limousine with its police siren.

The young man who enjoyed these unusual privileges was the star subject of the psi researchers, and in their scientific publications he was known only as Z. Before he had been made exclusively available to the scientists at the ISME, 19 scientists under Lin Shuhuang of the physics department of Beijing Teacher's College had conducted psychokinetic experiments with Zhang, whose speciality was truly amazing – he moved pieces of paper with identifying symbols, small chemically active objects and even marked living insects through the walls of sealed containers.[32]

In one of the experiments with Z, a chemically treated piece of paper was placed inside one half of a glass flask, which had been constricted at the midpoint by melting. Chemically treated cotton was inserted in the other half. If the cotton were to touch the paper, a detectable chemical reaction would occur. The top of the test tube was permanently sealed with a piece of special paper. The flask and its contents were in front of Zhang Baosheng for 5 minutes, while four monitors watched carefully from different positions. Then the paper lay outside the flask, which was completely intact, and the seal was also undamaged. The scientists had not seen the process. At one instant the glass flask held its contents; in the next the paper was outside the flask. An analysis revealed traces of a chemical reaction on the cotton. The scientists assumed that the paper had passed 'through' the cotton in order to get outside the flask.

In another experiment a marked living insect was placed inside a sealed glass test tube. If any attempt were made to open the flask, a fine hair that had been glued to the inside of the flask would break. Again two scientists watched Zhang, who stood next to the flask. Two minutes later the insect was merrily crawling about outside the hermetically sealed container.

On one occasion such an experiment was successfully filmed with a high-speed camera taking 400 shots per second. The film shows a pill moving through the wall of an hermetically sealed glass container.[33] On one exposure the pill can be seen as it is penetrating the glass wall, on the next it is half inside and half out, and on the third it is completely outside the container. If the effect really can be seen on only three exposures of a high-speed film, this would explain why the scientists could detect the objects only when they are inside and then outside the containers. The human eye is incapable of following so rapid a process. Unfortunately, it appears that no scientist outside China ever saw this film.

It is a significant indication of both the sources supporting this research and the importance attributed to it that in 1987 the military's

Spaceflight Department awarded this film the Scientific Research Achievement Prize of the second class.

Z was not the only subject at the ISME to have extraordinary abilities, but he was certainly the one about whom the most bizarre phenomena were reported. However, the scientists also had the opportunity to work with a man, Yan Xin, about whom truly miraculous deeds were rumoured in another area. In western terms, Yan was a sort of miracle healer. He is alleged even to have instantaneously healed people with multiple fractures, enabling them to go back to work immediately. His successes were so numerous that his patients began to write articles about him. Yan became famous throughout the country and began to give talks in front of huge crowds. His presentations filled arenas holding up to 30,000 people, but these were not presentations as we know them in the West. They normally lasted for between 6 and 14 hours without interruption. Most of the listeners did not leave their places during the whole of this time, either to relieve their bodily needs or to take nourishment. There are stories that paralysed patients got up from their wheelchairs and walked about with tears of joy in their eyes, that diabetics experienced relief, that gallstones disintegrated, that cancers went into remission and that pains disappeared.[34] All of this was the result of the external emissions of qi. Yan Xin is a master of qigong.

## 'TOP TECHNOLOGY' QIGONG

In recent years traditional Chinese medicine has gained a foothold in the West. The millennium-old treasures of the oriental knowledge of healing, however, are far from being widely known and even less from being utilized to any great degree.

Since the Han Dynasty (206 BC to AD 220), qigong (pronounced 'tshigung') has been regarded as one of the four major fields of medicine, and its roots are in spiritual and physical exercises that date back to Taoist and Buddhist practices. Qigong means 'work or exercise with qi'. Qi is a basic term in traditional Chinese medicine, in which it represents a natural force that permeates both the universe and man. Its actual meaning is very similar to the Hindu *prana* and the Greek *pneuma*, which refer to an energy that is both physical and mental, a power that both sustains life and shapes bodily form, and the direct expression of which is breath, a sort of link between the corporeal and the spiritual.

By means of physical exercises and mental concentration, which are taught in qigong, qi is supposed to become detectable in the body with the help of the spiritual power, yi. This is the precondition for being able to direct qi through the body. For example, qi can be made to circulate through the body along certain paths at various levels of depth, or it can be directed along so-called meridians to those parts of the body that are ill and collected at predetermined points. Exercises in movement[35] are practised by many Chinese as a way of ensuring the maintenance of good health. The accuracy with which they are carried out combined with the image of the qi stream through the body is supposed to facilitate the flow of qi.

According to Chinese teaching, a master of qigong has such a control over qi that he can direct, accumulate and transmit it. By means of his own qi, directed outwardly towards the patient with his hands – the so-called external emission of qi, *waiqi* – he can influence illnesses in the patient.

In his presentations, the qigong master Yan Xin astonished the whole country by his external emission of qi. It is hardly surprising that the scientists soon took him to their laboratories. Lu Zuying of the chemical and biological department of Qinghua University in Beijing conducted several extremely enlightening experiments with Yan Xin. In one series of experiments the scientist prepared a number of biological and chemical solutions.[36] Then Yan Xin directed his external emissions of qi at them for 10–15 minutes. In the case of ordinary tap water this influence resulted in a dramatic change in its spectral characteristics. Immediately following the 'treatment', the spectrograph registered a massive peak on a wavelength of $1970 \text{ cm}^{-1}$, which subsequently slowly declined and returned to normal after several hours. On a spectrograph, physiological saline (0.9 per cent) normally shows a characteristic peak on a wavelength of $246 \text{ cm}^{-1}$. Immediately after the transfer of qi, this peak disappeared or was shifted to $237 \text{ cm}^{-1}$. Influence on a 50 per cent glucose solution led to the disappearance of one characteristic peak and to the intensification of others. All of these effects gradually wore off and conditions returned to normal, but there can be no doubt that for a short time the molecular structure of the solutions was changed by the application of external qi.

The truly fantastic aspect of these experiments is that qigong master Yan exerted this influence from a distance – not a few metres, not from another room in the lab, but over distances of 7–10 kilometres! Successful results were even achieved over a distance of 2000 kilometres.

The experiments with Yan Xin were continued at ISME, and further systems that could be influenced by emissions of external qi were system-atically investigated. Among other things, Yan Xin was able to change the molecular structure of various substances, including the ultraviolet absorption characteristics of DNA and RNA preparations, the half-life values of radioactive isotopes and the polarization level of a light beam emitted by a helium–neon laser.

While psi research was being continued in secret, the public appear-ances of Yan Xin and other masters resulted in qigong quickly developing into a mass movement. At this point, scientists carefully avoided mentioning psi and qigong in the same breath, and the qigong movement did not, therefore, qualify under the Party ban against public discussion of psi. Quite the opposite, in fact, and even though it was prohibited at the time of the Cultural Revolution, many of the leading politicians accepted qigong as part of the spiritual heritage of their country and promulgated it themselves by publicly conducting qigong exercises.

At a meeting in 1987, Hu Qiaomu, the standing member of the Party's Central Political Bureau in charge of propaganda, announced: 'We should mobilize every unit in our society to study qigong science. I believe it is a very fundamental scientific effect and absolutely not superstitious fiction.'[37]

Hu Qiaomu even called for every possible effort to be made to spread qigong. These statements were in marked contrast to the Party's 1982 verdict on psi research, but they did help the study of exceptional func-tions of the human body, because the 'somatic sciences', which were to cause an unparalleled revolution, as Qian Xuesen had predicted, included not only qigong but also the phenomena of psi. In his initial statement in favour of anomalous phenomena, Qian had already pointed out that it was necessary to look at qi to find the roots of these phenomena. Now the official stance had shifted in such a way that psi found its way back into a large number of research institutes through the back door.

The Chinese Society for Somatic Sciences was founded in 1987, and *Ziran Zazhi* again began to publish articles on psi, although these were now almost exclusively related to qigong. Parapsychology mutated to become an accepted field of scientific research. In the same year, Qian Xuesen was elected Chairman of the Chinese Science and Technology Association, a semi-official commission for the coordination of the nation's scientific research. Qian had reached the pinnacle of power and was now able directly to influence scientific policies. He did not let this opportunity escape. Greatly influenced by the experiments conducted with Yan Xin, he supported the advancement of the 'somatic sciences' with enormous conviction: 'Chinese qigong is modern science and technology – high technology – absolutely top technology.'[38]

How should we evaluate contemporary psi research in China? Is a Chinese lead in the military application of psi to be feared? The enormous effort with which partially secret research is being undertaken in many places in China today is reason enough to raise such fears. Is there a real threat in this field?

In 1995 I had the opportunity to talk with Li Zhi Nan, a leading representative of the officially sanctioned psi research. Li Zhi Nan is the Secretary General of the Chinese Scientific Qigong Research Association and a member of the board of the Society for the Investigation of Qigong. He is a guest professor at Qinghua University in Beijing and is also an old Party member with direct connections to the political élite. If anybody knows how far Chinese research has advanced, it is Li Zhi Nan.

During our conversation it became clear that almost all the very heavily state supported psi research is secret. Li explained to me that the Chinese differentiate between paranormal abilities of the yang and yin kind.[39] Yang abilities can be acquired by practice (like qigong). Yin abilities, on the other hand, belong to the dark, uncontrollable sphere; they are inherited, mediumistic, shamanistic abilities. The political leadership is torn about the direction to take, at least officially. The demand for a witch hunt against the yin psychics who appear in fairly large numbers as, for example, the clairvoyant children, could be resisted. Meanwhile, there is even an intensive search for particularly talented yin psychics going on. These are sorted out and – as Li expressed it – subjected to 'internal' investigations. What he meant was secret research programmes.

The official point of view is one of scepticism. Internally, however, scientists are increasingly urged to study exceptional functions of the human body and qigong. As Li explained, China has adopted the outwardly projected image of sceptical propaganda in 'agreement with the officially negative portrayal of psi in the United States and Russia'. And then he smiled meaningfully. On both sides the playing down of really important issues as being mere curiosities appears to be part of the international game that those in power know how to play but that the population takes at face value.

How seriously these things are really taken in China can be seen from the fact that until recently a committee of only three politicians was responsible for the 'somatic sciences'. Since 1994 no fewer than nine politicians have taken over the job, a clear indication of the importance this research has assumed. A short time ago the Chinese Academy of Somatic Sciences was founded in Beijing as a centre for psi and qigong research.

As far as access to the projects and documents by foreign scientists is concerned, China continues to remain secretive. There were two large meetings in 1996, the Third World Congress on the Academic Exchange of Medical Qigong in Beijing and the Sixth International Qigong Symposium in Shanghai, and at both events, the Chinese scientists were practically on their own. Only a few Japanese scientists who have recently shown increased interest in qigong research reported on the results of their investigations.

Based on the Cartesian view of the world, western culture differentiates clearly between the material and the spiritual. For a long time consciousness was defined as being nothing more than an epiphenomenon of brain activity, with no causal force of its own. Only in recent years has this view changed, even among neuroscientists. It is becoming accepted that consciousness exerts a causal effect on the body. It even appears that the conviction is slowly gaining ground that consciousness can achieve effects beyond the body.

Chinese thinking is not handicapped by any such philosophical constraints. Traditionally, the Chinese recognize no dichotomy between the outer and the inner world, between body and mind. They have been able to preserve their unique holistic view of the world, while at the same time taking over the instruments of empirical scientific methods from the West. This may go some way to explaining why the frequency and intensity of psi effects is greater in China than in the West. From the investigation of this rich historical tradition by scientific methods, the Middle Kingdom might well provide a source of fresh ideas for the study of anomalous mental phenomena.

For the time being, however, we should be careful in our interpretations. The problem with research in China, as with that of the states of the former Soviet Union, is the methodological weaknesses of the experiments conducted. Often experiments are insufficiently prepared, they are not well designed and the precautions taken are inadequate. In publications, the experiments are mostly not described in sufficient detail. The multitude of activities is difficult to oversee, and much takes place that is not controlled. It is hard for an observer to separate delusion from fact, largely because an appreciation of the specific problems inherent in the investigation of extrasensory perception and psychokinesis is still generally lacking. Only after Chinese standards have reached those of American and European research will it be possible to take experimental data from these countries into our considerations on the nature of psi without any qualification. It would be highly desirable that this objective be reached soon, because not only is very active research being carried out in Russia and China but also the investigators can draw on an impressive fund of gifted subjects.

In the West, where psychics with extraordinary abilities appear to be less widespread, nobody has been idle during the past two decades. Parapsychology, which depends on strong, replicable phenomena, has made a virtue out of necessity. It has increasingly turned to the investigation of conditions that are thought to favour the appearance of psi, and in so doing, it has made important discoveries and achieved a quantum jump in its acceptance by orthodox science.

# Chapter Three
# ANOMALOUS COGNITION
## TRACKING DOWN THE MYSTERY

### WITHIN THE GANZFELD

Marisa lay completely relaxed on an Italian designer couch and took no notice of what was going on around her. She was completely in her own world. She heard only a uniform sound, which appeared to her like the distant murmuring of the sea. But Marisa was not asleep; her eyes were open. What she saw was a thick, pink fog completely surrounding her. And images arose from this fog as if in a dream, moving pictures of great clarity and intensive colouring. Marisa was in a 'ganzfeld'.

The murmuring in her ear came from earphones. Her eyes were completely covered by table tennis balls that had been cut in half so that they blocked her field of vision but allowed her to keep her eyes open without any difficulty. There was a red lamp above her. Behind the milky white of the table tennis balls was what appeared to her to be a pink sea.

Carefully, so as not to disturb her state of relaxation, I asked her to describe her impressions: 'There is a beach,' she began, 'a long empty beach ... and the sea, and a bright blue sky ...' Marisa did not notice the unrest growing around her, so deeply was she immersed in her dreamlike world.

We were in a hectic television studio at RAI in Milan, in the middle of a live programme, and a public notary had just selected one of four large sealed envelopes, opened it and taken out a picture that was shown to millions of viewers in the studio and at home. The picture showed a beach on the Adriatic coast.

This demonstration experiment took place in the mid-1980s. I had been invited to a TV series on parapsychology by my Italian colleague

Paola Giovetti and had intended to demonstrate one of the newest – and most successful – methods of psi research, the so-called ganzfeld procedure. This was an uncertain endeavour, like all demonstrations of 'psi abilities' on TV, because the phenomena can easily be disrupted and are not readily replicable. The intense expectations and the time restrictions of a live programme add to the difficulties. What is required is a sort of demonstration on demand, but these are far from ideal conditions for success. Nevertheless, I had decided to make an attempt, because the isolation from sensory stimuli offered some chance of success.

Several days before the scheduled appearance, I had conducted some exploratory ganzfeld experiments with a group of young people who had regularly practised meditation for a long time. For 10–15 minutes each of them was in a ganzfeld state, in which they heard nothing but the murmuring and saw nothing but the pleasant pink light. In this way the state of consciousness that precedes sleep, during which dream-like images appear, is experimentally created. After some time in this condition, those dream-like images surface, the hypnagogic hallucinations we have already learned about in Tart's investigations of out-of-body experiences. The ganzfeld stimulation appears to be a condition in which subjects are particularly receptive to paranormal impressions. Marisa proved to be highly talented in perceiving – as hypnagogic imagery – many striking elements of pictures at which I was looking. Nevertheless, that the demonstration on television would succeed so well still surprised me.

The ganzfeld experiments surprised many people. First and most notably, they surprised parapsychologists themselves, because they had no longer dared hope to find such a successful technique. However, the results also surprised not only scientists from other disciplines, who recognized the advance marked by this rigorous procedure, which involved strict shielding against any possibility of sensory leakage, but also even a fair number of persistent critics, who were forced to change their views in light of the successes achieved.

On 15 May 1993 the periodical *New Scientist*, which is well known for its scepticism, ran a title story on ganzfeld experiments that had been conducted at the University of Edinburgh: 'Psychical research has long been written off as the stuff of cranks and frauds. But there's now one telepathy experiment that leaves even the sceptics scratching their heads.' How had this unparalleled achievement come about?

# DREAM TELEPATHY

In the 1960s American psychologist Montague Ullmann and his colleagues at the Maimonides Medical Center in Brooklyn, Stanley Krippner and Sol Feldstein, succeeded in telepathically influencing dreams under controlled conditions. The team achieved impressive results in the transmission of paintings by famous artists as well as with other material.

In a typical experiment William Erwin, a psychologist and successful percipient, was asleep one night in the dream laboratory. He was awakened as soon as a dream phase ended[40] and therefore the time phase for the telepathic transmission of a picture was concluded. The target picture was *The Descent from the Cross* by the Expressionist artist Max Beckmann. During this experiment, the telepathic effort was to be reinforced by an intensive emotional involvement. The sender not only was to concentrate on the painting but also had the task of taking a small wooden cross, a picture of Christ, some tacks and a red marker out of a box. The instructions on a piece of paper read: 'Using the tacks, nail Christ to the cross. Using the marker, colour his body with blood.'

When he was awakened from his dream, Erwin first described a speech by Winston Churchill and then a ceremonial sacrifice by a tribe of natives at which he had been present: 'In the Churchill thing there was a ceremonial thing going on, and in the native dream there was a type of ceremony going on ... We were going to be sacrificed, or something, and there were political overtones ... what we would do is pretend we were gods ... in looking at the so-called king, chief, or whatever the native was ... it would be almost like ... looking at one of these totem-pole gods ... I would say the sacrifice feeling in the native dream ... would be more like the primitive trying to destroy the civilized ... It believed in the god-authority ... no god was speaking. It was the use of the fear of this, or the awe of god ideas, that was to bring about the control.'[41]

Besides the obvious connection to the target picture, a peculiarity of telepathic transmission is demonstrated here. In a dream something sensible is often expressed in a surprising, unexpected manner. What does the politician Winston Churchill have in common with the Crucifixion? By splitting the name we get 'church hill' and suddenly we have a symbolic relevance. Furthermore, between 1940 and 1945 Churchill was Prime Minister and First Lord of the Admiralty in a great war coalition, which puts him into context with the topics of death and sacrifice.

When Charles Honorton, fondly known as Chuck by his friends, joined the Maimonides team, he began to point the research in a new direction. Honorton, a short, roly-poly fellow with a sharp intelligence, was always on the look-out for new challenges, and he was sick and tired of spending sleepless nights in the small, stuffy laboratory in the cellar and painstakingly staging a dream experiment over many long hours. That telepathy was possible in dream had been sufficiently and impressively demonstrated. Now Honorton was searching for a condition similar to that of dreaming but that could be created artificially. He had long been interested in psi conducive states, and dreaming was obviously one such condition. It is not a coincidence that by far the majority of spontaneous extrasensory experiences occur during dreams.

## PSI IN THE TWILIGHT ZONE

Honorton had two colleagues whose research was going in the same direction, psychologists William Braud at the University of Houston and Adrian Parker at Edinburgh University. Jointly, they hit upon a method that had been developed in the early 1960s in a study on experimentally induced experiences similar to experiences shortly before falling asleep.[42] The study had been concerned with discovering how thoughts, emotions and images which occur in the waking condition find their way into dreams while asleep via the hypnagogic state. The investigators had used the monotonous sounds, so-called 'white noise', and the split table tennis balls for the eyes already described, and they had given this condition of unpatterned visual and auditory stimulation of the senses the German name *Ganzfeld*, meaning 'whole field', because it produced a uniform, homogeneous audio-visual field, which was accompanied by an increase in the mental imagery experienced by the subject.

Honorton, Braud and Parker wanted to know if images could be transmitted telepathically in a ganzfeld just as readily as in dreams. In their initial experiments they had discovered that the uniform stimulation quickly engendered a markedly different state of consciousness in their subjects – the attention was shifted inside, the outer world disappeared, and dream-like imagery arose. Because of its richness in images, emotions and free associations, this is a condition of heightened creativity.

At first, Honorton liked to work with series of transparencies on a given topic instead of with single pictures. A sender in a remote room looked at a series of stereoscopic slides through a binocular three-dimensional viewer. In one case, the topic of the slide series was 'rare coins'. After about 15 minutes in the ganzfeld simulation, the subject stated: 'Circles ... their sizes are not the same ... some are really large, and others are very tiny – no larger than a penny ... all these different sized circles ... Now I see colors, two in particular – gold and silver seem to stand out more than all the others.'

During another experiment at the Institute for Parapsychology in Durham, North Carolina, the target picture was a photograph from the *National Geographic* magazine. Taken from an elevated position, the photograph showed a country scene in Kentucky or Tennessee, with a lonely country road and a small truck. The female subject described her hypnagogic impressions in the following words: 'There was a road, but ... it wasn't a gravel road, it was a pebble road, a hard-packed pebble road ... And there was a very fleeting image of being inside a car and I could just see the rear-view mirror.' After this she also said that she had the feeling of driving through a wide open landscape in the country in a car.[43]

How good such results really are can often best be seen from the pictures that were not selected in the random process. In the foregoing case, these were a still-life with flowers, a Chinese noble in full dress and snow-covered cars on a parking lot. After the experiment, the subject has to arrange all four possible pictures in a sequence, putting the one that most closely resembles their impressions at the top and the one that does so least at the bottom. Without any hesitation, she pulled out the picture with the truck on the country road and said: 'That's what I saw.' A direct hit.

Charles Honorton had the good fortune to be able to leave the tiny, insufficiently equipped laboratory in Brooklyn in 1979 and continue his pioneering investigations at a university with the highest of reputations. With funds supplied by aircraft pioneer James McDonnell, he founded the Psychophysical Research Laboratories (PRL) at Princeton University, New Jersey. There, together with his team, Honorton developed a computerized, fully automatic process for ganzfeld studies.[44]

All sorts of target pictures were recorded on video tape. Some were photographs, others were video clips from films, cartoons and TV advertising. As a rule, the clips ran for less than 60 seconds. The volunteer subjects were prepared for ganzfeld in a sound-proof room and then locked in. For 30 minutes, during which the subject simply had to describe the pictures that appeared before his inner eye, the computer program selected a target picture, automatically wound the tape to the correct spot and then played the video clip six times in succession. The sender, normally one of the project leaders, looked at the pictures and attempted to transmit them to the recipient telepathically. At the end of the session, the subject was automatically shown the target pictures and three others that had not been selected. By means of remote control, the subject could automatically enter on the screen the picture they believed to be the one selected. This system kept contact between sender and percipient to a minimum and was designed to eliminate any possibility of information transfer by normal means.

At the 1982 Parapsychological Association convention in Cambridge, Ray Hyman voiced his criticism of the ganzfeld studies. He pointed out some of the weaknesses in the statistical analysis and in their methodological design. But Honorton found much of this criticism to be unjustified. In his detailed reply, Honorton summarized for the first time all the studies conducted to date and came to the conclusion that the results provided sufficient proof for the existence of psi.[45] This was the beginning of a controversy between the two scientists that lasted for several years and that has already gone down in the history of parapsychology as the Honorton–Hyman debate. It is thanks to the stubbornness of the protagonists in the debate that the analysis of psi experiments was elevated to a new level at which, in the meantime, a scientifically irrefutable mass of proof for the reality of psi has been amassed.

Critic Ray Hyman was the initiator of this development. In order to refute Honorton's findings he undertook a new form of statistical analysis, a so-called 'meta-analysis'.

## META-ANALYSIS: THE MAGIC FORMULA

Like many other sciences, experimental parapsychology has constantly piled study upon study, experiment upon experiment. Individual studies on many different questions have been conducted, and sometimes small answers have been found to big questions.

What do you do with a mountain of individual studies, each one of which is meaningful in itself but is difficult to compare with another? The traditional method was to collect all the experiments in an overview, and then to attempt to find common factors permitting all the different results to be summarized. This process naturally depends on the interpreter's ability to synthesize the information, and it always runs the risk of being adapted to some consciously or unconsciously preconceived hypothesis by means of the 'art of interpretation'. It is well known that syntheses of a field of science undertaken by different interpreters will result in widely differing interpretations.

For those sciences that depend on statistical experiments in their studies, everything changed in 1976 when Gene Glass invented methods by which the results of many different studies on the same question could be compiled and compared. This method was given the name 'meta-analysis' because it is, in a way, an analysis of analyses.[46] It is among the most important innovations in science in recent years, and meta-analyses have revolutionized the way science deals with data. Today, scientific controversies are settled by meta-analyses because they cannot be manipulated to fit preconceived opinions. At a stroke, their use made psi research acceptable. They were the missing piece in the proof puzzle.

A meta-analysis is called for whenever many studies on the same problem have produced different results. It is the method by which we can determine whether the sought-after effect is actually present and how strong it is. In a meta-analysis groups of research projects are compiled and uniformly described and the results of studies on comparable topics are systematically combined. The significance of the meta-analysis lies in the fact that it provides a measure for the degree of consistency of these results. It also makes it possible to reach conclusions about the replicability of phenomena that occur in individual studies to only a minor degree and are not statistically significant. This is exactly the case with psi experiments.

A meta-analysis is a fairly complex procedure, and not only because we are dealing with a mass of data. To begin with, all studies relevant to a defined question must be compiled. Not all experiments have been equally well designed, and it is therefore necessary first to evaluate the different studies – for example, to assess the protocol of the experiments, the quality of the study itself and so on – and in psi research in particular, to judge the precautions taken to exclude 'normal' effects. Ideally, this encoding is done by a scientist who is not too closely connected with the field of research in question. Only when this has been done can the studies be compared. One of the central questions a meta-analysis is able to answer is: if it is known that there is a statistical significance, what is the size of the effect that has been measured? The test statistics of the individual studies are mathematically converted into so-called effect sizes. The effect size is a measure for the degree to which a phenomenon occurs in a group of experiments. The calculation of a mean effect size for a certain class of comparable experiments can show the scientist what he or she can expect from future experiments.

Effect sizes give a more accurate picture of the consistency of a phenomenon in repeated experimental examination than can be provided by the standard statistical measures alone. A low effect size, however, does not necessarily mean that a phenomenon does not exist. The effect size must always be seen in connection with the calculated statistical significance, which is the measure for how unlikely it is that the result – in this case the effect size for a group of experiments – depended on chance.

An example may help to clarify this. A controversy arose in the mid-1980s about a medical study that was attempting to discover if aspirin could prevent heart attacks. The meta-analysis of 25 experiments came up with a clear effect in favour of this assumed property of aspirin.[47] One study was then broken off prematurely, because the effect had been clearly demonstrated and the scientists concerned did not feel it was ethically justified to continue to prevent the control group in the study from enjoying the benefits of the treatment. A look at the individual studies shows a surprising picture. Only five of them reached a value that supported, with 99 per cent certainty, the assumption that the result had not come about by chance. The majority of the studies did not reach such a level of assurance. An interpreter looking only at the individual studies would have come to the conclusion that aspirin did not possess the therapeutic effect in question. In the event, the meta-analysis produced a totally different picture and a medical breakthrough that was widely acclaimed. It was highly significant, even though the effect size of 0.03 was very low and is far lower than many effect sizes measured in psi experiments. The fact that such a low effect size yielded a highly significant result depends primarily on the large number of individual subjects tested.

The aspirin study shows that we should be careful not to overestimate the importance of the value by which an effect size is expressed. It says nothing about the consequences and the possible applications. As Robert Rosenthal of Harvard University, one of the leading experts on meta-analyses, quite rightly points out: 'Even though controversial fields of research are characterized by low effects, it does not follow that the effects are of no practical importance.'[48] This must apply to psi research as well.

For psi research the entry into the realm of meta-analysis was like the discovery of a new continent. Studies that had been slumbering in dusty cabinets suddenly appeared in a new light and could be placed in contexts that decisively extended the current understanding of psi and led to the development of more efficient research. Meta-analysis was a much-needed stroke of luck, because parapsychology was on the verge of failing because of the problem of replicability. The objection raised by most of its critics was that the phenomena could not be replicated at will. Meta-analyses have confirmed that psi phenomena can indeed be demonstrated in experiments and are replicable. Because the 'psi signal' is normally very weak, the phenomena are not replicable in the traditional sense. When the tool of meta-analysis is used, however, they proved themselves to be consistent and recordable effects, which can no longer be argued out of our view of the world.

In an isolated experiment, a phenomenon is considered to have been demonstrated if it reaches statistical significance. Meta-analysis, on the other hand, is based on the homogeneous distribution of the effect in question over numerous isolated experiments. If there is agreement, we can speak of the replicability of the effect. In order to achieve the homogeneity of the data, some studies have to be excluded from the meta-analysis. These are the outlier studies, which show either exceptionally good or exceptionally poor results. In meta-analyses in other fields of research, it is sometimes necessary to exclude as many as 45 per cent of the studies in order to obtain a homogeneous distribution of the effect sizes. Compared to this, parapsychological data normally achieve the necessary homogeneity without such drastic measures.

A further important advantage of meta-analyses is that they permit the easy identification of the effects caused by mistakes in the design of the experiment. Furthermore, the effects of variables within the database that appear to affect outcomes, so-called 'moderating variables', can be expressed numerically and the design of new experiments can thus be substantially improved.

A meta-analysis also deals with a problem that is familiar to all scientific endeavour but that is normally hushed up, namely the tendency to publish only those results confirming the hypotheses of the scientist involved. The critics of parapsychology are particularly fond of suspecting that negative research results are swept under the carpet and never reach the public. We can therefore never be sure, when an experiment with positive results is published, how many other unpublished studies remain in the files of the institute. If they were known, the successful experiment would have to be seen in relation to the unsuccessful ones, and the scientists' hypotheses would stand on far less certain ground.

Robert Rosenthal aptly describes this as the 'file-drawer problem'. A meta-analysis will show how many non-significant studies would theoretically have had to remain unpublished in order to cancel out the outcome of the meta-analysis. For a weak and not very homogeneous effect, it is possible that only a few file-drawer studies would be sufficient to make it disappear. But where the effect is significant, it is doubtful if there is a sufficiently large number of file-drawer studies – and sometimes an extremely large number would be necessary – to affect the results simply because there would not have been time to have conducted them.

# THE HONORTON–HYMAN DEBATE

Armed with this new method of analysis, Ray Hyman set out to perform the first meta-analysis of parapsychological experiments. He took the data from the ganzfeld investigations with the intention of proving that the much-vaunted ganzfeld experiments would show only an almost imperceptibly small and non-significant effect size. It is a proof of the honesty of scientific parapsychology that Hyman's article was published in the *Journal of Parapsychology*.[49] In fact, Hyman's conclusions were just as expected – that is, ganzfeld showed only a minute degree of replicability and was not capable of proving the existence of psi. In his analysis, Hyman did find a high degree of significance, but he concluded that this effect was eradicated by mistakes in the procedures and erroneous statistics used in the studies.

Honorton countered by sharply criticizing Hyman's interpretations.[50] The Honorton–Hyman debate, a milestone in the history of parapsychology, was on.

Honorton rose to the challenge and in his own meta-analysis came to the conclusion that there was no correlation between positive results and the quality of the work performed but that the highly significant effect size was indeed homogeneous. He also found proof for the replicability of anomalous information retrieval under ganzfeld conditions, even if this effect was low.

The debate escalated. The publishers of the *Journal of Parapsychology* sensed that here, at last, was a fruitful controversy between critics and proponents that was quite different from the usual below-the-belt blows the two camps had been exchanging for so long. They invited experts to give their opinions on the two meta-analyses. The December 1986 issue of the *Journal* was almost completely devoted to these comments. One of the most interesting opinions expressed was certainly that of the expert Robert Rosenthal,[51] who, as a well-known independent scientist, had been asked to pronounce a verdict on the debate. His own analysis led to the same results Honorton had found. The mean hit rate of all the experiments was 33 per cent, whereas on the basis of chance, a hit rate of only 25 per cent could have been expected. For the 28 ganzfeld studies that had been included in the meta-analysis, there would have had to be no fewer than 423 negative file-drawer studies in order to reduce the very distinct effect to zero, and that was an absurd assumption.

Critical opinions were also expected from Hyman and Honorton, but at that point something happened that was quite unexpected and without precedent. The two contestants got together and jointly wrote an article, 'A Joint Communiqué', which has since become well known. It contains the decisive sentence: 'We agree that there is an overall significant effect in this database that cannot reasonably be explained by selective reporting or multiple analysis. We continue to differ over the degree to which the effect constitutes evidence for psi, but we agree that the final verdict awaits the outcome of future experiments conducted by a broader range of investigators and according to more stringent standards.'[52]

Hyman and Honorton then set the standards for future ganzfeld experiments, from design to documentation, from rules for the randomization of the targets to the protocols for the evaluation of results. This jointly developed procedure led to a reform of the tests, which then became known as auto-ganzfeld (for automated ganzfeld procedure).

Before Honorton's Psychophysical Research Laboratories at Princeton had to close their doors in 1989 for lack of funds, his team was able to conduct a further 11 series of experiments, consisting of 355 sessions, according to the improved technique of auto-ganzfeld. These studies achieved very high levels of significance. They showed a hit rate of 34.4 per cent, which was even higher than the 33 per cent calculated by Rosenthal for the previous total number of experiments.

The results of the new studies and a comparison to the meta-analysis were published in the respected scientific journal *Statistical Science* by Jessica Utts.[53] Now even Hyman was impressed. He commented on Utts's article with the words: 'Honorton's experiments have produced intriguing results. If independent laboratories can produce similar results with the same relationships and with the same attention to rigorous methodology, then parapsychology may indeed have finally captured its elusive quarry.'[54]

Only a few years later Hyman, writing as an expert witness on the remote viewing experiments, noted: 'I want to state that I believe that the SAIC experiments, as well as the contemporary ganzfeld experiments, display methodological and statistical sophistication well above previous parapsychological research.'[55]

Words such as these from the mouth of this obdurate critic had a significant effect. Since then, ganzfeld studies, carried out following the auto-ganzfeld methodology, have been conducted at various laboratories, including the Institute for Parapsychology at the Rhine Research Center in Durham, North Carolina, and at the Koestler Parapsychology Unit at Edinburgh University.[56] Both laboratories achieved positive results with hit rates of 33 per cent. The ice had been broken.

Charles Honorton's methodologically impeccable procedures had caused a minor earthquake in the ranks of the sceptically inclined scientists. Two of these, Jessica Utts and psychologist and professional magician Daryl Bem of Cornell University, both of whom were highly respected in their fields, saw reason to change sides. It was quite obvious that parapsychologists were not a dedicated community of prejudiced pseudo-scientists but rather a small group of individuals who worked with extreme care and had an honest interest in applying the best available scientific methods and in taking the greatest possible precautions against fraud, deceit and misinterpretation in order to discover whether psi actually exists.

Bem and Honorton had convincingly answered this question in an article entitled 'Does Psi Exist?'.[57] They presented an extensive synthesis of all the ganzfeld studies and the meta-analyses based upon them, and submitted it to the respected journal *Psychological Bulletin*. Even though they offered proof in their article for the existence of an anomalous process of information transfer, all four independent judges, including Ray Hyman, recommended publication. After their paper had been accepted, the publisher of the *Psychological Bulletin*, Robert Sternberg, wrote to Bem: 'This is a blockbuster article and one that should generate great interest from the field ... You should look at this rapid acceptance as an indication of how important I think the article is.'[58]

Completely unexpectedly, 9 days before the article had been accepted for publication, Charles Honorton died at the age of 46. Parapsychology had lost one of its most creative brains. He left piles of research material that may perhaps show parapsychology the way to fulfil a dream – the 'early recognition' of gifted subjects based on personality traits.

# Chapter Four
# IN SEARCH OF THE IDEAL CONDITIONS FOR PSI

## THE PSYCHOLOGY OF ANOMALOUS MENTAL PHENOMENA

Honorton had wanted to employ the highly successful experimental ganzfeld technique to collect as much data as possible on promising subjects. Parapsychology's main problem was still the scarcity of the phenomena and the difficulty of replicability. Would it be possible to identify paranormally gifted subjects by means of appropriate tests and interviews in connection with ganzfeld experiments?

Honorton and his team collected the personality characteristics of hundreds of subjects by means of a widely used personality assessment test, the Myers–Briggs type indicator (MBTI), which is based on Carl Gustav Jung's model of the psychology of personality. The elements that go to make up a personality are recorded without any negative aspects. The MBTI's classification has four dimensions of personality, which are expressed in opposite pairs of types: extraverted–introverted, sensing–intuitive, thinking–feeling and judging–perceiving.[59]

After years of systematic data collection, Honorton and his colleague Ephraim Schechter were able to identify four factors that enabled them to predict successful psi results in the ganzfeld. People who possessed all four factors could be expected to produce very good results under ganzfeld conditions. The four factors were:

1. having already had psi experiences;
2. practising a mental discipline – for example, meditation, relaxation exercises or biofeedback;

3. showing the personality traits of feeling and perceiving, as opposed to thinking and judging according to the MBTI;
4. having previously participated in psi experiments.

The best results were therefore to be expected from people to whom all four factors applied. When they then went through their data, they discovered that of the many hundreds of people Honorton had ever tested, only four met all four criteria. These four, however, had achieved the unbelievable success rate of 100 per cent![60]

For practical purposes, the scientists then looked at the first three factors, and they found that 28 of their subjects met the requirements. On average, these had achieved the extraordinary success rate of 64 per cent. We must bear in mind that the hit rate expected by chance is 25 per cent and that the meta-analysis of the ganzfeld studies had shown a rate of 33 per cent.

At the Institute for Parapsychology in Durham, Richard Broughton had the ganzfeld experiments conducted over previous years checked according to the three-factor model. It was discovered that these factors also applied to 28 people, who on average had jointly achieved a success rate of 43 per cent. Thus, the model had been confirmed.[61]

For decades the search for the relationship between personality factors and psi has been one of the most important aspects of research. The phenomenology of paranormal experiences shows that people with certain personality traits report psi experiences more frequently than others. The valuable contribution the MBTI questionnaire made to the selection of subjects for ganzfeld experiments is an indicator that many discoveries are still possible in this field.

The best-known factor and one that plays a decisive role for success or failure is actually not a personality trait but an attitude – that is, whether a person believes in psi ('sheep') or does not ('goat'). Many studies had shown that 'sheep' achieve positive results in psi tests, while 'goats' sometimes score below even chance expectation. This phenomenon is known as psi-missing. There are indications that psi is being used subconsciously to avoid hits and thereby to confirm a conviction (that there is no such thing as psi). A meta-analysis of the 73 published studies on the sheep–goat effect showed a relatively weak effective size, but one that was still highly significant.[62] The estimated number of unreported file-drawer cases with null results required to make the effect disappear was 1726. Hence, the reality of the effect can be seen as having been clearly demonstrated.

Another personality trait that could be identified in many psi experiments as having an influence on the results has to do with whether the subject tends towards extraversion or introversion. Extraverts are people who are sociable, open themselves up and are generally more free of fears, whereas introverts are normally loners, are turned inwards and are often plagued by fears. Most of the studies showed that extraverts achieve better results in psi tests.

Initially, a meta-analysis confirmed a highly significant effect in the expected direction.[63] But the effect size proved not to be homogeneous. This is an indication that other moderating variables must have had a decisive influence on individual experiments. The search for the source of this lack of homogeneity brought the following results. Studies conducted according to the forced-choice method (guessing experiments) were significant only when the extraversion measure had been given after the psi test and the subjects knew how well they had done in the test. Studies conducted according to the free-response method were significant when the subjects were tested individually, even though the extraversion questionnaire was filled in before the psi test.

Here the analysis had shown that in measuring psi in correlation to the extraversion–introversion factor, the influence of moderating variables that were modifying the results had to be taken into account. Only the meta-analysis was able to uncover the type of relationship between extraversion and good psi results, which had long been considered to be a fact already proved by research, and thereby to demonstrate that the relationship in forced-choice experiments would appear to be artificial. In other words, the alleged relationship actually has nothing to do with the psi result but can be traced back to psychological factors alone. Apparently, the feeling of joy about having achieved excellent results in the test manifests itself in a generally more positive, and therefore more extraverted, self-description in the extraversion questionnaire, since those studies in which the extraverts had filled in the questionnaire before their test did not contribute to the significant effect.

In the free-response method, the correlation 'high number of hits in the psi experiment = tendency towards extraversion' appears to have been demonstrated in individual cases. The ganzfeld studies fall into this category, and Honorton asked his subjects to complete the questionnaires before the psi test. After the result described above had become known, he analysed his auto-ganzfeld data again. In 221 experiments of this sort, there was data on the personality trait of extraversion and indeed, in the auto-ganzfeld the correlation between extraversion and high scores in psi experiments turned out to be highly significant. This result shows how instructive meta-analyses can be and how indispensable a tool they have meanwhile become for interpretation and future research.

A relationship between personality traits and psi cannot be denied. But how does the brain deal with psi? Which physiological and neurological paths does anomalous information follow, and can appropriate measures, such as altered states of consciousness or techniques of self-regulation, assist the appearance of paranormal impressions?

## THROUGH THE ALPHA GATE

At the beginning of this century French philosopher and Nobel laureate Henri Bergson (1859–1941) had advanced the opinion that the brain and the nervous system have a dual function.[64] On the one hand, they detect and process sensory information; on the other, they serve as a filter that permits only some of this information to reach the level of consciousness. We are constantly bombarded by sensory information, and if we were to register all of it consciously, it would quickly confuse us and exceed our capacities. Bergson's filter theory is based on the assumption that although the selection of sensory information is based on criteria that are important for survival, it also depends on psychological factors, such as our motives. The filter mechanism can be demonstrated by examples from everyday life. You urgently have to post a letter and are driving down a street you know well and have often driven down before. Suddenly, a letterbox you have never noticed before comes into view. You have certainly 'seen' this letterbox before, but you have never recorded it consciously because you had no need and there was no motive.

Our nervous system primarily reacts to changes. The ganzfeld method takes advantage of this factor by presenting an unchanging sensory field. The underlying idea is that when our nervous system is deprived of opportunities to react to sensory stimulation it becomes avid for stimuli. A heightened sensitivity for weak, anomalous stimuli, which normally remain unrecognized under intense sensory stimulation, can therefore develop.

Ganzfeld is the temporary resting-place of a long search within parapsychology – the search for the ideal condition for the anomalous reception of information. But the search is not yet over, and the techniques of modern psychophysiology are only sharpening the sights that are aimed at the ephemeral world of the paranormal.

Ingo Swann and the remote viewers had discovered that the anomalous perception of an object, or a content of mind, was a problem of the signal-to-noise ratio. In anomalous information retrieval, the level of noise is generally so high that the psi signal is lost within it. While research in Russia took the path of strengthening the signal by transmitting the most radical and intensive stimuli possible, researchers in the West took a different route. The remote viewers attempted to penetrate the noise analytically by techniques of introspection, but because analytical mental effort is itself always a source of mental noise, Honorton and a number of his colleagues looked for the perfect conditions for letting psi enter the mind in as unhindered a way as possible.

The search for such 'psi conducive states' is as old as parapsychology itself – or perhaps it would be more true to say that parapsychology exists as a science only because man has, since the dawn of the evolution of consciousness, been searching for such conditions. At the beginning of the spiritual disciplines – at the beginning of all religions – lies the desire to escape the condition of everyday consciousness. The driving force is the yearning for a fundamental lost state of consciousness in which the gods and man communicated; a yearning for the state of paradise, the mythical beginnings, the golden age – a time when man had not yet become separated from the realm of the transcendental. Out of this desire, which sprang from the innermost soul, ways and methods were developed to alter consciousness in such a way that phenomena that have no place in everyday conscious wakefulness would manifest themselves. The shamans investigated dreams, set off on out-of-body excursions and travelled on the borderline between madness and reality.[65] Their successors investigated trance and possession, received divine inspiration as prophets or developed complex systems of self-discipline that would produce the desired result.

Among the latter, we number the teachings of the Indian philosopher Patañjali (second century BC), the founder of the philosophy of yoga, which was developed in the *Yoga Sutras*. Patañjali compiled a schedule of the various techniques of yoga known in his day[66] and presented them against the background of the metaphysics of Samkhya. He defined paranormal abilities as a necessary manifestation in the course of progress in meditation exercises. Patañjali dedicated most the third of the four chapters of the *Yoga Sutras* to the classification of the *siddhis*, the paranormal abilities. According to Patañjali, paranormal manifestations appear through persistent exercises in meditation. The adept of yoga can obtain information about previous lives, learn the thoughts and feelings of another person, become invisible, cause hunger and thirst to disappear, ascertain hidden and subtle things, free the consciousness from the body and submerge it in another body, obtain the strength of an elephant, gain an understanding of the world and the order of the stars and even attain an insight into the supreme being.

In their search for states that would be conducive to psi, parapsychologists quite naturally turned to the ancient concepts of meditation. Reports by psychics about their own experiences of internal conditions favouring psi information suggested such an orientation.[67] Most psychics described a state of consciousness that appears to be very close to that of meditation. A central factor was deep mental and physical relaxation and freedom from stress. In addition, a receptive state of mind – as opposed to an active one – was most important, and this had to be looked for in a deliberate rejection of the outer world. In this condition, the psychic must be able to silence his mind.

In new studies on personality traits and susceptibility for psi, a personality factor of a higher order was discovered, which correlates strongly with mystical and paranormal experiences.[68] This factor was called 'absorption'. People who tend to experience episodes of 'total' attention, who are completely absorbed by something, report not only paranormal experiences far more frequently than others but also transpersonal and mystic experiences. Such people are able to induce profound states of concentration and meditation.

Investigations into psi with yogis in the East and with students of meditation in the West did not lead to any extraordinary results, but the significance of such studies should not be overstated, for people who practise meditation as a process of spiritual growth are rarely interested in experiments on the concomitants of the process. They are likely to regard empirical research as a waste of time. It would indeed be difficult to convince an Indian yogi of the importance of an experiment in which he has to 'guess' randomly selected symbols that are hidden from his view. Under such conditions, we cannot expect good psi results. Similarly, experiments conducted with people who regard meditation as an 'exercise in relaxation' are not suited to teach us anything about the relationship between psi and meditation. At best, they can tell us something about whether conditions of relaxation can favour psi.

Interestingly enough, the descriptions given by psychics about the ideal 'psi condition' resemble not only Patañjali's description of yoga but also the introspective statements made by people who are able to produce strong and lasting alpha rhythms in their brains. It has almost become a truism that an alpha rhythm favours psi. Reality, however, is not so simple.

Alpha rhythms have been associated with conditions of lowered attention, reduction of thought processes and relaxation. People who are well advanced in the techniques of meditation show an increase in the amplitude of the alpha rhythm in their EEG, but laboratory experiments on the actual correlation between alpha waves and the results achieved in tests on anomalous cognition do not provide us with a clear picture. They are even contradictory. While some studies point towards a positive correlation, others show the opposite effect – that is, the results under increased alpha activity are poor. Quite obviously the presence of alpha waves is not itself necessarily favourable to psi.

In a notable experiment researchers were able to demonstrate that the increased appearance of alpha waves led to improved psi results only when the subject was able at the same time introspectively to gauge their internal state in accordance with the results of physiological measurements.[69] Apparently, the psi conducive state does not depend solely on the presence of alpha waves but also on the ability to produce a conscious feeling for the state of relaxation. While alpha waves may serve as a sort of 'carrier frequency' for psi, it is only the awareness of the internal state, which is gained by inwardly focused attention, that might lead to the identification of psi signals.

Studies conducted by American psycho-physiologist Edgar Wilson have led to new and illuminating insights into the role played by alpha waves in the brain.[70] They have also opened a physiological door to the problem of differentiation between paranormal and transpersonal experiences.

Wilson conducted his experiments with advanced participants in gateway courses at the Monroe Institute. During these seminars, altered states of consciousness are produced by use of the Hemi-Sync tapes with which the psychic spies had been trained. To begin with, his investigations showed that normally all forms of waves appear simultaneously. What is decisive is the difference in their density and location on the areas of the cortex. Wilson was able to prove that the massive appearance of alpha waves led to a suppression of very low-frequency waves (delta waves, 0–4 Hz), as well as of very high-frequency waves (gamma waves, 30–50+ Hz). As soon as alpha waves receded, delta and gamma waves again increased.

Wilson demonstrated that gamma and delta waves correlated with conditions of transpersonal, mystical and meditative experiences. He suspected that alpha waves serve as a sort of 'door keeper' for the entry and exit of such states.

The appearance of increased alpha activity can be compared to a motor running in neutral. The brain is in a state of preparedness, during which it shows a reduction in cortical activity. In a state of increased alpha activity, our time–space reality is formed. As soon as we let go of alpha during meditation exercises, we enter into an area of more immediate awareness of reality. As Wilson expresses it, we experience what actually is there at the moment and not what we expect to be there. Through the 'alpha gate', we move from a consciousness of time to a 'space expanding' state of consciousness.

It may well be, therefore, that psi impressions go hand in hand with alpha frequencies because they increasingly find entry into the conscious mind on the threshold between analytical attention (beta waves) and mystic insight (delta and gamma waves). Psi is a phenomenon on the threshold, and its EEG correlates reflect a transitional phase, moments in which the alpha gate is opened.

The scientists at the Bio-Emission Laboratory of the National Institute of Radiological Sciences (NIRS) in Chiba, Japan, have specialized in investigating the physiological concomitants of anomalous cognition. In recent years the laboratory has produced many interesting studies that provide new insights into EEG patterns and other electric activities of the brain during the psi process.

During an experiment in telepathy, the sender and the percipient were in separate rooms.[71] The percipient was supposed not only to attempt to perceive the content of what the sender was trying to transmit but also to identify the time intervals during which transmission took place. The image contents were not correctly reproduced nor was the percipient able to identify the correct time intervals, but an analysis of the EEG data showed that anomalous cognition is related to visual perception – that is, by an increase of the amplitudes of the alpha waves in the percipient's EEG in those areas of the brain in which visual sensory impressions are processed.

Moreover, characteristic wave patterns were identified in the percipient in the form of two isolated reactions. The first of these showed itself in the area of the so-called occipital and parietal region of the brain[72] and was terminated by a reaction in the frontal area.[73] This experiment indicates that the reception of extrasensory information can be detected by significant changes in the alpha waves, even though the contents transmitted are not consciously perceived.

In an experiment conducted by Mikio Yamamoto, a qigong master was supposed to transmit qi to a percipient. The qigong master was seated behind a screen that separated him from the percipient, and his hand was additionally screened by a metal box. The percipient, isolated visually and acoustically, sat opposite him and held his hand over the metal box. Both subjects were connected to EEGs. The task of the percipient was to state when he believed a transfer of qi was being attempted. In 20 attempts, the percipient was unable to recognize the time intervals in which qi was being emitted. In the EEG, however, between the phases of transmission and the control phases, the same statistically significant differences in the amplitudes of the alpha waves, which had already been noted in the experiments on anomalous cognition, were noted in those regions of the brain where sensory impressions are processed.[74]

The experiments at the Bio-Emission Laboratory indicate that there is no difference between psi and qi. The serious drawback of these experiments is that only a small number of individual tests have been completed. A statistically relevant result cannot be expected from only 20 attempts. It is essential, especially when dealing with such a weak effect as psi, to collect as much data as possible. The meta-analyses have shown that only when there is a vast amount of data can phenomena with low effect sizes turn into significant results.

An indication that anomalous cognition, like other sensory information, is processed in the brain was recently demonstrated in several very enlightening studies. They go back to an experiment that had caused a sensation among parapsychologists more than 25 years ago but had then been forgotten after an independent attempt at replication failed in another laboratory.

The complex experiment on the brain-electrical concomitants of telepathic transmissions was conducted in Canada in the early 1970s by a scientist who goes by the pseudonym of D.H. Lloyd. He applied the method of so-called 'evoked brain potentials'. In an EEG recording of the occipital region, the repeated stimulation by one and the same visual stimulus shows a characteristic curve. Because of the noise caused by the brain's electrical activity, however, this potential is not directly visible. The short EEG sections during which the same stimulus is presented repeatedly are then superimposed on each other, so that the noise can be eliminated by averaging out all of the curves. This leaves the signal as an ideal curve in which the evoked potential always shows the same characteristic track.

Lloyd applied the following procedure in his experiment. Every time a light signal appeared, a sender was supposed telepathically to send an image to a percipient in another room.[75] The percipient was connected to an EEG, and the recordings for the periods of transmission were subsequently analysed. The analysis showed that an evoked potential could be identified for the phases of telepathic transmission of the image. This means that a telepathically transmitted content is accompanied by a directly attributable electrical activity in the brain just like that of a sensually perceived stimulus.

Only a few years ago two research teams in the United States and Mexico[76] were able successfully to replicate this experiment. In the American study the brain waves of a psychic showed a different evoked brain potential when images were being transmitted than when there were no target pictures.[77]

The scientists at the Bio-Emission Laboratory in Japan also looked for elements in evoked brain potentials by which periods of anomalous information transmission could be differentiated from intervals without transmission. An experiment conducted by Hideyuki Kokubo and his team is of particular interest here, because for the first time Japanese scientists strictly applied the precautionary measures that Honorton and Hyman had developed in their Joint Communiqué on ganzfeld studies. What is understood to be a matter of course in western experiments appears to be a novelty in Japan. There, just as in Russia and China, the precautions that are regarded as essential in the investigation of paranormal phenomena had for many years frequently been taken far too lightly, with the result that many experiments must be interpreted with great caution. This is the reason the leading scientists in the field, who have followed research programmes in Russia and east Asia with a degree of goodwill, have not taken its results into their calculations. It is to be hoped that this will change in the near future.

In Kokubo's experiment subjects had to perform a remote viewing task. They were supposed to determine the position of a target person and what the person was doing.[78] The subjects were given nothing more than a photograph of the target person. The experiment lasted for about 90 minutes. During this time both the EEG and the so-called auditory evoked brain potential of the target person were recorded. The EEG data did not permit any clear conclusions, but the evoked brain potential showed a tendency towards a lower amplitude during the experimental session than in the periods immediately before and after.

At various times psi has been associated with the function of the right hemisphere of the brain. In general terms, the right hemisphere is more responsible for artistic tasks, listening to music, the recognition of faces and spatial arrangements, while the left hemisphere handles sequential tasks and is responsible for calculations, language and logical thinking.

Experiments conducted by American researchers Gertrude Schmeidler and Michaeleen Maher contradicted the opinion that psi is primarily a function of the right hemisphere. In their experiments the left hemisphere was first involved in a distracting task while – by an experimental device – the right hemisphere had to solve a psi task, and then the process was reversed. Right-hemisphere psi was tested through spatial and tactile perception, and left-hemisphere psi via verbal achievements. The results suggest the conclusion that psi information is not necessarily processed by the right hemisphere simply because it is associated with creativity and holistic perception but – depending on the nature of the task – is processed by the appropriate hemisphere.

During these experiments, the two parapsychologists uncovered an interesting fact: male subjects achieved better results in such experiments of cerebral specialization than female subjects. This is confirmed by the observation of neurophysiology that the specialization of the two hemispheres of the brain is more strongly developed in men than in women.

## CAN PSI BE TRAINED?

The still relatively new field of EEG studies permits us to draw the interim conclusion that the process of anomalous reception of information in the brain takes place in a manner that is analogous to the ways in which sensory information is processed. This processing occurs subconsciously. Psi signals are received by the body but are not consciously recognized and are processed in the central nervous system. The conversion of the information into conscious impressions is favoured by the conditions of inwardly directed attention that – based on a calm state of mind – lie on the threshold of states of deep meditation or mystic and transcendental (ecstatic) experiences.

Two recent meta-analyses provide insights into whether experiments under altered states of consciousness actually do lead to better psi results. British psychologist Julie Milton analysed free-response experiments in anomalous cognition in ordinary states of wakeful consciousness.[79] These experiments excluded ganzfeld, dreams and hypnosis, and she drew on 78 studies that had been published between 1964 and 1993. A few remote viewing experiments at the SRI were also included in the analysis. The probability in favour of a real anomalous effect lay at 10 million to 1. For the 55 studies finally included in the analysis, Milton calculated 866 file-drawer cases. This meta-analysis clearly indicates that successful psi experiments can be conducted in a state of normal wakeful consciousness.

The average hit rate of the anomalous cognition experiments analysed by Milton was only 54 per cent, against an expected 50 per cent, and it is significantly lower than hit rates achieved in experiments under slightly or strongly altered states of consciousness, indicating the efficacy of altered states of consciousness and of certain methods. The Maimonides studies of telepathy in dreams, for example, had a hit rate of 63 per cent, against an expected rate of 50 per cent. With ganzfeld, the mean hit rate of all the experiments conducted to date is 33.2 per cent, against an expected rate of 25 per cent.

In the 1950s and 1960s particularly good and stable hit rates were expected from hypnosis. Some scientists even believed that hypnosis could be used for training to achieve consistently better results in psi experiments. There are a number of problems with hypnosis, and this area of research has been largely discontinued in the West. Hypnosis is always related to the stigma of manipulation. Moreover, the talents required of a good hypnotist vary widely, and people show very different degrees of receptivity to hypnosis. While a meta-analysis indicated that there were distinct advantages for achieving good psi results under the conditions of hypnosis – as compared to the ordinary state of wakefulness – it also showed that the results varied very widely, depending on the experimenters and the hypnotists.[80]

Given this knowledge, we may now tentatively ask if there is an ideal inner condition for psi – still a burning topic for research. There are many who believe it has been found in ganzfeld. But can psi actually be 'trained' under such ideal conditions or are we doomed to live with psi as an unstable companion of our everyday lives?

The successes achieved in ganzfeld research and remote viewing have moved the possibilities of a regular application and the trainability of psi to the centre of attention. Ultimately, every science is applications directed. Even basic research is pursued in order to be able to apply new discoveries to everyday life. Nobody would deny that controllable 'psi abilities' would have far-reaching practical consequences. Nevertheless, the owners of gambling casinos or the managers of lotteries do not have to lose any sleep for the time being. Games of chance are always designed in such a way that the odds favour the bank. The rate of identification, particularly where numbers are concerned, lies at best only a few percentage points above chance. In the end, even a gifted subject would leave the gambling table as a loser.

Further, it has become apparent that the training of psi is not all that easy, and anybody who claims otherwise does not know the facts. Even Swann's meticulously designed system did not decisively improve remote viewing results. No doubt some of the participants discovered and perfected their talent for the reception of anomalous information by this system, but as soon as they had reached a certain degree of proficiency they levelled off. The more talented remote viewers were unable to improve their results by means of the system.

Charles Tart's attempts to train psi in guessing experiments with random sequences also have to be seen as having failed. Tart's point of departure was the classic learning theory of psychology. According to this, information is retained more readily if we receive positive feedback – a sort of psychological pat on the back, encouragement that says, 'Well done, carry on!'

Tart assumed that continuous feedback in the form of information on hit results would be an appropriate encouragement for the training of psi – that is, in cases of initially good hit rates, immediate information about the results could provide the necessary incentive to subjects to continue to 'guess' correctly above chance. Through self-observation, the subjects might possibly also be able to learn how to create an appropriate inner condition or to learn to distinguish between types of perceptions that went hand in hand with hits. By such means they might later be able deliberately to put themselves into the ideal state of consciousness or gain more confidence in making their choices.

Tart developed a piece of equipment that had ten lights arranged in a circle, the illumination of which was controlled by a random process.[81] The subjects had to push the button of the light they believed would light up next. As soon as the next light lit up, the subject knew whether they had guessed correctly or not. While there were some very good results, there was no learning effect in that improved results became deliberately replicable.[82]

The problem with feedback training is that in guessing experiments we never know whether a hit comes about by coincidence or if it can be attributed to a mysterious ability called psi. The subject therefore also receives positive feedback on chance hits that, from the point of view of psi, are misses. The ideal inner condition can hardly be discovered by such means.

We cannot hope for perfect control of psi. This will probably never be achieved and this is why I have always put 'psi abilities' in quotation marks. On the basis of all we know about psi, we are not dealing with an ability in the usual sense of the word. Psi cannot be learned like a foreign language or taught like the playing of an instrument. Up to a certain degree, however, we can learn to differentiate psi signals from other impressions, but this does not in any way mean that we can become 'clair-voyant'. Nor do psi signals occur more frequently through excellent achievements in introspection. Their being elusive and infrequent lies in the physical nature of psi itself.

If we are outside the frequency range of a radio transmitter, no matter what we do we will still receive only a weak and intermittent signal accompanied by a great deal of noise. We can turn up the volume on the set, but we only increase the level of static; we can tune down the high notes in order to reduce the noise marginally; and we can practise concentrating on catching the snatches of sensible information that appear in fragments among the static. Nevertheless, it will always only be fragments that come through to us. Even if we have a perfect inner access to psi, psi will never lose its ephemeral nature. Nevertheless, in the context of the fascination with the successes of remote viewing and ganzfeld, these problems with the very nature of anomalous cognition did not prevent some from attempting to explore the limits of applying psi in practice.

## PRACTICAL APPLICATIONS OF ANOMALOUS COGNITION

The entire remote viewing project had originated with an attempt to answer a single question: can anomalous cognition be applied in practice? The answer must be a clear 'yes'. But does this application actually have a practical use, a value exceeding other possible ways of achieving the same objective? Answers to these questions are far less clear. There are, however, some indicators that allow us to hope that progress can be made in this field. One of these has been presented by American clinical psychologist James Carpenter.

Carpenter asked himself whether coded messages could be communicated via psi. The people who took part in the experiment did not know they were supposed to decipher encoded messages. Before the experiment began, someone chose a word and encoded it by converting it into dots and dashes according to the Morse alphabet. Then several dozen students took part in a simple psi test. They completed several runs of guessing 24 binary targets. The target symbols were 0 and +. What they did not know was that 12 of these symbols encoded the message word. The subjects also had to describe their mood during the test.

Carpenter's complex procedure used the majority-vote technique, in which the guesses are summed across subjects to form a single composite set of guesses. The 12 target symbols for the encoded message were the same for all of the subjects. For each symbol, the selections of the digits 0 or + were added up. The symbol chosen most frequently was selected. In this way, Carpenter hoped to be able to 'extract' the weak psi signal out of a multitude of selections.

Then something very exciting was added. In previous experiments, Carpenter had discovered that from the statements made in the mood questionnaire it was possible to differentiate between people who consistently achieved good results in such guessing experiments and those who scored constantly below chance expectation. When the results from the questionnaire indicated somebody who would probably do well, Carpenter used the symbol the person had chosen. In the case of those where the indication was that they would do less well than expected from chance, Carpenter converted the symbol chosen into its opposite. In the end, Carpenter wound up with a series of 0 and + symbols that were then converted into the Morse alphabet, resulting in the letters P, E, A, C and E. The encoded target word had in fact been 'peace' and it had been identified with 100 per cent accuracy.[83]

Carpenter's work is still in its infancy, and we do not know if such impressive results can be stabilized. In any case, it will take a very long time before such a complex procedure can be simplified and shortened to such a degree that it will become useful in practice.

The idea behind Carpenter's experiment is fairly simple. We are confronted with a bulk of noisy information, in all of which the same weak signal is hidden. If we superimpose the recordings, the noise will always remain noise, but the signal will become more clear. Psi is no different. The key to success lies in the collection of large amounts of data on one and the same problem. In other words, many subjects must attempt to guess a target by anomalous cognition. And if there is also an independent measure available for anyone who is probably a gifted subject and for anyone who is more likely to produce psi-missing, the quality of the result can be improved.

Carpenter used the forced-choice method, but it was also possible to continually improve remote viewing data by the majority-vote technique. Optimists even believed this technique could be successfully employed in remote viewing. Stephen Schwartz of the Mobius Society in Los Angeles uses this procedure to locate unknown archaeological sites. Among other things, he claims to have found Cleopatra's palace off the coast of Alexandria by this method.[84] His claims, however, have come under fire from critics. It appears that Schwartz sometimes searched in places where he could count on making some sort of discovery, which he subsequently attributed to the impressions of psychics.[85] The majority-vote technique is far from being decisive and anything but infallible. Nevertheless, by a mixture of Carpenter's approach and the consensus of a group of remote viewers, it may be possible to develop a method by which anomalous cognition will be practically applicable in limited areas.

The practical application of psi plays a major role in the struggle of American scientists for the recognition of their field of research. In the United States anything that has a practical application is far more readily accepted as being 'real', and anything that can be converted into hard cash stands an excellent chance of being regarded as 'real' without demur.

In the early 1980s Russell Targ and Keith Harary founded Delphi Associates together with businessman Anthony White. The group intended to offer services of a special kind. By means of precognitive remote viewing, they intended to predict the movement of the price of silver on the commodity market of the COMEX in New York. Even the most famous financial paper in the world, the *Wall Street Journal*, wrote a positive article on the study.

Delphi Associates used the method of 'associative remote viewing'. The speciality of this experiment is to initiate the prediction of the actual abstract event by means of cleverly introduced illustrative material. In contrast to traditional RV experiments, a certain event is assigned to each target object.[86] In every single experiment there were four possible target objects – for example a frog, a miniature TV set, a medicine ball and a beaker full of ice cubes. Before the experiment began, the objects were assigned a subsequent event: the frog stood for a rise in the price of silver of more than 25 cents on Monday of the following week; the miniature TV set for a rise of less than 25 cents; the medicine ball for a stable price; the beaker full of ice cubes for a fall in price. Keith Harary, who acted as the remote viewer, did not know which target object had been selected nor which event it had been assigned by Russell Targ. Depending on how the price of silver moved on the coming Monday, Keith Harary would then be presented with the appropriate object as feedback. For example, if the price were to fall, he would be given the beaker with the ice cubes. The beaker would therefore be the actual target object, and the movement of the price of silver would have replaced the random process in the selection of the target object. Basically, this was classical precognitive remote viewing, in which the target is determined after the statements of the subject have been made.

If in his remote viewing Harary were now to described something that was slimy, green and moving and draw feet with webbed toes, the evaluators would not find it hard to identify the object as a frog. And now came the joker. Each time the monitors had the feeling a target object had been correctly identified, they placed the appropriate order corresponding to the target object on the exchange. If the target object was connected to a rising price, they bought silver futures; if it indicated a falling price, they sold short. By guessing correctly, you can make money in either case. And Delphi Associates made money, because in nine experiments they were right every time.[87]

Meanwhile Russell Targ and his colleagues at the Bay Research Institute in Palo Alto have been trying to improve the process of associative remote viewing. A system intended to detect errors passed the first test.[88] Two researchers acted as remote viewers and had a selection of two target pictures they knew nothing about. The other two researchers acted as evaluators. They associated the status of 'higher' with one target picture and the status of 'lower' with the other. As in the first silver price study, these two attributes were related to a rise or fall of the silver price on the following Monday. This time the group was more circumspect. The experiment remained theoretical and nobody bet money on the market on the basis of the results.

For nine consecutive weeks an experiment was run each week with both remote viewers. If they both correctly described a target symbol, one with the status 'higher', and the other with the status 'lower', the session was classified as a draw and not counted. Of the 12 recordings that were counted, 11 described the object the remote viewer was shown later.

Of the nine sessions run, two were not counted. Of the seven remaining predictions of the movements of the price of silver, six proved to be correct. Perhaps Russell Targ has found a way decisively to improve the hit rate. But a word of caution must be added here: this, too, is a new experiment, the initial success of which needs to be verified by replication.

# Chapter Five
# MENTAL INFLUENCE ON LIVING SYSTEMS

## INTENTION AS ACTION

It seemed as if it was going to be a relaxed afternoon. Rudolf was allowed to sit down in a comfortable chair in a semi-darkened room and to listen to an irregular sequence of clicks on his earphones. For Rudolf it was only another experiment, one among many for which the student had volunteered. Before the clicks began, a buzzer sounded. That was the signal. Rudolf was to concentrate on there being as many clicks as possible. The more the better. If he preferred he could also imagine that a hamster was keeping his treadmill running at speed and without pause. That was what the experiment was all about.[89] The hamster had spent a whole day in a narrow cage in which it could not move about freely. Shortly before the experiment began, it was put into the cage with the treadmill where it could exercise to its heart's content. Rudolf could not see the hamster – its cage was in another room – but with each turn of the treadmill, a click would be sounded that Rudolf would hear.

As the experimenter, I sat in a third room and saw none of this. According to a random key, I transmitted the buzzer sound and switched on the earphones of my subject when an experimental phase was on. In the control phase, I switched the earphones off. Then all Rudolf had to do was to relax and not think of anything. The analysis of the data showed that the activity of the hamster correlated to the intentions of my subject. This experiment was one of a series I conducted according to a concept that had initiated a new field of psi research at the end of the 1970s. The concept was called 'conformance behaviour' and had been conceived by American parapsychologist Rex Stanford and then developed further by his colleague William Braud. The basic idea is based on the fact that under some circumstances a system that shows a certain degree of disorder, randomness, weakness or noise modifies its organization in order to more closely match the organization of another system that is characterized by a lesser degree of disorder and a stronger structure. The instable system conforms with the structured system. The more various the possible states of the disordered system and the stronger the organization of the structured system, the greater the probability that conformance behaviour will occur.

This concept has the advantage of being able to overcome the demarcation between extrasensory transmission and psychokinetic influence, and it approaches the problem in a phenomenological way. What can be observed in effects of distant influence is a modification in the statistical behaviour of a system in correlation to the intentions or desires of a person. Consciousness directed by intention represents the structured system. For checking the concept, William Braud and a number of other scientist frequently chose as random processes living systems – humans, animals, plants, cell cultures. Living systems are much more sensitive, both as 'bio amplifiers' and as information-processing systems, than non-living random systems.

The concentration on living systems has opened a highly successful research programme with far-reaching consequences. In addition to the term bio-PK, Braud's team coined the abbreviation DMILS for direct mental influence of living systems. The distant influence of biological systems can assume many different forms. In the beginning attempts were made to influence the motor activities of mammals or the orientation of fish. When the success of such experiments became apparent, and the importance of the effect for anomalous healing was recognized, the focus increasingly shifted to the influencing of physiological responses in humans.

By far the greatest number of studies of this kind were conducted by William Braud at the Mind Science Foundation in San Antonio, Texas.[90] He and several other researchers systematically required subjects to influence shielded biological systems in remote rooms by means of simple mental intentions. The target systems included physiological parameters of humans, such as electrodermal activity, heartbeat, blood pressure, muscle tremor and ideomotoric movements, and also experiments *in vitro*, such as influencing the rate of haemolysis of red blood cells.

With special equipment – and without any psi – almost anybody can learn how to direct certain automatic physiological processes in their own body. It is relatively easy to reduce your pulse rate and heartbeat by listening to your pulse or heartbeat on a set of earphones. Without much effort, a condition of relaxation can be created by watching the appearance of alpha waves in the brain on a special monitor. This sort of self-regulation is known as biofeedback.

In a series of exciting and elegant experiments, William Braud demonstrated that biofeedback training is not necessarily limited to processes within one's own body.[91] A person to be influenced was connected to a biofeedback instrument which recorded the electrodermal activity – a measurement also used in lie detectors that tells us something about the degree of physical relaxation or excitement. During randomly selected experimental phases, the 'influencer' monitored the polygraph tracing with the intention of producing as few and as minor deflections as possible, which would equate to a state of relaxation. So far the experiment resembles a normal training session in biofeedback with the difference, however, that it was the electrodermal activity of another person that was being measured. The experiment succeeded – biofeedback relating to the physiology of somebody else.

A total of 13 series of experiments of this kind were carried out at the Mind Science Foundation, of which 12 were significant in the predicted direction – that is, the level of autonomous physiological activity of a subject correlated to the intentions of a monitor to either reduce or increase it. The effect is recordable and replicable.

The researchers approached this problem in the conviction that they might find a way mentally to influence life processes for the purposes of healing. The initial experiments looked very promising. Certainly, the effects were not overly strong – they lay in the order of 5 per cent – and naturally did not always succeed, but compared to a number of other techniques, this order of magnitude cannot be disregarded. It is comparable to the effects achieved in normal biofeedback training, the therapeutic effect of which has been proven.[92] The data also make it possible to conclude that the ability that manifests itself in this effect must be widely distributed.

What did the 'influencers' do to achieve these results? It was left completely up to them how they would mentally express their intention, but their efforts all followed one of three strategies: they tried to relax or activate themselves, or they imagined the subject in a relaxed or activated condition, or they concentrated on the tracings of the recording instrument and tried to direct it in the direction intended. None of these strategies proved to be better than any of the others, an indication – often observed – that psi is goal orientated and does not depend on mental strategies.

The psi effect can be aimed very selectively. In some cases it was possible to influence an isolated parameter of the autonomous activity without affecting others. It is obviously difficult to confirm this in an organism because physiological processes in the body are characterized by a high degree of interdependence and the modification of one parameter inevitably leads to changes in others. One study investigated whether the effect would be stronger in people who have a need to relax. Hyperactive people who were easily excitable were selected for the test, and in fact stronger calming effects appeared, apparently because such people could profit more from the effect than those in whom the need was not so pronounced.

A further insight the team gained had to do with the biofeedback process itself. Feedback does not appear to be a basic requirement for direct mental influencing. While feedback may be helpful for the control of imagery and therefore intentions, significant results were also achieved without feedback. The results confirm the insights gained in the analysis of the remote viewing process.

Braud's studies had been specifically designed to influence organisms in a positive direction. Obviously these effects can also be achieved with a negative intention. Ethnological observations show that shamans and medicine men use their 'psi abilities' for evil as well as for good. Death spells are just as much a part of their business as magic healing.[93] The inevitable question arises: is it possible to defend against an attempted influencing?

Braud conducted some exploratory experiments following a technique that is well known in occult literature. The subject is required to imagine that his body is protected by a shield or a cover of white light. The few experiments conducted appear to indicate that such a passive mental protection is possible. The earlier studies on paranormal interference of mental processes seem to show that an active disruption of distant influence is also possible. The question of what happens when one intention is set against another intention has not yet even been touched upon. One fact must be noted: all the participants in the DMILS studies knew that their autonomous physiological reactions were to be influenced at a distance and had consented to this, and nobody ever reported that the effect had been unpleasant.

Everybody has experienced the following situation: you are walking along, deep in thought, or you are sitting in an auditorium, and suddenly you have the feeling that you are being stared at from behind. You turn around and, there it is, someone is watching you. Sometimes it is not even a conscious assumption. An impulse, a feeling of unease, makes you look around, and you see a pair of eyes fixed upon you.

Braud believed this could also be due to a subtle psi effect. Because it often occurs as a subconscious reaction, he assumed the psi information 'I am being stared at' is registered as a weak stimulus, an activation of autonomous physiological parameters which then cause the unease, the hunch.

He checked this hypothesis in an elegantly designed experiment.[94] In order to exclude any possibility of sensual information transfer, the 'starer' was not permitted to observe his 'victim' directly. The staree, located in another room, could only be observed by the starer on a video screen. He was to attempt to attract the staree's attention. The staree did not have to report when he had the feeling of being stared at from behind. This task was taken over by a physiological measuring instrument which recorded the electrodermal activity. Braud and his team were able to observe that in the physiological recordings, being stared at manifests itself as emotional information, a sort of slight fear reaction of the organism.

Since then Braud's experiments on mental influence of autonomous physiological reactions have been replicated in several other laboratories with a similar degree of success.

## BIO-PK AGAINST RADIATION DAMAGE

The babies in the Laboratory for Psychosomatics in Kobe, Japan, had no inkling of what was to happen to them. In any event, they did exactly what infants at the age of 3 to 21 months like to do best: they slept. That was all that was wanted of them, with the minor difference that they had to carry some electrodes on their tiny limbs. These did not appear to bother them, however. And that was good, because they were not supposed to be aware that at various times during the night a hand was held over them with the intention of exerting a positive influence on their organism. All the while instruments were recording physiological data about the babies – peripheral blood circulation, micro-vibrations, electrocardiogram and breath frequency. In all of the experiments of this kind, distinct reactions were observed, which manifested themselves in movements of the body, deep breathing or a change in the sleep phase. The scientists concluded that 'this type of subconscious information transfer ability is common to mankind'.[95]

With these studies, we are entering a field of far-reaching consequences. Should the results of this research be confirmed, the clinical application of psi could no longer be rejected with a clear conscience. The fact that even people who do not feel themselves to be psychics or healers achieve measurable effects suggests that this ability is widespread. Is it really sufficient to pursue a certain intention in order to be able to exert a healing influence on organisms? How specific can these effects be? How strong and lasting are their effects?

The Russian researcher Dimitri Mirza and his colleague V.I. Kartsev recently provided us with an indication of the intensity of the interaction of consciousness with remote biological systems.[96] Mirza is head of the research department at the National Centre for Traditional Folk Medicine in Moscow. In his experiment mice were exposed to three sequences of lethal doses of gamma rays. The doses were increased from sequence to sequence. In the first series of the experiment, various healers treated the irradiation-contaminated animals for 15 minutes. The treatment took place without any contact with the mice. In the second series, the bio-PK effect was used as a preventive measure, and the healers treated the animals about 20 minutes before they were exposed to the lethal dose. In the third series, the animals were treated both before and after irradiation. The results of the second and third test series are of particular interest. The second series consisted of four control groups and four test groups of ten mice each. The death rate in the control groups was 100 per cent; all 40 animals had died within 19 days of irradiation. In the experimental groups, however, after 19 days the death rates were 90 per cent, 50 per cent, 40 per cent and 22 per cent respectively.

The surprising thing about this result is not only the fact that in all the groups where the healers attempted bio-PK there were animals still alive – as opposed to the control groups – but that the most successful healer had worked from afar. The healers for the first three groups treated the animals by simply holding their hands over them. M.B. Fatkin, the healer responsible for the fourth group, and the one who achieved the best results, exerted his influence from the town of Yalta in the Crimea while the irradiated mice were in Moscow – a distance of 1300 kilometres!

This astonishing experiment began in mid-August 1991. In January 1993 15 mice (38 per cent) were still alive from the experimental groups. In the third test series, when the mice were treated before and after irradiation, nine out of ten mice survived in one test group, and in another group all ten animals survived.

It is interesting to put this study into context with an experiment conducted by a team of the National Institute of Radiological Sciences in Chiba, Japan, under the leadership of Masatake Yamauchi of the Genome Research Group. The study dealt with the influence of healers on human cell cultures that had been exposed to lethal doses of an antibiotic or X-rays.[97] The healers were to attempt to make the cultures continue to grow despite the contamination. Although this was not successful in the cultures where the cells had been treated with antibiotics, in those exposed to X-rays, new cell colonies developed. From this pilot experiment the scientists concluded that in the constant presence of a lethal dose of a chemical, the assumed anomalous emission by the healers was not strong enough to counter the lethal effect.

The primary cause of cell death through irradiation with X-rays is double-strand breakage of genomic DNA. Organisms are able to repair such damage by a number of countermeasures. Apparently, the healers were able positively to stimulate the natural mechanisms that lead to the repair of damaged DNA.

From such reports, we should be able to conclude that healing by psi is possible. Nevertheless, some caution is indicated. We are still at a very early stage of research, and the numerous isolated results must first be brought into context and then verified in systematic comparative studies.

## ANOMALOUS HEALING EFFECTS

Ever since the sensational studies conducted by French allergist Jacques Beneviste on the 'memory' of water, we have known that water can store and transmit information. Beneviste regards the fact that water molecules rearrange themselves into different patterns several million times a second as the basis for storing information. The molecules can also arrange themselves in the form of a helix, which can form an electromagnetic 'circuit' of protons over the oxygen atoms.

These properties of water are apparently responsible for the fact that it is particularly well suited as a medium for the transfer of bio-PK effects. This was demonstrated in the 1960s in studies with the Hungarian healer

Oskar Estebany, who had emigrated to Canada, where he put himself at the disposal of the physician Bernard Grad of McGill University for carefully controlled laboratory experiments. This was the beginning of serious research into paranormal healing.

As part of his research programme, Grad had barley sprouts watered with a highly concentrated salt solution, over which Esterbany had previously held his hand for 15 minutes. By the ninth day, Estebany's plants had grown measurably higher than the control group. The healer was apparently able to influence the molecular structure of the solution and cancel its damaging effect.

Industrial research scientist Robert Miller of Agnes Scott College in Atlanta, Georgia, investigated water that had been treated by healer Olga Worral.[98] He discovered a highly reduced surface tension and modifications in the connections of the water molecules.

Recent experiments by Russian scientists L.N. Pyatnitsky and V.A. Fonkin involving light-scattering methods confirmed that the molecular structure of water can be altered by means of psychokinetic influence.[99] They were able to determine that this effect varies between different subjects.

A team at the Research Institute of Precise Mechanics and Optics at St Petersburg also investigated the effects of gifted subjects on the optical properties of water solutions.[100] These modifications resembled a change in the parameters of symmetry of organic molecules. They were also similar to the influence of electromagnetic, acoustical or temperature fields on the solution.

At the Division of Biophysics of Moscow State University the healer Igor Verbitsky was able to change the pH value of water (the pH value gives us a measure of the degree of acidity of a solution). In the beginning, Verbitsky succeeded in achieving only very minor changes in the pH value. More recently, he is alleged to be able to change the pH value of water in the order of 1.5 units of pH. In alkaline solutions (pH = 8.0–9.0) the effect is normally irreversible, whereas after treatment, acidic solutions (pH = 5.0–6.0) slowly return to their normal values.[101]

The influence of operators on living systems can be investigated in the living object or *in vitro* – that is, in isolated specimens. Both methods are necessary in order to reach a comprehensive understanding of the possibilities of influencing. The DMILS effect on healthy and sick tissue was investigated in a number of individual studies.

Human blood cells contain monoamine oxidase (MAO), an enzyme involved with metabolizing certain functionally important chemicals in the brain called neurotransmitters. MAO aids the degrading of neuro-transmitters, which are active in the junctions between nerve cells. It also plays a role in depression and other mood states. A healer who was not pursuing any specific intention sometimes achieved an increase, and occasionally a decrease, in enzyme activity compared with untreated cells.[102] It could not be determined why the psychokinetic influence varied. Nevertheless, the MAO study is of great importance as a point of departure for a healing effect. It indicates that healers may be able to change nervous functions directly and thereby cause the frequently observed alterations in the mood state of their patients.

If red blood cells are stored in a solution of similar concentration to that of body fluids, they can be kept alive for a long time. If they are put into a diluted solution, osmotic pressure leads to the cells swelling and rupture. The result is that haemoglobin is released from the cells. This process is known as haemolysis. The haemoglobin colours the solution, and its concentration can be measured with the aid of a spectrophotometer.

The famous English healer Matthew Manning attempted to reduce the rate of haemolysis in five out of ten samples.[103] This very carefully prepared and conducted experiment was highly successful, and the samples influenced by Manning, by nothing more than mental concen-tration, showed a statistically very significant reduction in their rate of haemolysis.

This result is of great importance for paranormal healing. It can be interpreted as an indication that the membranes of red blood cells can be strengthened by anomalous influence. It may well be that this is the site of action for healing, because cell membranes serve as both barriers and gateways between the cell and its environment.

Some 30 years ago scientists at the University of Santiago in Chile had demonstrated that subjects were able to slow the growth of artificially induced cancers in mice by aimed intentions.[104] In an experiment conducted by John Kmetz, Matthew Manning later succeeded in causing cancer cells in a test tube to disintegrate.[105] Healthy cells remain attached to the plastic surface of the glass by means of electrostatic forces. When the cells die, they lose their normal positive charge, free themselves from the negatively charged surface and diffuse into the liquid medium. Manning succeeded in effecting dramatic changes in the cancer cells. By the laying on of hands and also from a distance in an electrically shielded room, between 200 and 1200 per cent more cancer cells fell off the glass than without bio-PK influence.

Unfortunately, in many of these isolated studies of the direct effects on cells, the problem of replicability still remains. The initial successes achieved in pilot experiments frequently could not be repeated in subsequent studies under more stringently controlled conditions. Sometimes anomalous effects even occur that do not lie in the direction of the healer's intentions.[106]

This whole field is extremely difficult to research. The many experiments that have been conducted and of which I have presented only a small selection here need to be followed by comprehensive and long-lasting studies to look at all specific effects with the current state of knowledge. The fact remains that so many studies with important effects have been carried out that such a research programme is more than justified. American psychiatrist Daniel Benor has compiled an excellent overview, with critical evaluations of all the studies on psychokinetic healing.[107]

One result of these investigations is that no matter how complicated the assigned task was, psychokinetic effects could be detected. In order to achieve success, a healer does not have to know which processes in an organism need to be activated or toned down. Many healers or volunteer operators had no idea at all about the biochemical and physiological processes that must take place in the cells in order to produce a certain result. With this, we have an impressive confirmation of an observation parapsychologists had already made with PK on physical systems – namely, that the process of anomalous perturbation is goal directed. The intention to achieve a certain result is sufficient. Psi itself finds the necessary point of entry from which to direct the information to the right place.

Basically, this process reflects the mechanism of remote viewing. In that process too it had been discovered that anomalous cognition automatically adjusts itself to the intended target. The mechanism of being goal orientated appears to be inherent in the nature of psi.

## IN SEARCH OF SUBTLE ENERGIES

For a long time bio-PK was regarded as a mental effect on a material biological system. The underlying thought ascribes the ability to achieve a non-local effect to consciousness or the intention of a human. The key question is to determine how the mind achieves interaction with the remote material system. Is there only a transfer of information or are we dealing with a previously undiscovered form of energy flow?

As we have seen, psi research in recent years has been stimulated by a new concept, stemming from unorthodox medical investigations and the upsurge of qigong research in China and Japan. This concept assumes an exchange of energy. The idea is that the mind is able to mobilize a natural reservoir of energy in the body. Under certain conditions, this energy can be transferred to other organisms and material systems. Apart from the fact that the nature of such energy is still completely obscure, the effect itself remains paranormal. In some still unexplained manner, there must be an anomalous perturbation of a material or energetic system emanating from the mind.

On what levels should we look for possible carriers of the energies of the bio-PK effect? Until now science has paid little attention to the energies of the human body. Our knowledge is therefore very limited, and we know far too little about how these energies can be usefully employed. We know, for example, that organisms have fluctuating magnetic fields. In modern western medicine, human magnetic fields are used only for diagnostic purposes – in a so-called magnetocardiogram (MCG), for example, or in a magnetoencephalogram (MEG). Because blood contains moving electric charges, it modifies magnetic fields, and this is a means of measuring the speed of blood circulation.

In recent years it has been demonstrated that magnetic fields can play a certain, although still largely unclarified, role in anomalous effects in the healing process. In an experiment by biologist Justa Smith, Oskar Estebany achieved on the enzyme trypsin a bio-PK effect that was comparable to the effect of a magnetic field.[108] The same effect of an increased trypsin build-up caused by the healer was also achieved by means of a strong magnetic field. Had Oskar Estebany produced a 'virtual' magnetic field by paranormal means, as it were, or is the psi effect simply identical with that of a magnetic field?

Japanese researchers from the Department of Psychology at Showa University, Tokyo, have now demonstrated that qigong masters are able to radiate very strong magnetic fields when they are emanating qi.[109] A group of scientists at the Bioelectrochemistry Laboratory at the Mount Sinai School of Medicine in New York was able to ascertain that qigong masters who were attempting to influence a biologically relevant enzyme system caused an effect resembling that of a magnetic field.[110]

Magnetic fields certainly look promising as a point of departure, but as yet nobody knows where this will lead. Although many effects of bio-PK and the external emission of qigong have been demonstrated, they cannot be explained in terms of the influence of magnetic fields. Perhaps the generation of magnetic fields is only a side-effect, which by itself creates an anomalous effect in certain situations.

If a subtle energy actually does play a role in bio-PK healing processes, it must possess attributes that are as yet still undiscovered. One of the great mysteries is why the effects observed do not diminish, even over long distances. In fact, quite the opposite is true, for frequently the strongest effects are achieved from a distance.

Another question under investigation is whether DMILS works in such a way that it passes information to the cells via their normal channels of communication. It appears as if biophoton emission is primarily involved in this communication. In studies carried out by German physicist Fritz Albert Popp of the International Institute of Biophysics at the University of Kaiserslautern, it was demonstrated that food transmits information to the human organism via biophoton emission.[111] In other words, with the ingestion of food, the food's 'bio-information' is also ingested.

After Chinese researches had been able to demonstrate the photon emission of qigong masters,[112] Popp was able to confirm that this bio-information process might well be an important link for DMILS. In his laboratory he measured the photon emission achieved by healers.[113] The question under study was whether biophoton emission plays a part in the process of anomalous healing. For the test, the hands of the American healer Rosalyn Bruyere and Italian healer Nicola Cutolo were placed inside a specially designed instrument. A residual light amplifier detected, and quantitatively measured, the biophoton emission from the palms of the hands. Normally, people are incapable of regulating the natural biophoton emission from their hands. In all of the subjects Popp had tested, the light intensity of the hand was indeed far too low to be measurable by the residual light amplifier.

Quite the opposite was true with the two healers. When Rosalyn Bruyere attempted to send 'healing energy' through her hand, the photon emission immediately increased by a factor of three. Although it declined again within a minute, it then adjusted itself on a level that remained consistently above the level measured before her intention to emit energy. With Nicola Cutolo, a tremendously increased amount of photon emission was measured, with a minimum of about 1000 photons per second. This is approximately ten times as much as with normal people. The signals did not appear as a steady stream of light but as light flashes lasting for at least one-tenth of a second, an anomalous emission that does not occur continually, but in the form of eruptions.

According to Popp, biophoton emission plays an important part in the fundamentals of life itself. He defines life as the optimal ability to communicate, to build up databases and to use them. Life and health are closely related to the ability to communicate, and the result of disrupted biological communication is illness, but the provision of appropriate information can repair this disruption.

Is biophoton emission the key to the understanding of paranormal healing? Is it the measurable component of that life energy about which all cultures speak in the context of magic healing? Basically, we do not know what qi or 'life energy' is, nor do we know how biophotons might be involved in it. All we can say is that there are interactions over distance and these are normally equated with a form of energy.

Biophotons certainly play a part in the healing process, but that process is difficult to understand, if we can understand it at all. And we have only just begun to investigate how psi acts within these subtle forms of communication.

After decades of work and innumerable experiments on the self-regulation of internal, involuntary processes, one of the great pioneers of biofeedback research, Elmer Green, has increasingly turned to the study of the voluntary control of external processes (DMILS).[114] What interests Green is the possibility of measuring DMILS or the external emission of qi as an unknown, subtle form of energy. In theory, Green leans on ancient Indian concepts of the structure of the human body. Yoga claims that the physical structure of the human body consists of matter on seven different levels. There are three levels of density – solid, liquid, gaseous – and four levels of *pranas* (subtle energies). The seven levels are interwoven, so that modifications on one level are also registered on another. The mind is the organizing principle on all seven levels. The mind constructs 'thought-forms', whose subtlety is even greater than that of the seven levels of physical substance. The thought-forms do not depend on whether we possess a body or not. They are organized exclusively according to 'mental' laws. As long as we possess a body, the thought-forms produce resonances in physical matter. By such means we can move our limbs or, by our intentions, influence internal processes, such as immunological processes. Green believes that the four subtle physical energies serve as the link between mind and matter. By learning how to modulate the subtle energies so as to regulate autonomous processes within our body, we can gradually progress to the modulation of the same energies in order to control processes outside our body.

As far as Green is concerned, these concepts are no longer just pure theory. He and his colleagues have experimentally broken through into areas where the effects of the modulation of subtle energies are being studied with great success. For several years now at the Menninger Clinic in Topeka, Kansas, the 'copper wall project' has been pursued under Green's direction. He discovered the description of an obscure Tibetan technique of meditation in an article written in 1882. Meditation students were electrically isolated from the ground while they sat underneath a magnet and looked at their image in a plate of polished copper. He recognized this as being an attempt to create an electrostatic charge in the isolated body by means of meditation. Green had the 'copper wall' laboratory built, a chamber with four copper surfaces (one at the front, one at the back, one above, and one below), and in the centre a person, electrically isolated from the ground, can sit below a magnet. The subjects were connected to psycho-physiological measuring instruments, the recordings of which were transmitted to the control room.

In various experiments, modifications in body potential were recorded in people while they were meditating, and even greater variations were noted in healers, who achieved increases in body potential ranging from 4 to 190 V. The scientists define this enormous electrical phenomenon in terms of the modulation of subtle energies during the healing process, but they cannot offer an explanation for it. What was remarkable was that the modifications in potential corresponded to the intention to heal – that is, they were deliberately controlled by a mental process.

## CURRENT PSI RESEARCH IN JAPAN

For a long time parapsychologists in Japan have been regarded as outcasts by their colleagues elsewhere. The little that found its way into international publications from Japan consisted of reports on some rather ordinary and conservative traditional experiments. Outside Japan the impression was that the paranormal received very little attention in this highly technological country. It may be that this impression was based on a problem of perception, which makes the way Asian thinking, particularly Japanese thinking, works appear unknowable to the western mind. In recent years, however, we have been confronted with such a wealth of highly independent and vital research that we are in danger of losing track.

The most active scientific psi research in Japan is being conducted at the Bio-Emission Laboratory in Chiba, which has already been mentioned in connection with other projects. The head of the department is the physicist Mikio Yamamoto, who began investigating qigong and systematically studying anomalous cognition in relation to brain waves in 1993. The focus at the Bio-Emission Laboratory is on determining how subtle energies can be detected and how they can be controlled.

In 1995 the International Society for Life Information Sciences, which Yamamoto heads, received research funds of ¥100 million for a 5-year programme to assess exceptional functions of the human body by means of numerous simultaneous measurements. The principal objective of this research is the detailed study of the physiological concomitants of anomalous effects.[115] Yamamoto is confident that his application to the Japanese Ministry of Science and Technology for funds to study the emissions of living bodies will also be approved. Should this be the case, it would be one of the best-endowed research programmes in this specialized field of psi research. Yamamoto has applied for ¥1 billion.

Included in the programme was research on a form of remote influencing which is known as *tohate* in Japanese martial arts. *Tohate* is the Japanese variation of a sudden aimed external emission of qi as is done in qigong. Yamamoto investigated the claim made by students that they could physically feel a *tohate* action by their master.[116] In order to prevent any form of suggestive effect, a qigong master and one of his pupils were put into shielded rooms on different storeys of the laboratory. At randomly selected times, the master executed a *tohate* action. In six out of 16 cases his pupils reacted to this emission of qi within one second. In a second series of experiments, the pupils reacted to the master's qi emissions within ± 5.5 seconds in 16 out of 49 cases.

In further experiments of this nature, the pupils were connected to an EEG.[117] During the periods in which the emission of qi was attempted, the amplitudes of the alpha rhythm in the right frontal region of the brain showed significant changes. The scientists believe they have demonstrated that an anomalous transfer of information took place, although it was independent of any visible reaction.

New methods of representation – EEG topographies – permit the visual reproduction of the spread of EEG patterns across the brain, by showing in colour the majority percentage of intensity of brain waves in the relevant areas of the brain. Yamamoto believes that during *tohate* actions there is a correlation between the recorded topographical patterns of the beta waves of the sender and of the percipient.

Another interesting subject is whether the deliberate control of the flow of qi in the body correlates with physiological parameters. Should it be possible to prove such a correlation, it could be used in 'classic' psi experiments. It might then be possible to test whether psi and qi are only two terms for the same process, or whether the anomalous transfer of information can assume different forms.

Yoshio Machi, a physicist at Denki University in Tokyo, investigated physiological patterns in a special form of qigong exercise, the so-called 'minor circulation' (*xiao zhoutian*). During 'minor circulation', qi is circulated from the central channel at the back of the body (*du mai*) to the central channel at the front of the body (*ren mai*). Qi is directed upwards from the lower abdomen and along the spine to the top of the skull through the *du* channel, and from there back downwards in the middle through the *ren* channel, which runs centrally down the front of the torso. This qi circulation is accomplished by breathing exercises and concentration.

Machi's experiments brought a number of peculiarities to light.[118] The master's rate of breathing dropped from 14 breaths a minute before the exercise to six breaths a minute during qigong. This notable change in breathing frequency is alleged to have some relationship to the circulation of qi. In order to test this, Yoshio Machi recorded the EEG topographies for the alpha wave range. In the middle of the breathing cycle, when the greatest abdominal expansion occurs, qi effects the connection from the back to the front, between the *du* and the *ren* channels at the top of the head. At exactly this moment, the strongest intensity of the alpha waves occurred over the whole centre of the cortex, from the occipital to the frontal area. Machi is convinced that the alpha activity is a clear signal for the flow of qi in the body. If alpha waves actually do signal a state of preparedness for the extraordinary and serve as a sort of 'carrier frequency' for psi, this research could indicate a close connection between psi and qi. It could serve as a proof of the 'alpha gate' and the entry into a state of 'space-expanding' consciousness.

In many instances during qigong, an increase in the slow brain waves, particularly alpha waves of high amplitude,[119] and the occurrence of actual bursts of alpha waves were recorded.[120] Kimiko Kawano of the Nippon Medical School in Tokyo was able to observe certain adaptations between the EEG patterns of the master and his patient during the external emission of qi. In both, frontal alpha waves occurred and in total, the EEG showed a higher than normal degree of synchronization. In both, the frequency of alpha waves also increased. The beta wave range in the qi recipient showed the same topography as that of the qigong master.[121] The synchronization of the beta waves in particular indicates that an anomalous transfer of information connected to direct mental processes was taking place.

What is remarkable about the Japanese research is the casual, highly medical-technological manner in which it approaches the field of anomalous phenomena. Many interesting ideas are immediately acted upon and converted into experiments. Unfortunately, this conversion often takes place too quickly, without any attempt at the careful methodological consideration, planning and execution of the experiment that are so necessary in the field of the paranormal. In addition, things are often left at the stage of a pilot experiment. There is still no evidence of an overarching research programme that will follow a direction defined according to the current state of knowledge. The experiments remain a largely unconnected set of snap-shots in a very broad and extremely complex field, the worth of which has still not been determined.

The dedication, however, with which our Japanese colleagues pursue their work should not be underestimated. I am firmly convinced that in Japan – and China – an important support for the discovery of the secrets of anomalous mental phenomena will develop as soon as the scientific potential available is prepared to face up with determination to the methodological requirements of this field of research.

When we speak of 'qi emission' or of the 'external transmission of qi', we must be aware that science today still has no idea at all of what qi actually is. Here we are in the same situation as with the categories of attempted descriptions of psi. In scientific terms, we must define qi as a label for a group of phenomena the nature and functions of which are still largely unknown. Some of the phenomena remind us of anomalous cognition, others resemble anomalous perturbation, and others again cannot be described in existing psi categories.

There are many indications that subtle energies exist and permeate the living body and the cosmos, and that they can be deliberately directed by means of particular physical and mental exercises. But it is still much too early to be able to grasp these energies in theory and to categorize correctly the various forms in which qi manifests itself.

# Part 3

# A SELF-AWARE UNIVERSE? SILENT REVOLUTION IN THE PSI LABORATORIES

'Not once in the dim past, but continuously by conscious mind is the miracle of the Creation wrought.'

*Arthur Eddington*

'All the forces known to physics, like gravity for example, diminish with distance. And no forces in physics operate freely across time like this [psi]. It's as if consciousness is somehow able to direct its influence directly across space and time, and understanding that certainly poses a challenge for science.'

*Robert Jahn*

# Chapter One

# THE PHYSICS OF CONSCIOUSNESS

## DEVICES FOR CHANCE

Every human continues to have objectives and intentions, some that are pursued with great energy and consistency, others that are only fleeting and related to a particular situation. If all that is required for the direct mental influence of living systems (DMILS) effect is an intention, the question arises of whether our mind is not constantly exerting influence on our material environment through our conscious or subconscious intentions, without our being aware of this. Seen from such a perspective, psi would not be a special talent, possessed by the very few and applicable only in rare cases, but a function inherent in the biological system of organisms. Is it possible that there is a constant exchange by subtle psi interactions that normally take place below the level of consciousness and are so minute in their direct effects that they do not attract our notice? Psi could well be a fundamental biological function.

Starting from such considerations, American parapsychologist Rex Stanford developed a model that claimed that an organism constantly and subconsciously applies anomalous phenomena to optimize its contacts with its environment. He called this model psi-mediated instrumental response (PMIR).

In one of Stanford's classic experiments the subjects could terminate a terribly boring task only by psychokinetically influencing a hidden instrument.[1] On the basis of random selection, this instrument signalled the end of the experiment. The subjects, however, did not know the instrument existed or that they could influence it paranormally. Stanford's theory was that the organism, in order to shorten the boredom, would automatically extend its 'psi feelers' in the form of a psi-mediated instrumental response and cause the instrument to terminate the experiment sooner than expected. The study was successful.

In the past two decades Stanford's theoretical assumptions have led to extensive and highly successful research projects. They are designed to investigate the mysterious relationship between consciousness and matter – the interaction of the mind with its environment by the anomalous exchange of information. The most important piece of equipment for this research, which Rex Stanford's subjects influenced without their being aware of it, is the random-number generator, a machine for coincidences.

The difference between micro-PK and macro-PK lies in the fact that in some cases an effect can be seen with the naked eye (macro-PK), but in others a statistical analysis is required to demonstrate a PK effect on atomic particles (micro-PK). In micro-PK there is no visible change in an object, but there is a shift in the probability with which random processes will occur. It is not objects that are being shifted, but the probability of events occurring. Until recently it was believed that there is no fundamental difference between macro-PK and micro-PK. In both cases we are dealing with an unexplained mind–matter interaction (MMI).

The classic test for PK lies somewhere between macro-PK and micro-PK. Introduced by J.B. Rhine in the 1930s, the process attempted to demonstrate possible psychokinetic effects by means of rolling dice. The subject was asked to 'wish' that certain numbers would come up more frequently than others. Dean Radin and Diane Ferrari, formerly at Princeton University, recently subjected the extensive data from the dice experiments to a meta-analysis.[2] For this analysis they were able to draw on numerous studies conducted over a period of half a century. One of the advantages of these experiments lies in the fact that not only is there a probability value available as the measure for an anomalous result, but also baseline data exists – that is, control data from experiments that were conducted without attempted mental influencing. Although the probability always expresses a deviation only from the *theoretical* random distribution, the control data permits us to check whether the random system (in this example the rolling dice) corresponds to the theoretical expectations – that is, that it is actually working at random. When working with analogous macroscopic random processes, such controls are absolutely necessary, because minor faults, such as unevenly finished dice or inclining surfaces, can introduce systematic errors.

In order to obtain the necessary homogeneity in their data, Radin and Ferrari had to exclude 52 of their 148 studies. Of the studies excluded, 33 showed positive effects, and only 19 showed negative effects. Despite the exclusion of so many positive experiments, there remained substantial proof for a replicable anomalous mental effect on the roll of the dice. To cancel the effect, it would have required 20 times the number of file-drawer cases compared with the studies reported.

The modern equivalent to the experiments with dice is experiments with random-number generators. Since these instruments do not actually generate numbers but states expressed as numbers, they are frequently more appropriately called random-event generators (REG). An REG performs, on the micro level, the equivalent task of tossing of a coin on the macro level. The REG produces 'virtual' tosses of a coin in rapid succession. Depending on whether the coin comes up heads or tails, the number 0 or 1 – a sequence of bits – is shown. Modern instruments of this sort are based either on processes of radioactive decay or on electronic noise. Such physical processes produce electronic deflections that occur several thousand times a second and cannot be predicted. These random deflections interrupt a counter that, for example, switches from 1 to 0 and back 10 million times a second. Depending in which state the counter is (on 1 or on 0), the number is recorded as a random bit. This cycle can also be slowed down to produce random series of exactly 1000 bits a second. A computer makes exact recordings of these incredibly fast processes.

The first person to apply random-event generators in parapsychology was German-born American physicist Helmut Schmidt. Using this technical innovation, Schmidt replaced the old 'coarse' method of rolling dice in order to pursue a theoretical objective. With his instruments, the random process could be directly attributed to quantum mechanical processes. He was therefore able to study micro-PK as an effect of observers on quantum physical processes, an interpretation that is of central importance in quantum physics.

## PEAR AND THE ORDINARINESS OF PSI

Robert Jahn, a former NASA scientist and Dean of the School of Engineering and Applied Science at Princeton University, has made work with random-event generators (REGs) the focal point of a research programme that has now been going on for almost 20 years. It is one of the most exciting innovations in psi research. Neither Jahn nor his colleagues were parapsychologists when they set off on this adventure. They are physicists and psychologists, and they were able to establish their research at a respected university.

In 1979 Jahn founded the Princeton Engineering Anomalies Research Program (PEAR). It has only one objective: the rigorous scientific analysis of the interaction between human consciousness and sensitive physical instruments. The ultimate goal is a better understanding of consciousness in the framework of physical reality.[3]

Among Jahn's colleagues at the PEAR lab are Brenda Dunne, a developmental psychologist whose role is the integration of the various directions followed by PEAR research; Roger Nelson, an experimental psychologist and specialist in the design of PEAR's experimental protocols and controls, aids in statistical modelling and data interpretation; Johnston Bradish, an electrical engineer responsible for design, construction and the maintenance of the experimental instruments; and York Dobyns, a theoretical physicist who designs and implements PEAR's data processing and analytical strategies. The great advantage of the team that works with Jahn is that all the members are generously funded by various trusts and institutions.

Brenda Dunne describes PEAR's work in the words: 'Gamblers throughout history have believed that they could affect the outcome of a random process like rolling dice or shuffling cards. The phenomenon we're measuring is a lot more subtle, but it's the same idea and we've measured it in the laboratory.'

For its experiments, PEAR developed the so-called tripolar protocol. According to this, the operator – this is what PEAR calls its subjects – has to pursue one of three mental tasks with regard to the REG. In one phase, the operator is supposed to produce the number 1 more frequently ('aim high' ), in another the number 0 ('aim low') and in the third to pursue no specific intention. As soon as the operator activates a switch, they have to pursue one of these three intentions, and the instrument immediately begins producing a random sequence of bits.

The data collected over many years permits of only one conclusion: that the random distribution of REG outputs changes in relationship to the intentions of an operator. These are not dramatic changes, but rather extremely small effects in the order of 1 per cent, but the effects are recordable and appear over long periods of time and with many operators, so that they become statistically highly significant.

The PEAR team defines its databases as process-orientated material. What is important is to get as much out of the data as possible, and they therefore refer back to the constantly growing material time and again in order to find answers to new questions and problems by means of appropriate methods of analysis.

They recently submitted the results of 5.6 million individual tests out of 1262 series of experiments to an elaborate statistical analysis. The data had been collected over 12 years in experiments with different types of REGs. The analysis confirmed that the intentions of the operators are the primary correlation of the anomalous effects. What is remarkable is the substantial difference between the best operators and the rest of the subjects. The 30 best operators achieved a stronger and more definite symmetrical effect.

What came as a real surprise is that recording the effects reveals different distribution curves for different operators. Operators, particularly the best, apparently influence the REGs in individual ways, and this singularity is maintained in repeated experiments. The scientists call this a 'signature'. It is a sort of mental signature recorded by micro-PK in the data produced by an REG. There were operators, for example, who tended to produce low values even when their intention had been to 'aim high'. Others were able to achieve significant deviations from chance expectation in only one direction. Still others showed characteristic patterns of fluctuation.

A further unexpected result has to do with distance. The characteristic distributions and the 'signatures' remained the same, regardless of whether the operators were very close to the instruments or whether the REGs and the operators were far apart.

It is only among the group of superior operators that the type of feedback plays a particular role. The data for some subjects shows that the instructions they received were an important condition for the anomalous results achieved, whether the intention to be pursued was prescribed or whether it was left to their own free choice. Both the way individual runs in the experiments were set off (manually or automatically) and the duration of the runs sometimes also influenced results. The indications are that such factors should be seen not so much as influencing psi effects in general but as part of the 'signatures' that characterize individual performances.

The data collected at the PEAR laboratory permits us to define a hierarchy of effects, starting with the most important.[4]

1. A large number of human operators are able systematically to achieve anomalous deviations of the output distribution means of REGs.
2. The scale of the anomalous effects is always quite small (in binary machines only a few bits per thousand displacement from chance

expectation). With the large databases collected, however, these add up to highly significant statistical deviations.

3. The primary correlate for the anomalous effect is the intention of the operator – try for high values, try for low values, no intention – which has been decided upon in advance.

4. The form and the extent of the tripolar separation are operator specific. The graphic displays of the operators' results are sufficiently characteristic that they may be described as 'signatures'.

5. The dependence of the results on the machines employed is unclear. Some operators appear to be able to transfer their signatures to two or more devices; others show substantial variations depending on the machine used. In most cases the extent of the effect is preserved.

6. The sensitivity of the effect for secondary technical parameters – for example, the duration and speed of the test run or the type of feedback – is also operator specific. Some show themselves to be strongly affected; others do not react at all.

7. Two operators who jointly influence a machine do not compound their signatures, but produce a new, specific signature, distinctly characteristic of the pair.

8. The effects can be achieved over long distances (up to several thousand kilometres). With several operators the characteristics of the effects achieved over distances are very similar to those achieved close up.

9. In some cases effects 'remote in time' were achieved – retro-PK, when the machine was activated *before* the intention of the operator was formed; 'PK into the future', when it was activated *after* the intention of the operator was formed.

10. Even though the PEAR laboratory has as yet collected only a few systematic correlations with psychological and physiological determinants, the individual effects achieved do not appear to depend on the personality, style or strategy of the operator.

## THE INFERNAL MACHINE AND THE PENDULUM

Sometimes visitors and staff members who pass the PEAR laboratory wrinkle their foreheads. Many people consider the studies being undertaken by Jahn and his team to be crazy or at least a waste of time. Some may even suspect that there is something rather demoniacal behind the group's sober reports and articles. If they press their ear to the door of one particular room in the cellar, they regularly hear a rattling and banging, as if an infernal machine were being set in motion. However, anyone who entered the room would be astonished, or even amused, by this 'infernal machine'.

A few years ago some creative brains in the United States came up with a simple sales concept that they marketed with the slogan 'think big'. They made reproductions of everyday objects that influence the daily lives of Americans to such a degree that they are regarded as icons. What is special about these reproductions is that they can no longer be used for their original purpose because they are many times larger than the originals.

Whether the PEAR scientists got their idea from one of these stores is not known. In any case, the members of the team 'think big' in every respect. Their 'infernal machine' is an enormously enlarged version of the Galton board, a common statistical demonstration device, which is a conveniently sized transparent box with many evenly spaced pins on the upper part and, in the lower section, a row of tubes. Small balls are introduced into the box through a hole in the centre and pass through the rows of pins until they finally land in the tubes below. When all the balls have finished their trip through the pin barriers, they form a bell-shape, with the majority of the balls being in the tubes in the centre and the fewest in the tubes at the edges. This pattern is known as normal distribution or Gaussian distribution.

In the PEAR laboratory there are 19 long collecting bins with a matrix of 333 nylon pegs above, which the operator can see from a comfortable couch in the panelled room. It takes 12 minutes for all 9000 of the polystyrene balls to rattle through the lattice-work of this random mechanical cascade (RMC).[5] Photoelectric cells count each ball as it enters one of the bins. The actual ball count is constantly displayed beneath each tube so that in addition to the visual distribution of the balls there is constant feedback on the absolute number of balls in each container.

As in all experiments conducted by Jahn's team, the job of the operator is relatively 'simple'. Following the normal tripolar protocol, all they have to do is to wish that as many balls as possible should fall into the tubes on the left, or into the tubes on the right, or not to have any preference at all. And here again the operators were able significantly to shift the distribution of the balls in accordance with their intentions. While the degree of the effect is comparable to that achieved with the REGs, there is a strange variation. Here, the anomalous results show a curious asymmetry, with a tendency of the operators to shift the balls to the left. This is not the result of individual signatures but is displayed in the data of all operators. This asymmetry cannot be traced to a fault in the system, such as badly aligned nylon pegs or bins sitting at a slight angle, because control runs without operators or runs in which the operators had no intention to shift distribution all resulted in a baseline that equated exactly to the expected Gaussian distribution.

What is it that causes this list to the left? The PEAR team assumes the causes to be psychological or possibly even neurological, but so far it has been unable to come closer to solving the mystery.

In these experiments with the RMC the effects also proved to be independent of how remote the operators were. Some even achieved statistically significant results at a distance of several thousand kilometres from the laboratory.[6]

Another analogous instrument with which the PEAR scientists are investigating the interaction between mind and matter is a high-precision pendulum.[7] It is mounted in a transparent acrylic container and hung from a computer-controlled mechanism which always releases the pendulum from the same starting height. A high-speed binary counter records the swings of the pendulum at its lowest point by means of interruptions of photodiode beams, and it measures the velocity to the microsecond. During a series of 100 hundred swings, the operators have one of three tasks: to keep the swings as high as possible (that is, to reduce the damping rate), to increase the damping rate or not to exert any influence at all.

The 42 operators produced different results. With five of them, there were significant differences between runs in which the damping rate was to be increased and those in which it was to be reduced. A further five produced significant differences between those runs without influencing (baseline runs) and those with influencing, and these conformed to their intentions. When all the results are compiled the statistical significance is cancelled out because there were a number of outliers which produced astonishingly strong effects that were diametrically opposed to the intentions of the operators.

In analyses summarizing the results of digital and analogous REGs, the scientists found some peculiarities. They discovered that the anomalous effects themselves are not distributed at random but follow a certain law of distribution. Discovering the nature of this law will require further analysis.

# MIND AND MATTER INTERACTION

In 1989, in the respected physics journal *Foundations of Physics*, Dean Radin and Roger Nelson published a meta-analysis on all of the published studies on consciousness-related anomalies in random physical systems.[8] This work was based on the most comprehensive database that psi research has accumulated to date. The analysis consisted of 597 experimental studies and 235 control studies on the attempted influencing of micro-electronic REGs that had been conducted between 1959 and 1987. Almost half of the experimental studies (258) and more than half of the control studies (127) came from the data collected at the PEAR laboratory.

As could be expected, the mean effect size for each individual experiment proved to be very low but recordable. The probability that these effects cannot be attributed to chance is more than one trillion to one.

The scientists calculated the unbelievable number of 54,000 file-drawer studies, all yielding negative results, that would be required to negate the reality of an anomalous interaction between consciousness and micro-electronic random systems. These are numbers that astonish even the sceptics.

On the basis of the meta-analysis, it was predicted that future experiments would produce similar results. By 1996 the database at PEAR had grown to 1262 studies. A total of 108 operators took part in these experiments, of whom 30 contributed the major part of the data. The results equated exactly to the effects discovered in the meta-analysis.[9]

Jahn and his colleagues came to the conclusion that there are no current theoretical models to explain the anomalous effects. They believe their development will require a greatly expanded model of reality, a model in which the mind is granted an active role in its experiencing of physical reality. The PEAR group did not stop with the amassing of empirical data; it has developed such a model. Its basic assumption is that there is an elemental way in which the mind exchanges information with its environment, orders that information and interprets it. By this process, the mind is able to bias probabilistic systems and thereby to gain a certain amount of control over its reality. What we had already learned from the investigation of direct mental influence of living systems is now being confirmed. By its intentions, consciousness shifts unstable systems in material reality according to the order manifested within itself.[10]

This model regards many concepts of quantum mechanics – primarily the principles of complementarity and wave mechanical resonance – as fundamental characteristics of consciousness and not as intrinsic features of objective physical reality. On the basis of such a definition, we should actually expect anomalous phenomena of the sort demonstrated by the PEAR experiments to occur in systems where humans interact with machines or with other humans.

The complexity of the data means that we are still unable to define the psychological mechanisms behind these strange effects. Jahn and his colleagues have therefore advanced a holistic hypothesis based on the theory of information. Consciousness contributes a small additional amount of information to the technical system. The system uses it in the most efficient way to achieve the objective of the experiment. This is the technical interpretation of the psychologically motivated theory of psi-mediated instrumental response that Rex Stanford had already formulated.

Robert Jahn points out, however, that any model for the transfer of information necessarily includes the transfer of energy. As Jahn expresses it, there are three currencies in the physical world, substantial matter (mass), energy and information. The relationship between the first two currencies has been established by Einstein's theory, which largely dominated physics in the twentieth century. The relationship between energy and information, however, has been defined far less clearly. 'In our experimental situation,' Jahn and his colleagues write, 'the inversion of a small fraction of the information bits from their chance configuration or, equivalently, the shift in the apparent elemental probabilities, also has energetic as well as informative implications, although the former are of minuscule scale.'[11]

The human mind is a supreme information-processing system. Under the eyes of the PEAR scientists it uses this ability, with which it is outstandingly well endowed, to enter into active interactions with the physical world. It rearranges portions of its array of information and in so doing accesses its energy and, indeed, its very substance. By means of the third side of the mass–energy–information triangle, human consciousness finds a natural entry through which it participates in the construction of reality. This is where the interface between the subjective information of the mind and the technical information of the cosmos is located. Jahn and his hard-working team at Princeton are pursuing the investigation of the dynamics of the transfer of the one form of information into the other.

If mind–matter interaction (MMI) is a continuous process, we should be able to detect similar effects outside the laboratory. In the laboratory, the intentions are predetermined. Everyday situations frequently arise in which certain intentions, often of groups of people, are being pursued. Is it possible to detect phenomena of group consciousness as anomalous effects in random-event generators?

# FIELD RESEARCH WITH REGS

On 23 January 1997 thousands of people throughout the world took part in a 5-minute meditation. The event, organized by the Gaiamind Project, took place between 17:30 and 17:35 Greenwich Mean Time, a time that was chosen because it coincided with an unusual astronomical conjunction. The meditation was dedicated to the veneration of Earth as a living planetary being and to an exchange of spiritual experiences on a global level.

The fact that a large number of people throughout the world took part in a coordinated meaningful activity offered a unique opportunity to scientists to test whether this directed mental activity would modify the statistical behaviour of random-event machines. Several laboratories decided to switch on REGs during the meditation in a global experiment, which was made possible by the modern form of communication via the Internet. Roger Nelson at PEAR sent out experimental protocols via the Internet mailing lists that are read by professional parapsychologists, and he explained the planned experiment on the website of the Gaiamind organizers. The result was that parapsychologists ran three REGs in the Netherlands, three in Germany, one in Scotland and seven in the United States. In total, records were collected from 14 independent random-event generators in seven different places in the USA and Europe, and in summary, the data showed a marginally significant deviation from the theoretical random distribution. The hypothesis was confirmed, albeit inconclusively.[12]

The data of the PEAR laboratory experiments have been collected over a long period of time, and the effects recorded became apparent because such an unbelievable amount of data was available. During the field experiment, the machines were on for just 5 minutes. Was it reasonable to expect anything at all in so short a time? Nelson therefore submitted the data to a special statistical analysis. This was a mathematical operation that calculates what is known as a time-normalized yield. The data are analysed in such a way that it is possible to calculate how much time would be required to achieve a certain anomalous effect. The total time during which the 14 5-minute data batches were generated was 1 hour and 10 minutes. This is an extremely short period compared with the REG experiments in the laboratory, which ran for days, weeks and sometimes even for years. If we compare this data to the data recorded during the short time span of the global meditation, we get the astonishing result that the effect size of the global meditation experiment was nine times as high as the time-normalized yield of the total of all the REG experiments conducted in the PEAR laboratory.

What does the experiment tell us? During the global event, some sort of process or condition apparently correlated with a biased behaviour of the machines. It is possible that the participants in the global meditation were not responsible for the result. The effect could be traceable to the intentions of the instigators who ran the machines and knew the object of the experiment, and they certainly had the strongest motivation to achieve positive results. In this case, the experimenters would have become operators against their will. This type of psi-mediated effect – that is, one that is caused by experimenters – constitutes one of the most confusing problems of parapsychology (see Part 3, Chapter 6). As the time-normalized yield analysis showed, however, to reduce the experiment under discussion to an effect achieved by the influence of the experimenters would mean having to attribute far stronger effects to them than any previously observed effects. In all probability, therefore, we can trace the result to the interaction of a group consciousness with a material system.

Roger Nelson is a pioneer in the investigation of 'field consciousness effects', and to record continuous data sequences in the field, PEAR developed a portable random-event generator with software called a FieldREG. Nelson's research is based on the premiss that the degree of strength of consciousness fluctuates in relation to the focus of attention. Normal waking consciousness is characterized by a very low focus of attention. Special states of consciousness, such as meditation, contemplation, concentration and euphoria – that is, states in which we are virtually absorbed by or in something – show a very high degree of focused attention. There is no difference between a group of monks during communal prayer and a group of football fans during an exciting phase of a game.

In a group of people the strength of consciousness varies continuously as the focus of attention changes. On the other hand, groups of people

*Groups of People*

who pursue a common focus of attention generate a mental coherence within the group. The greater the coherence of a field of consciousness, the higher its order. Weak physical systems react to this by also assuming a higher degree of order.

Accordingly, the hypotheses of MMI ordered, coherent, focused states will produce comparable – ordered, coherent, focused – states in unstable (random) material systems. This effect will primarily be detectable on the micro-physical level, which is controlled by random processes, and will appear only rarely on the macro-physical level. The best means for testing this hypothesis are rapidly fluctuating natural processes, such as are ideally produced by REGs.

In contrast to the tripolar protocol for laboratory experiments, FieldREG measurements are not based on fixed intentions. All that is required is natural situations in which a structured group consciousness appears – for example, particular times during scientific conferences, when interesting new results are being reported that focus the attention of the entire audience on a single topic. The reflection of this mental structure on the REG can be demonstrated by a simple statistical method, namely a search for structural patterns in the machine's bit sequences, which would not occur in a genuine random sequence.

The PEAR team developed formal protocols for these experiments. These define the time spans during which the REGs are exposed to the respective field situation. The time factor is decisive in making it possible to compare the data. If we compare the field events with the periods during which data sequences were recorded that deviated sharply from the expected values, we find curious correlations with special phases of 'structured mental activity' within a group of people: attention, intellectual unanimity, shared emotions. In any case, there is a tendency for coherent qualities of groups to correlate statistically with anomalous deviations in the sequences of FieldREGs.[13]

In recent years Dean Radin, the former director of the Consciousness Research Division at the University of Nevada in Las Vegas, has investigated the effect of structured group consciousness on REGs in various situations, including a personal growth workshop, an Academy Awards ceremony, the announcement of the verdict in the O.J. Simpson case, a Superbowl football game and the opening ceremony of the Olympic Games in July 1996.[14] At all these events it could be assumed that small to huge groups of people would have a similarly focused attention during particularly noteworthy moments. For instance, the announcement during the Academy Awards ceremony of the winner of the award for the best movie was selected as being a moment of heightened interest. At this instant, approximately one billion people were tensely waiting for the result in front of their TV sets all over the world. Such a moment, at which the attention of close to 500 million TV viewers was similarly aligned, could also be identified during the reading of the verdict in the O.J. Simpson trial.

A total of 12 people took part in the personal growth workshop, which was a seminar at which strong emotions were released by means of a breathing technique developed by psychiatrist Stanislav Grof. After nine hours of continuous data emission, the FieldREG showed a statistically significant, constant increase in the degree of order induced into the random data.

During the final court session in the Simpson case, Roger Nelson at Princeton and Dick Bierman, professor of psychology at the University of Amsterdam, also turned on the REGs in their laboratories. The results showed that something unusual did occur in all five REGs activated during the reading of the verdict. The degree of order in the data emission of the machines increased rapidly, culminated exactly at the moment the verdict was pronounced and then immediately declined to the random level. At other events – the Academy Awards in 1995 and 1996, the opening ceremony at the Olympics and the final game of the Football league – unexpected increases in the degree of order in the REGs outputs could also be detected during periods that generated high interest as compared to periods of reduced audience attention, in which the REGs fell back to random behaviour.

'Never mind if we are having a period of bad weather, at the festival of St Peter and St Paul the weather is always good.' I often heard this saying while I lived in Bretten, Germany, and I took this to be a local legend that had, over time, developed into a firm belief or even into a pious wish. Nonetheless, I was astonished how often, just in time for the festival, the threatening cloud cover broke and the sun came out.

Similar stories are told all over the world. In Princeton people believe the ceremonies of commencement, which mostly take place outdoors, are always accompanied by good weather. Roger Nelson saw this as an opportunity to test the belief. Could the collective desire for good weather influence the complex meteorological system in such a way that the probability of rain decreased?[15]

Nelson analysed the weather for the days immediately preceding, during and immediately after commencement day and for similar ceremonies elsewhere, drawing on data collected over 30 years. In addition, he investigated rainfall in six cities in the vicinity of Princeton during the same period. He wanted to find out if there was actually more sunshine and less rain on the days of the ceremonies than on the days preceding and following. Nelson's assumption was confirmed, even though the probability lay at only 20 to 1 against chance.

Curiously enough, the average amount of rainfall on commencement day itself was slightly higher in Princeton than in the neighbouring cities on the same day. This was due to a massive cloudburst on 12 June 1962, which had been far milder in the surrounding areas. However, members of the class of 1962 vividly remember that the downpour set in only after the ceremony on the lawn was over.[16]

We should not underestimate the cultural significance of the discovery of the interaction between mind and matter or the effects of field consciousness. For millennia religions have promulgated the close relationship between all forms of beings, and for mystics this is the only true picture of the universe. Modern man, who has abolished the gods and who regards religion as a pastime for insecure and intellectually weak people and mysticism as a benevolent form of insanity, does not know how to deal with spiritual truths. The new gods are technological, economic and pragmatic, machines that generate money and everything and anything that enables humankind to make ever more wonderful machines and ever more money. The technological proof of the interaction between mind and matter that has been revealed by the scientists at PEAR stands like a monolith in the monotonous landscape of approved scientific models of thought. Now there are tangible results, and wonderful machines producing incontestable data, that prove the existence of subtle connections beyond space and time.

It is far from certain if this fact will really lead us to revise our view of ourselves and our relationships with others and the universe in which we live. Robert Jahn is convinced it will, and he believes that this revision will also bring about a change in our values, our priorities, our sense of responsibility and our lifestyles.

I do not believe that a superior cultural ethic will necessarily develop from all this. The productive reunification Jahn expects of those 'long-estranged siblings' science and spirit, analysis and aesthetics, intellect and intuition, can at best be a distant goal, a goal that will be attained only if the results of modern psi research find their way into the consciousness of mankind, if people are no longer faced only with the choice of admiring the dubious miracles performed by alleged mediums or of condemning psi as an adjunct of occultism and esoteric nonsense, and if the belief prevails that psi is an expression of a feeling, an instinct, a hidden sense, that connects us to everything around us at a very deep level.

## PSI DIRECTION-FINDING

Although space and time are not obstacles, the major problem in FieldREG experiments is the correct allocation of intention and effect. In such field experiments, the participants are normally unaware that they are supposed to 'influence' a random-event generator. They do not even know they are taking part in a psi experiment. In a laboratory test the allocation can always be based on the clearly obvious connection between operator and machine. The subject *knows* they have to direct their intentions towards a certain instrument in the laboratory. We have already seen that psi effects are goal orientated, and in the laboratory, psi has no problem in finding the connection between mind and machine.

Since this effect, which is not localized and may not even not be constrained by time, can be demonstrated by perturbations in random sequences even without the knowledge of the subjects, the question arises of whose effects are actually being measured in the field. How does the 'consciousness of the field subjects' know it has to interact with a certain REG? If it does this automatically, however, because the exchange between mind and matter is not localized or affected by time, it would be difficult to allocate the bit sequences to the mental activity of a given collective. Somewhere on earth there are always groups of monks or other religious communities engaged in meditation, contemplation or prayer in one form or another; there are always mass meetings, such as sporting events, political rallies and so on, taking place. We can safely assume that at any given time there are different groups of people together somewhere who have an intensively directed, uniform and ordered field of consciousness, which should find its expression in any REG measurement.

The major proponents of FieldREG experiments believe that these effects cancel each other out, because countless other people are occupied with completely different things, so that the structuring and the chaotic mental influences counteract each other. If this were true, it would be impossible to conduct any meaningful FieldREG studies at all, because the assumption would always have to be that any given ordering field of consciousness would have its effects negated by a chaotic field.

Another major problem is posed by the timeless nature of the effect. How can we determine, for example, whether the significant results actually recorded during the global meditation in January 1997 did not continue to affect experiments conducted days, weeks or even months later?

Should we even assume that intensive meditative efforts such as those undertaken by the followers of Maharishi Mahesh Yogi in 'transcendental meditation' (TM), with which (or so they believe) they intend to modify global consciousness, do not lead – over time – to an 'accumulation of aligned consciousness', which must necessarily influence all future FieldREG measurements? Such an effect would be similar to that of 'morphic resonance' postulated by English biologist Rupert Sheldrake. Indeed, the efforts of the adherents of TM would then be an expression of 'morphic resonance', and FieldREG studies would be a means of measuring its effectiveness.

Reality, however, appears to be quite different. Nothing in the studies conducted to date permits us to conclude that the REG results measured in the field are entirely independent of the time factor. There is no indication that we can prove a cumulative effect of 'large' and repeatedly occurring 'fields of consciousness'. It is not even possible to document the effect's absolute independence of space. Nevertheless, there is no question that the effect is real, measurable and replicable.

This raises the fascinating prospect that it is possible that this effect actually is (largely) independent of space and (largely) independent of time and that it does not occur at random but according to something akin to a deliberate selection. As in laboratory experiments, which permit a clear attribution of the operator to the machine by way of the operator's knowledge that they are directing their efforts towards a specific instrument, FieldREG experiments would not be possible without any such 'internal connection'. This is provided by the experimenter. His knowledge is the missing link between the field of consciousness and the machine. If you like, it is necessary to state a sender and an address in order for the right package (structured field of consciousness) to reach the correct target (REG).

The problem is similar to the one Ingo Swann attempted to solve for the application of remote viewing to espionage. He discovered that it was sufficient for the mind to be able to find its target if it was fed with coordinates. In a FieldREG experiment, the experimenter formulates the 'coordinates' by defining the objective of his experiment. As soon as this has been fixed, the connection is made. Sender and address have been formulated. Against this background, we can now also understand why it was later found that coordinates were no longer necessary in remote viewing, why it was sufficient to use encoded coordinates or even no coordinates at all. The link to the target object had already been established, either by the experimenter, who knew it, or by the client. The selection of a target for psi takes place on the same level on which psi functions; it is psi-mediated.

# Chapter Two
# SUBTLE CONNECTIONS

## GEOMAGNETIC INFLUENCES

Some people feel the weather in their bones, others sleep badly during the full moon, but who considers that our behaviour is influenced by particles on the sun's surface or by other planets? No, I am not talking about astrology, I am talking about the measurable physical influences to which the earth and the humans who live on it are exposed.

The earth is surrounded by a magnetic field composed of an inner and an outer part. The inner part, which makes up the greater part of the geomagnetic field, consists of the permanent field and of magnetic fields caused by electric currents approximately 3000 kilometres inside the planet. To a minor degree, the outer part of the geomagnetic field is also determined by variable fields of electricity in the atmosphere. Finally there is an influence on the magnetic field resulting from rock formations in the earth's crust. On a global level this influence is very minor, but it can lead to important local variations.

The earth's principal field has been subjected to gradual changes in direction and strength over many hundreds of years. On the other hand, the magnetic field in the atmosphere shows rapid variations in periods ranging from 1 second to more than 24 hours. These are caused by the activities of the sun, the so-called sun wind, a constant, outwardly directed flow of charged particles. The global variations in the magnetic field are called magnetic storms. The interaction with the magnetic fields of other planets also influences the geomagnetic field.

Several indices are used to measure geomagnetic activities. One of the best known is the aa-index, the antipodal index. It is recorded twice a day for each hemisphere and has the advantage that it has been continually recorded for over a century.

Michael Persinger, professor of neurology at Laurentian University in Sudbury, Canada, is the leading authority on the influence of geomagnetic and electromagnetic radiation on man. In the course of his work he discovered that unusual events are related to fluctuations in the geomagnetic field.[17] Persinger began to investigate this subject and in a series of studies compared the times of spontaneous experiences of extrasensory perception with the index data on geomagnetic activities. For this he drew upon the famous historical collection *Phantasms of the Living*, which was compiled near the end of the nineteenth century by Edmund Gurney, Frederick Myers and Frank Podmore from the Society for Psychical Research.[18]

Persinger made the interesting discovery that spontaneous telepathic experiences occurred more frequently on a day of low geomagnetic activity that had normally been preceded by a day of high activity.[19] These results were confirmed by a series of subsequent investigations based on large collections of data on spontaneous phenomena. It was shown that these spontaneous phenomena occurred on days that were geomagnetically calmer than preceding and subsequent days, and moreover, that showed a lower level of activity than the average calculated for the respective month.[20] The same effects could also be demonstrated in the data of experimental studies on extrasensory perception.[21] The geomagnetic effect occurred only in those sets of data in which psi effects were also shown, an indication that spontaneous and experimental phenomena follow the same mechanisms.

Working with Persinger, Stanley Krippner, one of the dream researchers at the Maimonides Medical Center, submitted the results of year-long experiments in dream telepathy to an analysis. They discovered that the best results were achieved on nights with low geomagnetic activity.[22] Their investigation also provided a preliminary answer to the question of whether the decisive factor was the absolute level of activity or the relative decline of geomagnetic activity compared with preceding geomagnetic storms. It would appear that an absolute, not a relative, low level of activity favours the psi phenomena.

In the data from 97 ganzfeld studies conducted at the Koestler Parapsychology Unit at Edinburgh University only marginal proof could be found of a dependence of psi effects on geomagnetic activities.[23] Some indices showed the assumed correlation, whereas others even tended in the opposite direction, although they did not reach a significant level. In other studies with ganzfeld experiments, an anomalous correlation was discovered for the day preceding the experiment – that is, when geomagnetic activity was high on the day before the experiment, the subjects achieved better psi results.[24]

To these already rather unstable results we must note that as far as psychokinesis is concerned the results were even more confusing. Based on observations of spontaneous psychokinetic phenomena, the assumption was made that PK would be accompanied by an increased geomagnetic activity. Unlike anomalous cognition, which benefits from conditions of relaxation, the psychokinetic effect appears to be favoured by conditions of bodily arousal. The assumption was, therefore, that subjects would do better in PK experiments if they were stimulated, for example by geomagnetic activity.

It was possible to discover a cautious indication of this in some experiments on psychokinesis.[25] A research team headed by Stanley Krippner recently took continuous measurements of the local magnetic field during experiments with the Brazilian psychic Amyr Amiden.[26] Amiden claims that he can make objects appear and disappear ('apports'). During the sessions held in Brazil, rings, brooches and medallions with religious motives appeared seemingly out of nowhere, and although the researchers could not exclude the possibility that this was a trick, they still believe that at least some of these phenomena were anomalous. Stanley Krippner and his team classified the phenomena according to various criteria in order to obtain a measure of their assumed anomalous origin, and it was, in fact, shown that those phenomena that had been rated 'apparent anomalous phenomena' displayed a significant correlation to periods of increased geomagnetic activity.

Even though the geomagnetic influencing factor expresses itself only weakly in the data and has sometimes led to contradictory results, the opinion held is that a physical influencing factor has finally been discovered, and this could be of major importance for our understanding of the psi process.

A calm field increases the probability that anomalous cognition will occur, while an active field decreases the probability.[27] There are two possible ways of classifying this effect. It could well be that it is in the nature of anomalous cognition to closely correlate with geomagnetic fields. In this case, geomagnetic storms would disrupt the relationship. The other possibility is a direct effect of the geomagnetic field on the sensitivity of the brain for psi signals. From this point of view, psi is omnipresent in space and time, and it is only our ability to find an entry into its potential that is modulated by environmental influences and psychological conditions.

# THE PSI SWITCHBOARD IN THE BRAIN

The organism constantly reacts to electromagnetic influences. A German research team at Giessen University succeeded in artificially reproducing very weak electromagnetic impulses such as are normally produced by atmospheric discharges (lightning).[28] The influence of these impulses affected the electric waves in the brain and continued even after the stimulation was over. The importance of this study is the indication that the human organism reacts to minimal magnetic stimulation. How these reactions relate to psi is a question currently under heated discussion and empirical investigation.

Persinger argues that the key to psi experiences lies hidden in geomagnetic activity. His starting point is the reproduction in the brain of electric activities that can artificially create psi experiences. The electromagnetic fields he uses are not dangerous – they are weaker than those of an everyday hair-drier – but the problem lies in the translation of the messages contained in them into the language of the brain. To achieve this, Persinger attempts to copy the way this is achieved in nature and the way it directs many aspects of human behaviour via geomagnetic activity. Many species of fish, for example, communicate by means of electromagnetic fields, pigeons orientate themselves according to the geomagnetic field, and bees use electric fields to collect information from their environment. Persinger believes that telepathic phenomena are caused by an interconnection between all existing brains via the geomagnetic field.

Neurologically speaking, there is one area of the brain that appears to be predestined to respond to geomagnetic influences – that is, the temporal lobes. Persinger was able to prove that electrical activities in the deeper structures of the temporal lobes are in accord with global geomagnetic conditions. An increase in geomagnetic activity suppresses the production of the hormone melatonin in the pineal gland. It is known that melatonin plays an important role in dysfunctions connected to the temporal lobes, such as depression and seizures. Crisis hallucinations and psychokinetic effects could be related in some still unexplained way to these biochemical processes in the brain. Religious and mystic experiences could also be the result of electric phenomena in the temporal lobes.[29] By controlling magnetic fields, Persinger was able to simulate brain wave patterns by which he could evoke strong emotions as well as hallucinations, vivid feelings of being touched and of movement, even the appearance of spirits of the deceased.[30] The implications of this discovery are enormous, because we now know that such experiences have their origin in a specific area of the brain.

What functions do the electrical phenomena in the temporal lobes perform in order to transmit such experiences? Ultimately, our brain 'translates' all of our experiences, but even though we know this, it does not detract from our perception of our daily environment as real. Geomagnetic activity might possibly be defined as a modulating effect that controls the brain's preparedness to receive psi information.

The human temporal lobes are divided into three gyri, the superior, the medial and the inferior. Electrical stimulation, particularly of the superior or medial gyrus of the temporal lobe, leads to auditory hallucinations, *déjà vu* experiences and dreams. An experiment with monkeys revealed that the medial and inferior gyri of the temporal lobes are involved in the processing of visual information. Visual information is passed on from the primary projection area in the occipital cortex via the medial and inferior temporal gyri. This region of the temporal lobe is therefore now being called the 'second visual association cortex'. We know today that information from all of the modes of sensory perception is received in the temporal lobes.

In a clinical context, the temporal lobes first became known through what is known as the temporal lobe syndrome. The first person to describe it was Norman Geschwind of Harvard Medical School.[31] It is caused by injuries (lesions) to the lobes and expresses itself in a reinforcement of religious certainties, a compulsion to write (hypergraphy) and the practice of bizarre sexual habits. The actual religious belief held is of no importance; the syndrome makes the person receptive to any sort of religious teachings, which often vacillate within quite short periods of time.[32]

Disorders in the temporal lobes are often indicators of a special kind of epilepsy, psychomotoric or temporal lobe epilepsy (TLE). It occurs when there are lesions in one or both of the temporal lobes, and 20–30 per cent of all forms of epilepsy are TLEs.

Towards the end of the 1960s South African neurologist Gordon Nelson made EEG recordings of trance mediums and found specific disorders in the temporal lobes. South African psychiatrist Vernon Neppe noted that people who were reporting psi experiences also described other unusual experiences that were remarkably similar to those connected to disorders in the temporal lobes.[33] Patients with dysfunctions of the temporal lobes often experience anomalies of smell (olfactory hallucinations) and report *déjà vu* experiences. Many of Nelson's patients who reported subjective psi experiences also reported such effects. In most cases these are pleasant smells, whereas with disorders of the temporal lobes, the olfactory hallucinations are normally of unpleasant, rotten or burned odours.

Scottish psychiatrist James McHarg described the phenomena of one of his patients that had all the characteristics of being paranormal but that had been triggered by a TLE.[34] The patient had been visiting a friend in his new house, and she noticed the symptoms normally preceding an attack – a 'milky' odour and the feeling that her surroundings were becoming unreal. When she was in this condition, the woman normally experienced visual hallucinations, and this time she saw a woman with brown hair standing before a stove. The apparition threw a startled glance at the patient and disappeared. As was subsequently discovered, there had formerly actually been a stove at that particular spot. One of the two sisters who had previously owned the house was identified by McHarg's patient as being the woman she had seen in her hallucination.

It is possible that psi information finds its way into the temporal lobes by the same path that normal sensual information follows. There it is filtered and only passed on to the higher cognitive regions of the brain in certain cases. Electric discharges in the temporal lobes could well cancel the inhibition of information that occurs there, so that psi information reaches the conscious mind more readily.

Two structures closely associated with the temporal lobes could well hold a unique position as transmitters of psi experiences. These are the amygdala, an almond-shaped structure in the temporal lobe, and the hippocampus, a curved elongated ridge of grey matter extending from the olfactory lobe to the posterior of the cerebrum. The amygdala, the central element of the limbic system, is responsible for autonomic and emotional reactions. The limbic system controls our emotions, and the reason that it is primarily emotionally exciting information that reaches our consciousness via psi is probably to be found here. Emotionally charged information, anomalous or not, acts upon the fragile memory and inhibition system in the temporal lobes and causes some information to be recorded subconsciously and some to be raised to the level of consciousness.

Brain activity can be measured not only by the electrical activity in the cortex but also by means of blood flow in the various regions of the brain. Blood circulates more in regions that are metabolically active in order to supply oxygen to the cells. Positron emission tomography (PET) is an imaging technique by which from eight to ten cross-section images of the brain are produced in a very short time, permitting regional cerebral blood flows to be monitored. The images permit us to draw conclusions about which areas of the brain show heightened activity at certain times.

EEG recordings of qigong masters in conjunction with PET images of regional cerebral blood flows have shown that the temporal lobes and the hippocampus are activated during qigong, while the cerebrum remains calm.[35] The structures of the limbic system, the amygdala and hippocampus, are related to slow (alpha, theta and delta) brain waves. The investigators also found activities in connection with alpha waves in a specific region in the right temporal lobe, where discharges during temporal lobe epilepsy (TLE) led to hallucinations.

Recent research on the functions of the amygdala and the hippocampus supports their importance for processing psi signals. A group of hippocampal cells, known as CA3 cells, play a special role in relating external stimuli to internal associations through a process of inhibition and selection. Stress can lead to a change in the way the CA3 cells function. Paranormal talents frequently report that they had gained their abilities after having been subjected to extreme physical or mental stress, often after near-fatal accidents or illnesses or, as in the case of epileptics, during puberty. The stress-induced changes in the CA3 cells can lead to a reduction of the inhibitory function and therefore to an increased permeability for psi signals.

Of particular interest for psi is the ability of the hippocampus to build up long-term potentials – the first step to developing memory. An electrical stimulation lasting only 1 second of a frequency of 400 Hz can lead to an almost permanent change in electrical activity. Furthermore, within a period of 10 minutes, it causes the growth of dendrites (branch-like extensions of the nerve cells). These are a sign that new, permanent connections have been established.

This extremely rapid plasticity indicates that only a few seconds of an appropriate psi stimulation would be sufficient to cause permanent changes in the micro-structure of the brain and thereby to modify memory. As soon as the new information has become consolidated, it is just as 'real' and normally accessible as memories obtained by conventional means.

I have already explained that psi impressions are more readily comparable to memories than to sensory impressions, and the conscious reproduction of extrasensory information has been equated to subliminal perception. New studies have shown that the temporal lobes play an important role in the processing of subliminal stimuli.

A team working with Manabu Tashiro of the Division of Nuclear Medicine at Tohoku University in Sendai, Japan, was able to demonstrate that visual subliminal stimuli initially cause an increase of cerebral blood flow in the occipital lobe.[36] The flow of blood then moves to the region of the superior and medial gyri of the temporal lobe. The study shows that the temporal lobes play a key role in the processing of information that remains subconscious.

In investigations of psychological automatisms, particularly of automatic writing, it was demonstrated that people are sometimes able to report on matters about which they could not actually know anything. During his early experiments with automatic spelling, German parapsychologist Hans Bender had the following curious experience while he was working with an ordinary housemaid as his subject. In what are known as glass-moving experiments, the index finger is laid on an upturned glass, and the letters of the alphabet are arranged in a circle. Without any involvement of the conscious mind, the glass moves – often very rapidly – and touches different letters in turn, and these together form a meaningful sentence. During Bender's experiment, the sequence of letters initially appeared to make no sense at all, until it was discovered to everyone's surprise that the words were in English. The housemaid, however, knew no English at all. The text was finally identified as the opening passage of D.H. Lawrence's short story *The Woman Who Rode Away*. The solution of the mystery was as simple as it was astonishing. The lady of the house where the maid worked had a book of Lawrence's works on her bedside table. The girl had seen the open book and the optical impression of the words had been fixed in her memory. Such cases are called *kryptomnesia* (from the Greek for 'hidden memory'), when memories are experienced of never consciously perceived, but nonetheless recorded, information. From this we can see what an enormous storage capacity the human brain possesses and how great the disproportion of the consciously perceived fraction to the sum total of all perceptions must be.[37]

In historical experiments in automatic spelling it was discovered that extrasensory information frequently appeared in the texts. This is apparently due to a process by which previously stored anomalous information can be made available by the activity of the temporal lobes, enabling the threshold of wakeful consciousness to be bypassed. The subjects do not know what they are spelling automatically, and in this way subconsciously arriving psi signals can be stored and possibly become recallable at a later date. Investigation into the anomalous transfer of information during dreams confirms this theory. Extrasensory impressions that were unable to overcome the inhibiting barrier during the day become available during the more favourable state of consciousness that obtains during periods of dreaming.

Everything seems to indicate that the manifestations of spontaneous psi phenomena are dominated by the temporal lobes. They appear very frequently during dreams or in fantasies during wakefulness and are accompanied by intense emotions, which give these experiences a lasting personal importance.

The electric instability of the temporal lobes suggests that certain stimuli can cause experiences that are *similar* to psi experiences. The only condition of the brain during which spontaneous, psi-like experiences are produced is temporal lobe epilepsy. If an epileptic electrical charge remains inside a lobe and does not reach the motor centres, there is no epileptic seizure, and an observer would not notice that a person is undergoing an epileptic attack. Normally, an epileptic performs some sort of routine activities. Sometimes this is only the simple repetition of certain movements of the body, but it can take the form of longer-lasting and more complex acts. During these periods, which last from a few seconds to several minutes, and sometimes even much longer, an altered state of consciousness occurs as a result of the sudden change in the electric activity of one of the temporal lobes. We could, therefore, easily confuse such a 'pseudo-psi' experience based on an epileptic discharge with a real psi event.

It would be a mistake to assume that psi experiences are a form of temporal lobe epilepsy. The trigger for a psi experience is an external event, whereas an epileptic attack is caused by an internal event. Extrasensory experiences are most frequently reported as occurring during normal nightly dream phases, which have nothing to do with epileptic phenomena.

Persinger discovered that most of the reports about spontaneous extrasensory perceptions stated that these had occurred between 2 o'clock and 4 o'clock in the morning. The period with the second most frequent appearance of psi was between 9 o'clock and 11 o'clock at night. Before appropriate medicines were developed, these were exactly the time intervals in which most epileptic attacks were observed. But there was also a third significant time for psi, around 4 o'clock in the afternoon, which does not coincide with the data on TLE.[38]

The relationship between psi and 'religious' or 'spiritual convictions' could be explained in terms of the function of the temporal lobes, particularly since the intensification of religious certainties has been described as an aspect of the dysfunction of the temporal lobe. Recent studies on mystic and transpersonal experiences have confirmed the role played by the temporal lobes in this context.

EEG patterns during mystic and transpersonal experiences show a sharp two-part split of the wave patterns into very high-frequency and very low-frequency waves.[39] This split equates to an excited condition of attention (high-frequency waves) and a condition of deep relaxation (low-frequency waves). When such conditions develop, initially low-frequency waves of 1–6 Hz (delta and theta waves) occur in the centre of the cortex. Presumably this switches off our normal space–time perception. As soon as we descend more deeply into a transcendental condition, the wave frequencies separate. The decisive electrical activity shifts from the centre to the temporal lobes – an effect more marked in women than in men – where there is an increase of high-frequency beta and extremely high-frequency gamma waves.

The normal brain wave frequencies in the temporal lobes are hardly ever more than 20 mV power, but in transcendental states, virtual eruptions of from very low to very high voltages can be measured. It is almost as if fireworks were constantly being set off in the temporal lobes. During examinations of the 70-year-old healer Rod Campbell, the EEG recorded extremely high-frequency gamma waves of 18–32 Hz at 9.7 mV, of 32–64 Hz at 29.9 mV and 64–128 Hz at 39 mV in the temporal lobes. People in ecstatic states have even reached eruptions of gamma waves with 120–150 mV.

Gamma waves appear to be the hallmark for the loss of the normal ego demarcations. It could well be that the concentration of these extremely high-frequency waves in the temporal lobes cuts off the normal input of sensory information and 'switches over' the brain to the passing on of extrasensory and mystic experiences.

It is possible that the key to understanding the relationship between paranormal, spiritual and some abnormal experiences is hidden in the temporal lobes, where sensory stimuli, including subliminal stimuli, are integrated, filtered and stored, and from where they can then appear via internal or external electrical phenomena as outwardly displayed internal images – hallucinations, apparitions, visions – or as spontaneous psi experiences.

The most exciting thing about this region of the brain for our understanding of psi is the fact that it can so readily be influenced by electromagnetic waves. Individual neurons or groups of neurons within the hippocampus show periods of electrical activity during which they can be relatively easily influenced by external electromagnetic fields of a similar pulse or a natural frequency. This appears to be the point at which environmental influences, such as geomagnetic fluctuations, can produce a condition of receptivity for, or the suppression of, psi signals.

# UNDER THE CHANGING MOON

When it comes to beliefs about the powers of the heavenly bodies to influence humans, the most ancient are those involving the moon. The importance of the moon among all peoples and cultures can be deduced from their cults and myths. The moon's phases were seen to have a close relationship to 'increasing' and 'decreasing' natural processes on earth: growing and prospering, the fertility of plants and animals, illness, birth, love, marriage and death. In ancient times, Pliny the Elder claimed that a waxing moon caused the blood in the human body to rise, while a waning moon caused it to fall. Modern science has been able to demonstrate that ancient beliefs were not necessarily superstitions; it has been shown, for example, that post-operative bleeding is most pronounced at around the time of the full moon.

For a long time it was believed that the moon primarily acts on the condition of the human mind. In English the word lunacy was used for insanity, particularly if it was intermittent, and in German, somnambulism was called *Mondsucht* (moon obsession).

Even today many people still believe that their emotions and feelings are influenced by the moon. This is one explanation for the recent extraordinary success in Germany of a book by a farmer's wife from the mountains of the Tyrol, in which she recorded the knowledge handed down to her about the influence of the phases of moon on everyday life.[40]

Andrija Puharich conducted experiments in telepathy in accordance with magical concepts, and he expected that psi results would increase with a full moon and decline until half moon, only to increase again with the new moon.[41] The results confirmed his hypothesis. Dean Radin believes that he has found an alternative explanation for this result. It is not the phases of the moon themselves that influence psi results, but fluctuations in the geomagnetic field caused by the phases of the moon. Numerous studies investigating the problem of moon phases and geomagnetic fields have not been able to provide a clear result. Some indicate that the relationship can actually be traced to fluctuations in the sun winds, while others suggest that there is a direct influence of the moon on the earth's magnetic field.

Whatever the underlying cause may be, Radin intended to uncover the moon's effect on psi, and he approached the problem empirically. Proof of precognition and psychokinesis, even though rare phenomena, should be easiest to find where chance reigns and masses of data can be collected. Such conditions are found, of course, in a gambling casino, and not for nothing was Radin's laboratory at the time of the studies located in Las Vegas, the gambling capital of the world.

Radin analysed the average pay-outs in five different games of chance in relationship to the phases of the moon and geomagnetic activity.[42] His hypothesis was that the highest pay-outs would occur on days around the full and new moons and on days when there was low geomagnetic activity. He was able to confirm his hypothesis without, however, reaching an impressive statistical significance. The detailed analysis showed that the six largest pay-outs on slot machines all occurred on a day of full moon or on a day preceding or following – a result that is highly significant. He was also able to demonstrate similar moon and geomagnetic effects based on extensive data on lottery pay-outs. The daily fluctuations in the winnings of the casino guests could not be traced back to pure chance. They showed a close relationship to the daily fluctuations of the 'psi abilities' of the players. These are, in turn, determined by environmental influences. The results have important consequences for our understanding of the role played by psi in fields of consciousness. Psi is more widespread than we had believed and is – subconsciously – employed in everyday life.

Dean Radin brought the casino into his laboratory via the website of his Consciousness Research Division. There he runs several virtual games of chance in which you can test your own 'psi ability'.[43] The data on the points in time of the individual attempts are recorded. A questionnaire explores your own estimation of your momentary run of good or bad luck. The initial results of about 2000 Internet experiments confirm Radin's findings in his casino and lottery studies. Achievements in precognition tests show a positive correlation with the 'creativity' factor and a negative correlation with geomagnetic activity. The results of the second and larger on-line study are still being analysed, but several interesting relationships are already appearing.

# THE FUNDAMENTAL PSI FUNCTION

We have now reached a point where we should reflect a little about the nature of psi. Everything seems to indicate that in its most fundamental form, psi is a still unknown, subconscious and biologically determined constant anomalous exchange of information. Psi functions by the extraction of information (anomalous cognition, AC) and by the transmission of information (anomalous perturbation, AP), which indicates that AC and AP are not fundamentally different from each other. They are complementary to each other and appear to be two manifestations of the same basic function.

Moreover, psi is part of an autonomous process in the organism, which is modulated by geophysical variables. This could be defined as a reciprocal process of observation between the organism and its environment, during which consciousness and physical reality affect each other. The basis for this interaction is a sort of universal scanning mechanism with which the immediate space-time environment of the organism is constantly being scanned or recorded. I call this basic expression of psi the fundamental psi function (FPF).

If the FPF actually is a basic biological mechanism, you would expect it to have appeared early on in the process of evolution. As a sort of intuitive instinct, it would have been an excellent tool for ensuring the survival of a species. The numerous case studies and experiments on psi in animals confirm this assumption. Animals are probably better able to employ FPF than humans because their response to the exchange of information is completely automatic. These responses are reflexes that take place on the level of the autonomic nervous system. An example will illustrate how the fundamental psi function works among animals.

During the 1970s French engineer Pierre Janin developed a robot for PK experiments, the tychoscope. The cylindrical instrument is directed by a random-event generator and performs 'random walks', which are recorded on paper by a stylus attached to its base. The follow-up model, tychoscope II by Roger Tanguy, operates by remote control directed by an external random-event generator and directly linked to a computer for statistical analysis.

In his experiment, René Peoc'h exploited the biological fact that during the early stages of development of many bird species, the young are imprinted on the mother and follow her about. This biological mechanism is essential for their survival while they are unable to feed themselves. In an experiment that became famous, the behavioural scientist and Nobel laureate Konrad Lorenz imprinted some goslings on himself. From then on the animals followed the scientist about as their 'substitute mother'.

René Peoc'h used tychoscope II as a substitute mother. He imprinted some chicks on it and then put them in a cage on the edge of a rectangular surface. The tychoscope was activated in the centre of the surface. And then something astonishing happened – the randomly directed robot moved towards the cage with the conditioned chicks 2½ times more often than during a control run without chicks in the cage. If chicks that had not been conditioned to accept the tychoscope as their substitute mother were placed in the cage, it performed the expected random walk. The only explanation for this behaviour by the robot was that apparently the conditioned chicks used psychokinetic abilities in order to move the robot into their vicinity more often than could be expected.[44]

In a further experiment Peoc'h used 80 groups of 15 chicks each aged between 1 and 7 days, which were raised in total darkness. Chicks do not like darkness during the day, and as soon as a light was switched on they stopped peeping. The scientist mounted a candle on the tychoscope as the only source of light in the room. At different times the chicks were placed in transparent cages at different sides of the rectangular space on which the tychoscope moved. In 57 out of 80 individual runs – 71.25 per cent – the robot moved towards the chicks more often than away from them. During control experiments without chicks, the choice of direction lay absolutely within random expectation.[45]

These experiments support the suggestion that a fundamental psi function is inherent in organisms, and it appears to be more freely available in animals than in humans. Further investigations are required to determine if a dependence on geophysical influences exists in animals or if this is only the case with humans, where it might play a role in the translation of psi information into the conscious mind. Psi experiments conducted by René Peoc'h, Sergei Speransky, Natalia Yanova and others suggest that the fundamental psi function is also modulated by previous experiences, such as the way the animals were raised, bio-emotional ties and so on.

This is not the place to discuss why evolution did not choose the fundamental psi function and improve if it is such a useful ability. All we could contribute to this extensive topic would be some hypotheses or, rather, some speculations. The physical characteristics of psi as a channel for the extraction and supply of information may be basically different from those used by the other sensory systems. All forms of energy used by living beings diminish with distance and convey only a limited part of the information of their source. In principle, psi does not appear to suffer from such limitations – it is neither diminished by distance nor is there a reduction in the information being transported. If there were such a constant anomalous contact between all organisms and their environment, however, the bombardment with anomalous information would become a single enormous noise. The ratio between signal and noise would, for all practical purposes, become infinitely small and make it impossible to isolate sensible information directly.[46]

The intentions of humans and the needs of animals as the sources of such a constant interaction of mind and matter would, in effect, cancel each other out. We do, however, sometimes experience clear psi phenomena, and in principle, therefore, the unfavourable ratio between signal and noise and the interference could be overcome by goal-orientated anomalous perturbation. Evolution would have had to prefer these special cases and to perfect them.

A possible reason why this was not the case lies in the advantages that are offered by concentrating on the known sensory organs. Through evolution these could be adjusted to any requirement that the species in question had to fulfil. For example, some species preferentially 'see' objects that move at a particular speed, which is the typical speed at which their prey moves.

An important reason for the evolutionary 'neglect' of psi could be precisely that the organic substrata on which the mechanisms of evolution could have intervened are lacking. The fundamental psi function has no organ of entry at its disposal in which the essential structures could have been developed to select the signals necessary for the needs of the species. A reduction of the signal bombardment could, therefore, be solved only on the level of the central nervous system – that is, it would be a task for the brain – but the basic form the solution took is apparently that the weak psi signals were weighted according to their importance for the individual. The weighting itself has to consist of a physical, emotional response.

On the other hand, as we know today, the psi channel dep( external influences. In this context we might have expected that the sensitivity in the organic structures that were appropriate for modulating environmental influences favourable to psi would have been given evolutionary preference. Biological development obviously chose a different route.

The development in humans of the better – because more accurate – means of communication by signs (language and writing) on the basis of the known sensory organs may have pushed FPF as a mechanism for survival into the background. The specific evolution of consciousness finally led to a separation of the fundamental psi function from the conscious life of humans. In the process of becoming conscious, humans also perceived their subtle interconnection to all other things, which finds its expression in the fundamental psi function. But humans were no longer able to react automatically to the subconscious processes, because their dawning consciousness had opened an abyss between themselves and the subconscious psychical and autonomous physical processes. The interaction with FPF led to an increased 'spiritualization' of the anomalous system of exchange, by which the conscious mind increasingly developed into a barrier for reflexive responses to the system.

And so, as a sort of compensatory behaviour, humans began to develop magic and occult systems in order to explore these unknown relationships. People also began to examine their inner lives for answers to the questions they were asking about a world they did not understand. Humans soon recognized that dreaming was a condition in which fragments of the anomalous exchange of information could be lifted into the conscious mind, and dreaming developed into the state of consciousness *par excellence* that permitted a certain understanding of the subconsciously arriving signals. People also experimented with other altered states of consciousness in order to profit from the possibilities of the fundamental psi function. But in the end, psi has remained a subtle, unreliable sense.

## IN THE REALM OF CONFUSION

In recent years environmental influences and electric phenomena in the temporal lobes and the limbic system have led to a re-evaluation of a highly controversial class of phenomena: those that can be observed in what are known as poltergeist cases. Such phenomena are among the most mysterious and bizarre ever investigated by parapsychology, and they are a delicate subject even for psi researchers.[47] Here we distinguish between poltergeists associated with people and those associated with locations (hauntings).

The principal criteria for this distinction are the following. First, poltergeists associated with people are limited in time, the average duration being only a few weeks. The phenomena appear in the surroundings of a person and follow that person around. The phenomena in question consist primarily of unexplained movements or the breaking of objects, loud raps, electrical disturbances and the lighting of fires. Second, poltergeists associated with locations are often observed at a place – a haunted house – over many generations. In addition to loud raps, they are primarily characterized by 'apparitions' of people.

For the most part, parapsychologists have concentrated on investigating poltergeists associated with people. In such cases the mysterious phenomena appear over a period of a few days to several weeks in the immediate vicinity of the 'focus person' or 'poltergeist agent', and most parapsychologists believe that the manifestations are subconsciously triggered by the focus persons themselves. The manifestations are due to stress and psychological tensions, which are expressed through psychokinesis. Focus people are frequently young people going through puberty.

What is remarkable about poltergeists associated with people is their mischievous, impish behaviour. The basic structure of poltergeist disturbances normally follow a similar pattern: the phenomena begin outside the house and resemble a prank. Knocking sounds on doors and windows are heard. Pebbles are thrown against window panes, which sometimes shatter. Then the phenomena enter into the living area, so to speak. Doors open and close by themselves, and objects begin to develop a life of their own. Although the flight of such objects may be directed towards particular people, the flight paths are strange. Sometimes they follow the contours of furniture and fragile objects fall to the ground without breaking. Objects fly towards a person at high speed and are stopped shortly before impact as if by a ghostly hand, causing no damage. In other cases, things constantly break. Sometimes vases or glasses are shattered as if the base or stem had been cut through by a laser beam. Pieces of heavy furniture are moved about as if they were made of kindling. Among the typical phenomena we find the inexplicable appearance of water, the spontaneous starting of fires and the mysterious appearance of stones, which often first become visible on the ceiling and then fall to the floor.

The mischievous character of these events is the central problem for the scientists who attempt to understand it – the poltergeist is clothed in the garments of an imp. For a time people take the events for the pranks of a rascal, and by the time those involved have begun to realize that something monstrous and uncommon is going on around them, it is normally too late for the parapsychologist. The poltergeist is already over.

Until now poltergeist research has had to depend mostly on unreliable testimony by witnesses. In many investigations of poltergeist cases that Professor Hans Bender and I were able to conduct in the late 1970s and early 1980s,[48] the same central problem kept surfacing: it was impossible to determine whether the reported phenomena were, at least partially, of a psychokinetic nature. It is improbable that poltergeists are nothing more than a sort of massive discharge of PK in a certain social framework, as parapsychologists assume.[49]

Today researchers are pursuing alternative paths. These are based on FieldREG research and the discovery of the geophysical influences on the psi process. If anomalous perturbations in the form of micro-effects on a field can be measured, such effects should also be recordable in poltergeists.

American parapsychologist William Roll, who is well known for his poltergeist investigations, has long believed that dysfunctions in the temporal lobes are somehow connected to such manifestations. Roll, together with neurologist Elson de Montagno, advanced the theory that poltergeist disturbances correspond to disorders in the limbic system and particularly in the temporal lobes of poltergeist agents.[50] It was demonstrated in some cases that the focus person showed a disposition towards states akin to seizures. In 1975, for example, Roll examined a case in Michigan, in which the escalation of the disturbances was directly related to attacks of epilepsy in the focus person. It was demonstrated in other cases that the focus persons also showed signs of epilepsy or, at least, a disposition to epilepsy. In the temporal lobe epilepsy appears as a sort of 'chaos condition' within the electrical apparatus of the nerve cells. As far as Roll is concerned, the chaos in the central nervous system finds its equivalent in the psychokinetically induced chaos of the poltergeist disturbances. He assumes that increased geomagnetic activity, or electromagnetic and electrostatic fields, as well as ionizing radiation, trigger discharges in the temporal lobes, which, in turn, are supposed to lead to the psychokinetic effects.[51]

The first investigation of a haunting using REGs was conducted in the late 1980s by Michaeleen Maher and George Hansen.[52] They ran REGs in various areas of a haunted house in New York and a haunted mansion in New Jersey. They wanted to find out whether the machines' data output would change in those places where 'ghosts' had been observed. The results were sobering. In New York the random-event generators showed only a slightly higher variance in their data after they had been installed in the places of the 'apparitions', and in New Jersey the data sequences showed nothing remarkable at all.

Are FieldREGs useless as detectors for anomalous phenomena in connection with poltergeists associated with locations or do they just have to run for sufficiently long times to react to a fleeting, invisible presence? In May 1995 Dutch psi researchers Johan Gerding, Rens Wezelman and Dick Bierman were given an opportunity to investigate a poltergeist case in a Turkish family in the Dutch city of Druten.[53] Police officers were among the witnesses to the inexplicable events, and the investigators were also fortunate in that they arrived on the scene only five days after the first phenomena had been reported. Five days later and the whole thing was over.

The central aspect of the phenomena was the 'stone throwing' that is familiar from many reports on such cases.[54] On 14 May the two police officers, Cramer and Van Deursen, observed the rear of the house from two different vantage points. As already noted earlier, stones flew towards the house. The officers reported that they would certainly have caught the culprit if there had been anybody there. These stones, however, appeared to 'come from nowhere', and, as is usually the case, the team of investigators was unable to record the anomalous phenomena on video film.

Dick Bierman, one of the pioneers in FieldREG research, hoped that the random-event generator would prove to be a better detector. He installed an REG, which was linked to a computer and produced a steady flow of random bit sequences. The members of the family were able to record the exact times an anomalous event occurred by pushing a button on the computer keyboard. After the haunting was over, the random sequences were checked for any deviations. The analysis concentrated on two methods currently favoured by science by which it is possible to determine whether the machine was no longer producing random sequences at the times in question. In the first method, the first-order non-randomness is checked. A first-order non-randomness occurs when an excess number of either 1 or 0 bits are produced. In the second method, the total data sequence is divided into eight-bit segments, which are then checked for recurring distribution patterns appearing with a greater regularity than pure chance.

The Dutch investigators compared the periods in which a member of the family had entered an anomalous event in the computer program with those periods when no disturbances had been observed. And they struck lucky. The data output showed an unusual pattern: there was a significant *decrease* in the first-order REG coherence.

Randomness is actually a rather strange thing. In our daily lives we do not give it much thought, and only call an unexpected event that has no causal connection to another event 'a strange coincidence'. In a science where the answers to experimental questions in so many areas depend on random events, randomness is a highly complicated mathematical quantity. A sequence of two different states, or bits, is only truly random when it shows no patterns at all and appears in the form of the expected random distribution. If these theoretical conditions are achieved precisely in practice, when almost as many 1 bits as 0 bits are produced without the normal deviation predicted by the theory of probability, then there is something wrong with the random sequence. The decrease in first-order REG coherence discovered during the Druten poltergeist disturbances means that during the periods in question, the machine 'worked too well'. As paradoxical as this may sound, the sequences were 'more random than random', producing nearly exactly the expected frequencies of 1 and 0 without the normal expected deviations.

How can we interpret such behaviour by the machine? The Dutch psi researchers did not know and restricted themselves to predicting that in similar cases we could also expect a decrease in first-order REG coherence. We can note that there was an effect which was in direct opposition to the increase in order based on a directed group consciousness such as had been discovered in FieldREG research. In view of this singular result, this might be a daring speculation, but it is possible that the findings correspond to an increased 'disorder' during poltergeist events – in the phenomena themselves, in the psychological structure and in certain functions in the brain of the focus person.

In any event, one problem still remains unsolved and that is that there is a high degree of probability that not only were psychokinetic events recorded in the log but there were certainly mistaken observations, maybe even manipulations, involved. Much noise will be found in this recording system. Which log entries were actually anomalous effects will forever remain a mystery. What was the REG data actually compared with? We do not know.

We must also consider a second, possibly decisive, problem. If random-event generators react to intentions and emotional changes, the appearance of significant patterns in FieldREGs during a poltergeist incident does not necessarily indicate the presence of psychokinesis in the sense of a non-specific PK field. During poltergeist phenomena an extraordinary event, be it paranormal or not, always causes emotional unrest in those involved. It is therefore quite possible that the output of the REG does not reflect individual spontaneous PK effects. In reality, it might be recording the change in consciousness of the group of people concerned based on their *perception* of an apparently or allegedly strange event.

REG correlations to such psychological changes are no less interesting. They only require a shift in perspective. They could be micro-perturbations which occasionally lead to macro-effects because of the influence of appropriate physical or psychological conditions that are transmitted by one or more persons. The appropriate conditions could consist of predispositions of the temporal lobes or the influence of geomagnetic activity.

In two cases of hauntings, Dean Radin and William Roll intended to find out if they could detect geophysical singularities.[55] The targets of their investigation were Dragsholm Castle near Copenhagen, Denmark, and Engsö Castle in Sweden. Roll decided in favour of conducting the investigation because he believed the witnesses to be quite trustworthy and because the foundations of both castles were made out of granite. Granite? Is that a good reason for the appearance of anomalous phenomena?

There is some speculation that blocks of granite at sacred sites, such as the megalithic stone circles, have a direct influence on transpersonal impressions experienced there. How are we supposed to interpret this? Granite is a source of ionizing radiation which can trigger unusual physiological states. In its turn, this could lead to apparitions being perceived. Another theory claims that geological stresses on granite lead to large-scale piezo-electric effects. A piezo-electric effect is the appearance of electric charges on the surface of ion crystals as a result of mechanical deformation. The effect on granite would lead to local electromagnetic fields of high intensity. These fields may affect the assimilative mechanisms in the temporal lobes of certain people and produce neurological states under which apparitions are induced.

In Dragsholm there is a tradition of reports about recurring apparitions in and near a certain room. 'Light forms' and a 'grey lady'[56] are seen and the proverbial 'cold draught' is felt, while inexplicable booming sounds can often be heard in the inner courtyard. Legend has it that several centuries ago the Count of Dragsholm had his daughter buried alive in a wall of the castle. To many people's surprise, during renovation works a few decades ago, the skeleton of a young woman was discovered in a wall on the fourth floor of the castle.

Electric field measurements taken in all the rooms and corridors of the castle did not show any anomalous deviations. In the 'grey lady' room there were no remarkable measurement results either. What was rather unexpected was an increase in the radiation level near a partition wall on one side of the 'grey lady' room. This result cannot be attributed to a higher concentration of granite in the wall, because the 3-metre thick exterior walls of the castle – where no such increase in radiation was measured – certainly contain a far greater amount of granite. Radin was unable to offer an explanation for this strange measurement.

At Engsö Castle they tell a legend about a 'cursed stone', which claims that whoever touches it will die within three days. It is a smooth, metallic-looking stone, and it can be admired on a stand in the castle church. A few years ago an unsettling incident occurred. The priest of the church, who wanted to demonstrate to his flock how senseless it is to cling to old superstitions, touched the stone. Three days later he died in a mysterious manner. Small wonder that today more people than ever are ready to believe in the magic effect of the 'cursed stone', and hardly anybody is daring enough to touch it.

Radin assumed the stone could be a meteorite with unusual properties or an atypically high level of ionizing radiation, which could be responsible for a lethal dose of radiation contamination. The readings did not show any irregular results, but nevertheless, Radin took great pains not to touch the stone.

There was one place on the third floor of the castle where the owner had seen the apparition of a woman three times. Outside this 'ghost room' Radin was able to detect a weak positive correlation between electric fields and magnetic fields, which turned into a highly significant negative correlation inside the room. This fact is all the more remarkable because there is no electricity in this part of the castle – no electric cables, sockets, lamps or anything of the kind – that could have caused unusual changes in the field. A second, more prolonged measurement at the same spot two days later showed no significant correlations. This can mean one of two things: either the result is not remarkable at all but came about by coincidence, or singular events that appear as significant field changes and correlations occur sporadically (like the apparitions) and can therefore be measured only on rare occasions.

We are still a long way away from theories explaining macro-PK effects. PK phenomena in connection with poltergeists and hauntings could be partly the result of unusual static electrical effects, which are subject to the subconscious control of one or more people. Normally, the modulation of the information by the human mind remains an unnoticed micro-PK effect. Only under certain conditions does it turn into a macro-PK effect. These conditions are still largely unknown. They appear to exist in some mysterious relationship to external influences, something that has been neglected to date. The mechanisms of psychokinesis appear to be based on an internally and externally modulated organizing principle, which permits normal forces to be applied selectively and by which minute changes in the marginal conditions of a physical system – the delicate shifts in the probability distribution we know from micro-PK studies – may lead to enormous, surprising macro-effects in the complete system.

# Chapter Three
# THE FINGERPRINT OF CONSCIOUSNESS

## BEYOND THE CONCEIVABLE

At a time when our daily lives are increasingly determined by computers and microchips, the voluntary or involuntary penetration of consciousness on the microscopic level is of prime importance and has far-reaching consequences. As Robert Jahn puts it: 'It's something science cannot afford to simply ignore any longer. And besides, it's such an exciting challenge to our whole way of thinking about the physical world.'

Anomalous effects could have important repercussions on many systems of information processing, particularly on those that depend on random reference signals. The most important are aircraft cockpits, intercontinental ballistic missile silos, surgical facilities, environmental and disaster control technologies – that is, all sensitive technologies where the controlling instruments and processes might be affected by an interaction with the human emotions. Ultimately, this also includes the sophisticated instruments with which are gathered the fundamental data on which modern sciences depend. We cannot trust blindly in the results, but must always take into account a possible interaction with human desires, ideas and concepts, particularly those of the person who is carrying out the experiment.

One of the key tasks for the future will be to find methods by which we can exclude consciousness-related interference. In future, information gathering and processing systems will continue to increase in importance and the role they play in our daily lives will continue to grow. Their capabilities will increase to a multiple of what they are today. In such machines and systems, the most minute interference could have untold effects.

There is also an optimistic way of looking at things, which takes science fiction plots out of the realm of pure fantasy: the development of a machine that is controlled by cognitive processes. The search for the bio-chip, which can be implanted in the brain so that it will form a network with the neurons, will turn out to be of only secondary importance, and interest will be concentrated on the development of a totally new generation of sensitive instruments that will react to individual psi-mediated signatures. Such machines would allow for creative applications and could possibly even be taught to learn by means of mind–matter interaction (MMI).

It is when we begin to think about the possible applications for psi, if – yes, if – the ephemeral fundamental psi function could be technically harnessed that our minds refuse to grasp what is being suggested, but it is precisely this technical application of psi that Dean Radin has set his sights on. From this starting point he has dared to go far out on the psi front, to where only a very few of his colleagues are prepared to follow him.

Radin possesses an incredibly agile mind, and he is always prepared to describe his complicated and innovative experiments with a touch of humour. He is a master of incomprehensible scientific jargon as well as an accomplished conversationalist in that relaxed way that is typical of a mentally agile American intellectual. There is no phenomenon too astonishing that he will not confront with the weapons of modern science, none too seemingly bizarre for him not to try to make it technologically useful. In October 1996 he was quite rightly awarded the Alexander Imich Prize, which goes to the scientist who made 'the most important experimental contributions to parapsychology during the preceding five years'.

Radin assumes that MMI is based on an exchange of information on a very low energy level. Not much energy is required to achieve disproportionately large effects if the right sort of information is transmitted. Given the right sort of information, Radin intends to develop a *psibot*, a robot that reacts to the mental intentions of a person. Such a machine, for example, could help the handicapped. It could be a hybrid between a conventional robot, a recording instrument and various REGs which are adjusted to react to human intentions. These components would be controlled by advanced software which would interpret the entry data and direct the robot's mechanics.

For many, such a degree of optimism about the technical application of psi might only flourish in an atmosphere where the willingness to take risks is part of normal business. As we already know, Radin developed many of his ideas while he headed a laboratory in Las Vegas, the centre of gambling in the United States. Yet this versatile scientist is a far cry from being an uninhibited speculator in this field. He worked at the respected Bell Laboratories of the communications giant AT&T, at the Stanford Research Institute, at the Contel Technology Center and at the GTE Laboratories. After a short time at the University of Edinburgh, he worked for a time at Princeton University, until he finally became Director of the Consciousness Research Division at the Harry Reid Center for Environmental Studies at the University of Nevada in Las Vegas.

Radin had worked on psi research while he was at Bell Laboratories. He based his research on the argument that AT&T should have an interest in uncovering the reasons for inexplicable breakdowns in its systems. The observation is made time and again that sensitive technical equipment will work very well with some people but will tend to break down more frequently than can be expected by chance with others. Physicist Wolfgang Pauli is an example of this. Every time he came into a laboratory, his colleagues would throw up their hands in horror. It was almost certain that some piece of equipment would conk out, fall down or simply stop working. We know from several poltergeist cases that negative thoughts and feelings – dissatisfaction, hatred, aggression – can have a destructive effect on objects in the vicinity. In the macro-world such effects are extremely rare. But in the micro-world, where intentions are in constant interaction with physical reality, they are far more common than is generally assumed.

Radin is looking for the hidden link in the interface of man and computer, or man and machine. The major part of AT&T's telephone system is controlled by computers and machines, and the prospect of discovering the potentially damaging influence of consciousness did not appear to be ridiculous to the company's management, and they supported Radin's investigations.

In Japan industrial companies have also recognized the importance of modern psi research. In 1991, on the order of its president, electronic giant Sony founded the Extra Sensory Perception and Excitation Laboratory (ESPER) under the direction of computer scientist Yoichiro Sako.

The starting point for Radin's research is the individual 'signatures' that the Princeton Engineering Anomalies Research Group (PEAR) had discovered in their REG data. Based on modern computer applications, a way might be found to 'train' a software program so that it would correctly allocate individual REG recordings to the right subjects. Should different and replicable individual patterns actually occur in the data, the program would be able to identify these. When effects achieved by the same subjects are subsequently displayed, the program should be able to attribute each of these to the correct subject.

A successful experiment of this nature would be a big step forwards in psi research. Not only would this be proof that psi micro-effects appear as the individual characteristics of a person, it would also be a first step towards a possible technological application of psi. In pursuit of this objective, Radin fed the data into an artificial neural network.

## THE IDENTITY CODE OF THE MIND

Modern computer technology has made it possible to compare different data on complex problems in order to discover interrelations. Neural networks are a class of computer applications that are able to learn from such data and to adapt to changing situations while these are being run.

The structure of an artificial neural network is based on the organization of nerve cells. It attempts to copy the way in which the brain encodes and processes information, and it consists of a large number of similar units (also known as neurons or nodes), which are normally arranged in layers and interconnected by channels of communication. The nodes process input data locally and then pass it on in the form of signals to the nodes to which they are connected.

The individual nodes are interconnected in a network that has several layers. A three-layer neural network consists of an input layer, a middle layer and an output layer. The middle layer is also known as the hidden layer, because it cannot be directly observed from outside. The input and output nodes shape the specific problem of association that requires solution. The secret of the neural network lies in the hidden nodes, which form the mathematical space in which the network attempts to interrelate the input and output signals. This is the level on which the decisive calculations take place by which complex, non-linear relationships are learned and the best solution to a problem found.

Neural networks therefore possess the ability to store knowledge gained by experience and to use it. They are similar to the brain in two respects: knowledge is gained by a learning process, and the strength of the connections between the neurons is used to store it. Neural networks are particularly useful for approaching problems that can tolerate a certain degree of inexactitude, as when we are dealing with very 'noisy' data and do not know which patterns are hidden in the noise. Neural networks are also appropriate for dealing with data to which 'hard' laws cannot be applied – data of the sort gained in psi experiments, when the underlying process is largely unknown.

In 1988 Dean Radin achieved his first construction of a neural network based on the PEAR database.[57] With this exploratory attempt, Radin was on virgin territory. He had to find out whether the network would be able to learn anything from the input data. He also had to determine whether it would be able to apply that knowledge for the correct allocation of future data to the same subject. He entered the data from 32 subjects into the network. In the end the neural network was supposed to recognize a binary code as the 'operator identity' of each subject, a unique code as the 'signature' of the person concerned, a signature that had only come about through mental intention related to random machines. A mental seal, so to speak. The fingerprint of consciousness.

What happens within a neural network when it is fed with data? As a 'teacher signal', the program is presented with an arbitrary but unique five-bit code for each subject. After the data has been fed in, it compares the actual continuous-valued results residing at the output nodes with the predetermined five-bit codes. The difference between the observed signal and the arbitrary code is then propagated backwards through the network and again processed by the network as new input data. This process is repeated between 1000 and 3000 times. In the course of this procedure, the network constantly looks for, and finds, new 'solutions' to its problem. In the end, it learns to associate randomly appearing input data with the predetermined identity codes.

As soon as this process had been completed, the really exciting phase began. Would the network, which had learned to associate data from the experiments with the subjects' identity codes, be able to identify the person responsible for the material when it was given other data produced by the same person? That is, would the data prove to be so individual and different that the neural network was able to differentiate and would the data from each operator appear as such an identifiable intrinsic pattern that the network would recognize it?

Imagine an art expert who has been asked to attribute paintings by Rubens, van Gogh and Vermeer to the correct artist. Normally this will not be a problem for the expert. If we have coded Rubens as 00001, for example, van Gogh as 01110, and Vermeer as 10100, the expert will unhesitatingly allocate the correct five-bit code to the appropriate paintings. This would be the ideal case for our neural network – it would just associate the new data with the correct identity codes.

In reality, things are not as easy as in our example. An allocation will be difficult for even an art expert if he or she is confronted with unknown paintings by the artists concerned. The question arises whether a painting is truly an original or has only been signed by the master. Rubens, for example, produced an enormous number of paintings and employed many students in his studio. As art experts have recently discovered, there are very many forgeries of van Gogh, and for decades these have been taken for originals. Vermeer had a very original style of painting and left us only a small oeuvre of 40 paintings. The art expert will look at any alleged new discoveries with great scepticism. It all depends on how good the art expert's criteria for differentiation are, because these will enable him unequivocally to attribute a given painting to a particular artist. If the expert is not able to clearly commit himself to whether an alleged Rubens was actually painted by him, or whether parts of the painting, or the whole painting, were produced by a student, or even by a contemporary copyist, instead of the Rubens code 00001, the expert could allocate the code 00011. By having four out of five bits agree with the identity code, he is indicating that there is a high degree of probability the painting is by Rubens but that the origin cannot be attributed to him alone with 100 per cent certainty.

Let us make life even more difficult for our expert for a moment. Let us give him the task of allocating paintings from an era in which individual characteristics in painting – such as developed from the Renaissance onwards – had still not become widespread – a painting from the Gothic or Romanesque period, for example. Or let us have the expert judge works of art from a culture where the artists are completely unknown and the work can only be classed into a school or a style based on certain common features. Here it would be far more difficult, often impossible, to make an exact attribution, even if the origin of some of the works could be clearly established. The reason for this is that the input data is characterized by heavy 'noise' – there are far too many paintings from an era, a school or a style, and they are too similar to each other for us to be able to recognize the individual features.

The signal is too weak, and the poor expert will show us that, while there are some similarities, there is no hope of making a clear attribution of the work.

The neural network for the psi data was faced with similar problems of heavy noise and weak signals. The question was whether the high-tech memory of the network would work better than the low-tech ability of an expert. The trained network was presented with the 32 sets of transfer data. Ideally, given perfect recognition, the result for each set of data should have been the display of the correct identity code. As we have seen, with the input data in question, we were far away from the ideal situation. It would have been regarded as a success if the network had been able to show more correct codes, or parts of codes, than could be expected by chance. If we were to count it as a success if four out of the five binary numbers were correctly rendered, we could expect five correctly identified people out of the 32 subjects. In order to achieve a direct means of comparison, Radin also fed the network with random data and let it compare transfer data based on this senseless input.

On average, for the real MMI data from the PEAR laboratory, the network was able to identify 6.02 identity codes with 80 per cent accuracy. For the random data, an average of 4.91 codes were 'recognized'. Consequently, the quota lay exactly within the range of chance expectation.

The network had learned something – not much, but something. Signatures in REG data are not chimeras. After Radin had found that repeated training of the neural network with several selections of data of a given individual led to improved results, he was able, a few years later, to achieve better results in recognition based on new network configurations.[58]

# SIMULATION OF PSI

In order to improve its performance, it would be possible to provide the network with additional individual indices that it could process together with the psi data – for example, environmental influences, which are known to modulate psi performance – and by such means we could achieve a recognition rate approaching practical applicability. And this is what Radin is after.

Radin sees one possible application in the development of a 'mental lock'. He calls this instrument of the future a *mock* (from mental lock), a system that combines an REG with a neural network and that reacts to mental intentions. The network would be trained to recognize the signature in psi data of a given individual. As soon as a person approaches the lock, they are detected by a conventional detector. At present, the REG produces a random sequence and the network compares it with the learned pattern. If it finds correspondence, the lock opens.

Radin does not regard such things as pie in the sky schemes. Supported by the unusual abilities of former psi spy Joe McMoneagle, Radin works intensively on the technical applicability of his results. McMoneagle had 'seen' these instruments of the future in visions, and Radin hopes to apply for patents for psi-based machines before the turn of the century.

A few years ago Radin investigated whether the recognition of individual signatures could be improved by the provision of further variables. The task in a long-term project was psychokinetically to reduce background ionizing radiation (as measured by a Geiger counter) during certain phases of the experiment.[59] In these phases all the subject – in this case Radin himself – had to do, as in the PEAR experiments, was to intend that the background ionizing radiation would diminish. At the same time, a large number of environmental variables were recorded, including the temperature of the surroundings, humidity, atmospheric pressure, weather conditions, body temperature, local magnetic field, number of sunspots, geomagnetic activity, activity of the sun, background X-ray radiation, self-evaluation of the physical and psychological state and the results achieved in the experiment.

The experiment ran every day for 65 days (between 26 August and 3 November 1992). In the experimental phases Radin succeeded in significantly reducing background ionizing radiation, thereby demonstrating the possibility of an interaction between mind and matter in this specific case. But how did all the other physical variables Radin had measured behave? It was discovered that certain values – notably environmental influences, which act as modulators on MMI – correlated with the psi performance.

A second aspect that resulted from the analysis was so-called rebounds of the MMI effect in space and time. If a Geiger counter registered a lower background radiation during a phase of influencing, another Geiger counter in the same room, but further off, showed a higher rate (space rebound). Similarly, on the same Geiger counter a diminished phase was immediately followed by a phase of increased radiation activity (time rebound). In the context of considering the statistical equilibrium in random systems, this effect could lead to a new understanding of the subtle interaction between mind and matter.

Radin entered the recorded data on the environmental variables into a neural network. It learned the complex relationships and was soon able to predict the results of mind–matter interactions based on eight variables. This means that, based solely on the external influences – geomagnetic fluctuations, air pressure, wind, fluctuations in background X-ray radiation and the emotions and confidence of the subject, for example – the characteristic nature of the anomalous effect could be correctly predicted.

Psi has passed its baptism of fire. It is encouraging to find that there are lawful principles at work behind the erratic nature of psi.

# Chapter Four

# THROUGH THE
# TIME BARRIER

## SHADES OF THE FUTURE

Physiological studies have shown that anomalous information is often registered by the body but does not reach the threshold of consciousness. In many conventional experiments in telepathy, clairvoyance or precognition in which targets are to be reported, there may be a subconscious anomalous gaining of information even though the experiments apparently fail.

Let us consider what we have been able to observe phenomenologically. Information in a remote system is accessed; the access primarily takes place by a physical reaction; in all probability, the temporal lobes and the limbic system that is related to them play a role in the storage of such subconsciously perceived information; emotional factors (the limbic system is responsible for the processing of emotions) act as internal censors in the selection of psi signals; and there is a physiological response to the emotional weighting of relevant information. From this, we can formulate the simple theory that the stronger the emotional charge of a psi signal is, the greater is the probability that it will lead to a response or reach the threshold of consciousness.

Emotions also convey a class of psi experiences that number among the most astonishing experiences the science of anomalous mental phenomena has to offer – that is, precognition or knowledge of future events. As unbelievable as it may sound, precognition is one of the most thoroughly proved facts in psi research. Excellently documented and confirmed spontaneous experiences are piling up in the archives of the institutes. In the laboratory the phenomenon of precognition has been experimentally investigated with the most up-to-date techniques, and it is recognized as a real experience.

One example comes from the hundreds of anecdotes on the paranormal. There are many reports of incidents involving the German physician and writer Friedrich Wilhelm Weber (1813–94), author of the epic

*Dreizehnlinden*, which illustrate his precognitive talents. One night while he sat reading in his room, he heard noises and the voice of a farmer he knew, who had come with his wagon to fetch Weber because his mother had broken a leg. Weber made ready to go and called out that he would be down shortly. When he stepped outside his house there was nobody to be seen, though he looked far and wide. An hour later the farmer really did appear in his wagon to fetch Weber to his mother, who had broken a leg. In many cases, however, the future event is not perceived concretely but experienced only as an ill-defined feeling. We call this a presentiment or a premonition. Presentiments are often experienced as an unexplained oppression, an inner unrest, a faint and not definitely identifiable 'knowledge' of an often upsetting event. A presentiment is an emotional reaction based on a subconscious, precognitive impression, which sometimes induces the person experiencing it to carry out certain acts without knowing why they are doing so.

A woman told the following story at the Institute for Border Areas of Psychology and Mental Hygiene in Freiburg, Germany. During the 1930s a flood had cut off her village on the Baltic coast from the railway station 10 kilometres away. Her husband had gone to Königsberg for several days. On the evening of the fourth day she was seized by an inexplicable fear and a feeling of unease. The fear was so strong that she dared to go out onto the railway embankment, which was the only thing still above water although it was in danger of disintegrating. As if compelled to do so, she walked along the embankment for over an hour without knowing why, until she came across her husband, who was close to collapse. A high fever had forced him to break off his trip, and he had tried to reach home on foot. He would probably never have made it without his wife's presentiment.

Having carried out a careful analysis, William Cox came to an interesting conclusion.[60] Looking at the records over a long period, he compared the numbers of passengers in trains that had had an accident with the average number of passengers on ten other days. On the days of an accident there had been statistically significantly fewer passengers on the trains than on the other days. Apparently, many people have presentiments without being aware of this and allow themselves to be guided by these premonitions.

Working with psychologist Diane Ferrari, Charles Honorton subjected the controversial issue of precognition to a meta-analysis. They drew on 309 precognition experiments conducted between 1935 and 1987.[61] All of these had been run according to the forced-choice method, the subsequent random selection of which had to be predicted. The data fed into the computer consisted of almost 2 million sessions with more than 50,000 subjects. The mean effect size for each individual run proved to be low, but at the same time it was consistent, so that the total effect could be termed extremely significant. In order to cancel it out, the parapsychologists would have had to make no fewer than 14,268 file-drawer studies yielding negative results disappear. In other words, during the 52 years in which the 248 precognition studies had been published, they would have had to conduct a further 23 studies each month that were not published, and this is clearly an impossibility.

Honorton and Ferrari identified four moderating variables which showed a systematic relationship to the results:

1. Studies with subjects who had achieved positive results in previous psi experiments achieved significantly better results than subjects who had not been pre-selected.
2. Subjects tested individually achieved more hits than subjects tested in groups.
3. There is a close relationship between feedback on hits and the hit rate. The more immediately and the more detail in which the subject is informed about their actual hit rate, the better they do.
4. There is a close relationship between the hit rate and the time interval between the naming and selection of the target – the shorter the interval, the higher the hit rate.

The time effect mentioned above is of particular interest. At first glance we might assume that we could formulate a sustainable argument for precognition on the grounds that the further we want to look into the future, the less we will 'see'. But Honorton and Ferrari found this time effect existed only among unselected subjects. Those who had previously been successful in psi experiments were not affected by the 'time barrier', and their hit rate even improved slightly with increasing time intervals.

As far as the nature of feedback is concerned, we have to be careful in our interpretation. The subsequent feedback about a hit is obviously not totally independent of the selected time interval in the test. If a larger group of subjects were to do less well in longer time intervals, the reason might be the necessarily delayed feedback on their success or failure. In such a case, feedback would have to be given priority. On the other hand, it is not clear if the time factor itself plays an important role in precognition among those we might term the 'non-psi-trained'.

# IN EXPECTATION OF THE UNFORESEEABLE

If psi is a fundamental biological mechanism in the form of an autonomous bodily function, we would expect it to be easier to grasp psi effects if we shut off the conscious mind. In the field of extrasensory perception, conscious reproduction can lead to psychological defence mechanisms and prevent the very impressions we intend to study.

This is by no means a new idea for parapsychologists. In the early 1950s a few successful experiments were conducted in which telepathic transmissions were measured not by the conscious reproduction of images or the guessing of symbols, but by autonomous physiological reactions. If impressions of the future are actually transmitted by means of their emotional undertone, autonomous physiological measurements that take this concomitant effect into consideration would be particularly appropriate.

We know from psychological tests that reaction times increase when we are asked to name a colour that is associated with contradictory information – a green patch of colour, for example, that has the word 'red' written on it. The cause of this is known as 'cognitive interference' – that is, the sensory impression of the colour is simultaneously overlaid by the word shown.

What happens, however, if the colour spot is seen first and the name of the colour is shown shortly afterwards? In one study, all the subjects had to do was to name the colour as quickly as possible and then to pronounce the word shown. The analysis of the reaction times demonstrated a curious effect.[62] Where the colour shown and the colour name following it matched, the reaction time to the first stimulus – the colour spot – was shorter than for those colour spots when the following colour name was mismatched. Is this a 'time reversed' cognitive interference? It would seem that the word that appeared later acted retroactively on the ability to react. Or to put it another way, the subconscious psi sounding had already identified the word by precognition.

Ever since the sensational findings of Benjamin Libet, the renowned physiologist from San Francisco State University, California, decision-making processes have been the focus of attention for research on consciousness. The results of his famous study are easy to describe, but their content is sensational and hardly credible for many people. Our mind functions in a largely unconscious way. Libet had found that we make decisions first and only subsequently become aware of the decision taken.[63] Our responses to the outside world are completely unconscious, but we are convinced we have taken deliberate decisions. When Pete Sampras returns a serve by Boris Becker, he does not consciously perceive the tennis ball. This happens only after the ball is back on Boris Becker's side of the net. We become aware of the outer world about half a second after our response, and on the neural level half a second is a long time. How does it come about, then, that we still believe we perceive stimuli exactly at the moment they actually occur? A curious mechanism in our mind arranges for the pre-dating of our decision, or of an external stimulus, to the exact moment of the stimulus or the decision, and it is even spatially shifted to the exact spot of the stimulus. Libet called the first of these effects subjective temporal referral; the second he called spatial referral.

The consequences of this discovery have still not been completely digested. Libet's results mark a revolution in our understanding of consciousness and have extended the philosophical discussion about free will in a new direction. If it is not our conscious mind, what hidden mechanisms are at work in our reactions? Has the fundamental psi function found a window through which it can supply our routine actions with additional information?

Recently a team of psychologists investigated decision-making aspects of intuitive hunches.[64] When it was their turn, subjects had to draw a single card out of one of four packs of cards. The choice of which deck of cards was left to them. With some cards they would 'lose', with others they would 'win'. The subjects did not know that two of the packs contained more losing cards, while the other two contained more winning cards. Whoever chose to draw from the 'winning' packs more often would win in the end. During the game, the participants were connected to physiological measuring equipment, which detected the anticipatory effects in the electrical skin activity that always occur when a decision that could be risky has to be thought through. It was also discovered that the subjects showed increased anticipatory effects in the skin conductance response before they drew a losing card for the first time, and even before they were aware of their decision strategy when, without knowing it, they drew a card from a losing deck. There is apparently only one possible explanation for this result: the players had presentiments that could be measured physiologically but that did not reach the threshold of consciousness.

Human emotions are one of the forms of expression that are particularly easy to detect by means of physiological measurements. From psychophysiological studies we know the effects of a 'signal stimulus'. When fearful people are shown alternately exciting or neutral pictures and they know that the next picture will be an emotionally exciting one, their heartbeat increases remarkably even before the next picture appears. But what happens if they do not know what sort of a picture will appear next?

An experiment intended to clear up this very question caused much furore in modern parapsychology. It was performed – and it is tempting to say, 'Where else?' – in Dean Radin's laboratory.[65] The object was to find out whether people react with physiologically recordable presentiments to target symbols that are only shown to them in the future.

## THE PRESENTIMENT REFLEX

On 15 April 1997 American newspapers reported the story of a woman who had won a fortune from a slot machine in Las Vegas with a single go. She claimed she had had a hunch that one particular machine would come up with the jackpot. She did not play at any of the many other machines, but lined up behind the other people waiting in front of this one machine. After an hour her turn came, she played, and the machine paid out the $12 million jackpot.

Are such presentiments coincidence or are they based on precognitive information? Radin developed his experiment to find out.

The orienting reflex is a physical reaction to new and important stimuli. The body signals its readiness to recognize and react to a novel impression. Investigations have shown that the orienting reflex is accompanied by a short-term increase of sensual perception and that this immediately follows the new stimulus. Radin pursued the question, asking if, for appropriate stimuli, a similar reflex might be observed before stimulation occurred. This would reflect a presentiment. He defines this postulated presentiment as a differential anticipatory response.

In Radin's experiment the subjects were seated in front of a computer screen.[66] Five seconds after a click with the mouse, a colour picture appeared on the screen, then the monitor screen remained dark for 10 seconds. With another click of the mouse, the process could be repeated. The computer program chose pictures at random from a pool of 150.

The selection of a picture occurred only at the end of the 5-second delay during which the screen remained dark, and the selection process took 0.1 seconds. Each subject had 40 turns, during which their physiological parameters were recorded. There were pictures with calm, not emotionally charged contents, such as landscapes, portraits and pictures of fruit, trees or animals, and some with emotionally charged contents of an erotic or aggressive nature. Radin decided that the pool should include only 50 pictures with an emotional content and 100 neutral pictures to avoid the habituation effect that would result from the too frequent appearance of exciting pictures.

Because of the wide range of possible reactions to emotionally charged images, a weak anomalous presentiment effect could disappear if the results of all the subjects were summarized. Radin decided, therefore, to include the individual forms of the reactions in his study. It was to be expected that the familiar orientating reflex would be detected after a picture appeared on the screen, but that this would vary quite strongly from subject to subject. A person who – physiologically speaking – reacts to aggressive contents relatively calmly will show similar relatively calm reactions in his presentiments. More important than the differences in the subconscious reactions to neutral or exciting pictures is the individual constancy of the reaction itself. Radin postulated that the physiological effects measured after the presentation of a picture would be the same as the physiological effects immediately before presentation.

In order to achieve a uniform measure, a complicated procedure was followed to impose three physiological parameters. The graphic display of the results already showed remarkable differences in the reactions to emotional or to neutral pictures, not only during and after viewing, but also before. The effect became particularly clear in the differences of the physiological reaction between neutral and emotional pictures – blood volume in the fingers showed the strongest effect 3 seconds, heart rate 2 seconds and electrodermal activity about 1 second *before* the emotionally exciting picture appeared. The change in blood volume showed the strongest reaction to the presentiment. The physiologically recorded presentiment effect was even stronger when, from the emotionally exciting pictures, only those were shown that other subjects had classed as being extremely negative or positive.

A further finding was also remarkable. Those subjects who showed a strong orienting reflex on all three physiological parameters after having looked at an emotionally exciting picture, also showed a much stronger presentiment reflex than the other participants. Interestingly, the presentiment reaction proved to be stronger in people with little psi experience than in those who had often had psi experiences. Moreover, the influence of geomagnetic activity on the data proved to be astonishingly clear. Only presentiment studies that were conducted on quiet geomagnetic days reached statistical significance.

Finally, Radin also submitted the raw data of his study to an analysis by artificial neural networks. The networks were trained to associate four and three input variables respectively (lunar phase, planetary geomagnetic flux, gender and presentiment response before the stimulus) with the orientating reflex after the stimulus (as the one output variable). An interesting learning effect came to light. While the correlative relationship between the presentiment reflex and the orientating reflex was relatively weak, the neural network was able to learn to predict the nature of that reflex. The neural network had learned to establish meaningful relationships between environmental factors, gender and the physiological reactions before stimulation with the physiological reaction after stimulation. This was a highly promising result, and also a confirmation that the effects measured are real and not due to chance. It may be that psi researchers are not all that far away from identifying the best variables with which to develop pragmatically useful models for prediction.

## THE GAMBLER'S FALLACY

Gamblers are familiar with the effect that if the 'wrong' number comes up in roulette, the expectation rises that on the next go, the 'right' number will come up – the number the player intends to bet on. If a red number has come up three or four times in a row, many players assume that the probability of the ball stopping on a black number on the next turn has increased. This assumption is a fallacy. The probability of which number will come up or to which colour it will belong remains the same for every turn of the wheel. Even if a red number has come up ten times in a row, the probability that on the eleventh turn a black number will come up remains exactly the same. It is only our own concept of the order of things that is misleading us.

If only that were all there was to it! Gamblers become tremendously excited when they believe that the time has come when 'their' number must come up. Everyone reacts more or less strongly to expectations with involuntary physiological changes, particularly when these are accompanied by intense emotions. As soon as the hoped-for number has come up, the state of excitement is allayed, and the player would be nonplussed if it were to come up again straight away.

In experiments on presentiment such states of excitement based on normal false expectations have to be carefully excluded. Subjects quickly realize what the experiment is all about. There are boring pictures, and occasionally ones that arouse some kind of emotion. If a series of neutral pictures has been shown, the subjects will automatically assume that an emotion-evoking picture will soon turn up, and they will begin to build up the appropriate, gradually increasing physiological expectation reaction. As soon as an extreme picture appears, the purely psychologically motivated expectation reaction will fall off again.

Dick Bierman designed his experiments in such a way that this effect could be identified and excluded.[67] Among other things, the subjects did not know what the experiment was about, and as soon as the first emotionally charged picture appeared, the experiment was considered to have come to an end. This prevented the subjects from being able to build up any expectations. On the other hand, Bierman created a problem for himself because he needed a large number of subjects, since each individual test was of very short duration. In general, Bierman's experiments confirmed Radin's results, even after expectation strategies had been excluded. This is an additional decisive argument in support of the thesis that a real anomalous effect had been recorded.

These excellent studies on the presentiment effect are among the most important milestones in modern parapsychology. They cannot be overlooked by the 'hard' sciences, and they have opened the way into a long-neglected field to which psychology is increasingly turning: intuition. Intuition can be defined as a form of subconscious problem-solving.[68] It would seem that the process of intuition profits from the fundamental psi function, and it is even possible that intuition is its most direct expression, albeit clothed in the mantle of thought processes, creative problem-solving strategies and emotional weighting.

# Chapter Five
# COSMIC CONNECTIONS
## PSI, THE EARTH AND THE SKY

### THE PSI CATALYST

Hard to grasp, fleeting and weak – that is the reality of psi, even if we are now able to claim that the question of the existence of anomalous cognition (AC) has been positively answered. Modern psi research no longer needs to be interested only in proofs. After numerous environmental variables were shown to correlate with psi in a more or less remarkable manner, there was only one more element to be identified: a physical influencing factor that strongly and dependably correlates with psi.

James Spottiswoode, director of research at the Cognitive Sciences Laboratory in Palo Alto, has now discovered this factor – a parameter that increases the quality of anomalous cognition by a multiple.[69] Has the parapsychologists' dream come true? Has the science of anomalous mental phenomena now found the means to link psi to the forces of nature?

Spottiswoode, a mathematician, computer expert and former adviser to the World Bank, is the man everyone is talking about. The announcement of his discovery burst into the parapsychological community like a bombshell. 'It may end up being not *the* breakthrough, but *a* breakthrough,' commented Richard Broughton, director of research at the Rhine Research Center in Durham, North Carolina. Everybody had hoped for such a discovery. Nobody had expected it in this way.

We know very little about the physical mechanism of anomalous cognition, and identification of physical parameters that clearly modulate AC performance is an important step towards getting closer to a solution. The problem of investigating AC in relationship to influencing factors is hidden in the hard-to-understand psi process itself. With comparative data we never know if psi is actually at work or if a comparison is being made to a random event that is being interpreted as psi. This problem is more pronounced in forced-choice studies than in free-response experiments, but in the end, every study of the relationships to psi comes up against this barrier. The isolation of psi is still, at present, impossible. Psi always appears only as an approximation. It is embedded in a phenomenological complex, but the exact point at which psi could be clearly identified cannot be located.

This is why many studies of the correlations of physical parameters to psi performance have been able to discover only very weak relationships or even no relationships at all. A series of variables seems to influence the quality of psi, but it is scarcely possible to nail down such an influence. There is a weak indication of one physical influencing factor: shielding from electric fields by means of a Faraday cage leads to improved AC results.[70] Another promising area for research is fluctuations in geomagnetic fields. As we have already seen, relatively calm geomagnetic activities favour the appearance of anomalous cognition, but there is still no definitive answer to whether geomagnetic activity acts as a 'carrier' for psi or whether it modulates the centres in the brain for processing anomalous information. As interesting as the studies on geomagnetic variables may be, the relationship to anomalous cognition remains tenuous.

In their search for physical factors that influence psi, parapsychologists have gradually 'taken off'. They are moving increasingly further from the earth. First they discovered the influence of the geomagnetic field, then they cast their eyes towards the changing moon, recently they are considering the rotations of the sun. And in the meantime, hard though this is to credit, they have directed their sights at the stars. Is this just superstition? Have the psi researchers turned to astrology?

The answer to this is no, they have not. In a database consisting of 1468 free-response AC experiments, James Spottiswoode found a remarkable correlation between psi performance and local sidereal time (LST). The experiments, which had been conducted within a certain time window of local sidereal time, showed an increased effect size of, believe it or not, 340 per cent. Spottiswoode then analysed a further database containing 1015 similar experiments, which showed an increase of the effect size during the time in question of 450 per cent.

Is it possible that the location of the percipient in relation to the stars in the firmament can influence the ability to perceive paranormal impressions? The question sounds odd and one that can hardly be taken seriously.

Alignments in the sky are determined by spheric coordinates. There are several methods of dividing the sky above our heads by systems of coordinates. The most common form is known as the equatorial system, in which the geographic coordinate system is projected onto the firmament. Imagine that the earth's rotational axis was extended so that it became the celestial axis. If the earth's equator were extended in the same way, you would have the celestial equator. The position of a star is determined by two angles on the spheric coordinates, declination and right ascension (RA). If we project the earth's coordinate system into the sky, the right ascension equates with longitude.

As a reflection of the daily rotation of the earth, the equatorial system rotates around the celestial axis once in 24 (sidereal) hours. For any point on earth, the stars return to their starting position at the end of a sidereal day. Because the sun moves about 1 degree each day contrary to the daily rotation of the firmament, a sidereal day is about 3 minutes and 56 seconds shorter than a solar day.

We can therefore define a sidereal time for the celestial coordinate system that is counted from 0 to 24 hours, just like solar time. And just as we can determine local solar time for any point on earth, we can also determine the appropriate local sidereal time. At an identical LST, the exactly identical firmament appears above the head of an observer. Because of the unequal time measurements between solar time and sidereal time, solar time and sidereal time are almost exactly identical only once a year. This happens each year on 22 September, at exactly 12 noon world time.

Since most of the data comes from experiments conducted in Europe and the United States and was recorded at various times of the year – mostly during the day – the information encompasses the whole range of LST values.

## SIDEREAL TIME: 13:47

Spottiswoode's analysis was initially based on remote viewing and ganzfeld studies, and the necessary exact data – location, date, time – was available from these experiments. When an experiment is conducted, the starting time is normally recorded. The actual statements about the remote viewing of a target or the hypnagogic impressions in a ganzfeld normally occur between a few minutes and a quarter of an hour later.

Spottiswoode fed the location coordinates and the time of the experiment into a computer, which automatically calculated the appropriate values for local sidereal time. Then he projected the data into windows of 1 hour duration each. The result was a dramatic increase of the mean effect size for experiments conducted between 12:00 and 14:00 hours local sidereal time.

In a second step, Spottiswoode subjected those studies to a special analysis, which consisted of the upper half of the culmination point between 12:00 and 14:00 hours LST. He wanted to find out at which point in local sidereal time the maximum effect size appeared. Spottiswoode found that the absolute culmination point occurred at 13:47 local sidereal time. The experiments in anomalous cognition conducted in the time window of ± 1 hour of 13:47 LST showed an effect size of 0.507. Compared with the effect size of the total data of 0.148, this represented an increase by a factor of 3.42.

Spottiswoode could not believe his eyes. He certainly had not expected such a strong effect. He was so puzzled that he decided immediately to subject a further compilation of experimental data to the same analysis. Either coincidence had decided to play him an extremely nasty trick or he had struck a rich seam. The additional data from various institutes confirmed his findings in a most convincing way. Again, Spottiswoode detected a remarkable increase in AC performance at around 13:00 hours LST, and the culmination point again lay at exactly 13:47 local sidereal time.

On the basis of this impressive finding, Spottiswoode was now able to subject the complete data to an analysis. The result was that extrasensory perception works best at 13:47 local sidereal time – and this result has a statistical significance that takes it into the realm of the stars, for it would require 60 billion sets of data of this sort in order to hit upon this result only once by chance.

In future, the clocks in the psi laboratories will be adjusted to local sidereal time. Experiments that take place during the ideal time window have a three to four times greater chance of being successful than those conducted at other times. Incidentally, the most unfavourable time for psi is the evening of a sidereal day – between 17:30 and 19:00 hours LST, psi goes to bed. If, for example, psi researchers had planned to conduct an experiment in London on 1 August 1998, in order to profit from the time window 13:47 LST, the ideal time for anomalous cognition would have been at 5 o'clock in the afternoon.[71]

The next step is obvious. In future psi researchers will put the exact locations and times on their experiments, particularly for the phase during which extrasensory perceptions are actually being described. In addition, as far as possible they will attempt to conduct them during the favourable time span. It is a tremendous advantage for them to have been given such a simple variable with which the psi performance of their subjects can be greatly enhanced. Many of the attempts to investigate anomalous mental phenomena in relation to various influencing factors failed because psi did not appear at all. If the probability of success can now be increased by a multiple, we can expect rapid advances in para-psychology.

How can we interpret these results? At first glance we are confronted with an unknown causal connection between a certain right ascension in the sky and the ability for anomalous cognition. If it is a causal effect, then it must come from outside the solar system because interplanetary space is dominated by solar and planetary effects. Moreover, the planets of the solar system alter their positions.

The influence may be due to a number of factors. The greater part of the electromagnetic spectrum, from gamma rays all the way to low-frequency radio waves, can be traced back to known cosmic sources. There are, in addition, particle fluxes, the origin of which can be determined. It might be possible to detect one factor among all these emissions in the sector of the firmament that appears directly above us at 13:50 hours right ascension. Physical influencing factors from this sector would have to be related to the psi-enhancing effect.

One possibility is that a signal coming from this direction in space increases anomalous cognition. Since the enhancing effect does not take place at any other time, this signal must at least be partially blocked by the earth. We could also assume that a signal coming from the opposite point of 13:50 hours right ascension inhibits anomalous cognition. In this case, the shielding from this detrimental influence would be responsible for an increased appearance of extrasensory perceptions. In any event, it appears that the earth plays an important role in this mechanism, either by absorbing or by reflecting the signal.

It is also possible to look at the results from the point of view that certain cosmic influences prevent the production of AC or at least keep it down to a weak level. Their disappearance around 13:50 hours LST would then be responsible for the 'psi surplus'.

# A TIME WINDOW FOR THE GEOMAGNETIC EFFECT

The studies on the geomagnetic influences on psi have produced many different indications and a number of contradictory results. In an unpublished meta-analysis of 21 published studies, James Spottiswoode came to the conclusion that the effect would be more readily detectable if a large database with high effect size was available. The meta-analysis revealed that the correlation between low geomagnetic activity and superior psi results during experiments on anomalous cognition was disappointingly low and not significant.

After having discovered the time window in local sidereal time, Spottiswoode set out to again check the studies on geomagnetic activities.[72] The LST effect is a physical factor for which cosmic and earthly determinants play a central role, and Spottiswoode thought that there might be some type of relationship between the LST effect and the effect of the geomagnetic field.

For this analysis Spottiswoode again drew on the data of the past few decades collected in free-response anomalous cognition studies. These were the experiments in which the greatest effect sizes had been recorded: ganzfeld studies from the Psychophysical Research Laboratories in Princeton, from the Institute for Parapsychology in Durham, from the Psychology Department of the University of Amsterdam, from the Institute for Parapsychology in Utrecht and from the Koestler Parapsychology Unit at the University of Edinburgh. Also used were the remote viewing experiments at the PEAR laboratory, the SRI, SAIC and RV experiments that Marilyn Schlitz and I had conducted, as well as some of his own experiments.

Spottiswoode discovered a pronounced correlation between AC and a geomagnetic index dependent on local sidereal time. Maximal effect size appeared at 13:00 hours LST, with a statistically very significant correlation to reduced geomagnetic activity. The remarkable relationship showed itself only in the narrow time band of three hours around 13:00 hours LST. Outside this small time window the relationship is nil. The correlation could also be detected in individual series in which experiments fell into the respective time window. In the extensive studies at the PEAR laboratory, for example, there was no correlation between psi performance and geomagnetic activity, but as soon as only the data from the decisive time window was selected, a strong correlation could be detected.

When high scores in psi tests are achieved in the time window of ± 1 hour around 13:47 LST, we also find a particularly calm geomagnetic phase. An analysis of the transcontinental remote viewing experiments that I performed together with Marilyn Schlitz (see Part 1, Chapter 2) is of interest under these new considerations. I had to visit the randomly selected places in Rome at a time when it was still light; the time had to be one that would be convenient for Marilyn Schlitz. Because of the 6-hour time difference between Detroit and Rome, we decided that I would go to the target places in late afternoon. That equated to a time of between 11 o'clock and 12 noon local time in Detroit. When Marilyn Schlitz made herself comfortable on 3 November at 11 o'clock in the morning in order to note her impressions during the subsequent 30 or more minutes, it was about 13:16 local sidereal time in Detroit. The final experiment of the series took place on 10 November and began at about 13:45 LST. Therefore the whole RV experiment series took place during the ideal time window. Furthermore, an analysis showed that at the time in question there was very little geomagnetic activity. Coincidence had provided us with the two known external factors that favour psi, and they obviously contributed to the great success of the series of experiments.

In Spottiswoode's analysis there are only 4 hours in local sidereal time during which the relationship between the effect sizes of experiments in extrasensory perception and geomagnetic changes appears at all. This helps to explain why the search for geomagnetic influencing factors on psi had previously produced such varying results. Apparently geomagnetic activity exerts its effect only in connection with the time window discovered in local sidereal time.

James Spottiswoode asks us to consider that global geomagnetic indices such as the ap-index measure fluctuations in the magnetic field of the whole planet. The fluctuations last from a few minutes to a few hours. In centres of population the fluctuations in magnetic fields can be far more pronounced and occur more rapidly because there are buildings and concentrations of iron. Since most parapsychological experiments take place in cities, Spottiswoode claims it is improbable that geomagnetic fluctuations themselves are responsible for the modulation of psi results. It should be assumed that anomalous cognition depends on complex interactions between particle emissions of the sun and the earth's magnetic field.

Spottiswoode's work has led to the establishment of order in the confusing field of the influence of physical factors on paranormal impressions. It has also demonstrated that there are two such factors: 'AC effect size is strongly dependent upon the LST of the receiver and the limited region of LST where effect is enhanced, the effect size is likely modulated by solar activity, as reflected in the GMF [geomagnetic fluctuations] index.'[73] The underlying mechanism must have a causal reason. Its right ascension must have remained more or less constant during the 20 years from which the data analysed stems. The search for the mysterious factor behind the sidereal time window and the quiet geomagnetic phases can now begin – somewhere out there in the cosmos.

# Chapter Six
# THE PARSIFAL EFFECT

## WHOSE PSI?

When we are dealing with such fragile phenomena as psi, which are modulated by psychological and physical factors, various subtle influences by the experimenter can affect the results. Sometimes these effects can be purely psychological. It may be, for example, that subjects from whom good psi results are expected receive better treatment from the experimenters than others. But in psi there is another experimenter effect that demands attention. In the 1950s two British parapsychologists, G.W. Fisk and D.J. West, noticed in jointly conducted experiments that West's subjects normally produced poor results in psi tests, while Fisk's subjects did well, even when neither of them had any contact with their subjects.[74] This marked the discovery of a psi-mediated experimenter effect, an effect that is still a mystery for parapsychologists.

Marilyn Schlitz recently conducted some DMILS experiments with the sceptic Richard Wiseman in which the non-local psi-mediated experimenter effect appeared – Schlitz achieved positive results, but Wiseman did not.[75] During an investigation of the phenomenon of dowsing, German psychologists Harald Walach and Stefan Schmidt also accidentally ran into the same phenomenon.[76] It was discovered that only those dowsers who had received their instructions from one and the same of three instructors achieved hits significantly above chance expectation. In parapsychology, the experimenter is apparently an integral part of any experiment. He or she transmits anomalous information that causes varying results. It is still unclear if this information reaches the subject subconsciously and puts them into a condition of readiness for, or inhibition against, psi or if the subconscious effect directly affects the experimental outcome.

Some surgeons enjoy a good reputation, others do not. A few people achieve virtuosity on the piano, while others who practise just as hard always remain mediocre. Any sort of achievement requires great skill and a talent that cannot be acquired. In psi experiments the experimenter is so intimately integrated into the experiment that he cannot be isolated from it.

If we combine the subtle experimenter effect with what we discussed in connection with the 'ranging system psi' in FieldREG research, the perspective shifts. As soon as an experimenter has conceived his experiment, refined it and taken it up, the fate of the experiment may already be sealed. If we are dealing with a successful experimenter, one out of the 1 per cent of the population who are able to apply psi particularly well, we can expect significant results in support of his (or her) assumptions. These reflect his desires and his intentions. The intention of the experimenter is what tips the scales and directs psi in the right direction.

One burning question remains unanswered. Is the experimenter's intention in his experiment sufficient to bring about the desired effect or does his knowledge act only as the link between the subject and the measuring instrument? Put in more general terms and going beyond psi research, we must ask whether every thought process about real objects or other people does not contain an anomalous interaction on its content, simply by the content being addressed. Do our thoughts and feelings about the world at large not adjust the fundamental psi function anew at any given moment? Could this be the mechanism by which we subtly interact with things and moderate reality?

Robert Jahn and Brenda Dunne offer an example borrowed from physics. The physicists named a recently discovered particle 'anomalon' because different properties of the particle appeared in different laboratories. The manifestation of the anomalon is apparently so closely linked to the person who happens to observe it that it adapts to him or her in a completely specific manner. In fact, Jahn and Dunne even go so far as to claim that physicists do not discover new subatomic particles; rather, they create them. For psi, which also works on a very subtle level, such mechanisms are particularly valid.

The 'old school' of parapsychology thought in clearly differentiated categories: clairvoyance, telepathy, precognition and psychokinesis. Today psi appears to be a single ability that manifests itself in different ways. While this may sound odd, it almost appears as if psi phenomena are adapting themselves to the attempts by scientists to explain them and not the other way around. Ever since we abandoned the old patterns of classification and began to search for new ways to describe them, the data appears, willingly, to follow this trend.

We have seen how close is the link between mind and matter and that there is a constant anomalous stream of communication between humans and their environment. We should not be surprised, therefore, that the field of variable, weak and ephemeral phenomena that we have decided to call 'psi' is the one that reacts most clearly to this link. Just as the scientists are constantly informed subconsciously by their psi interactions, so do the ideas and concepts of the scientists inform the psi process itself.

## BEGINNER'S LUCK

In the mid-1980s C.M. Pleass and N. Dean Dey, two marine biologists from the University of Delaware, conducted experiments that are of great importance for our understanding of the subtle psi-mediated experimenter effect.[77] They wanted to find out if the human mind could influence isolated single-cell microbes.

In their first experiment they used cultures of the marine alga *Dunaliella tertiolecta* in an elegantly designed arrangement. At certain intervals, an opto-electronic system measured the movements of the algae according to speed and direction. During the experimental phase the movements of the microbes were to be influenced by focused attention and intention in such a way that they would alter their behaviour to a degree above chance expectation. The experimenters did not decree whether the influence exerted should express itself in an increase or decrease of movement. All the subjects had to do was 'to be with the algae' – that is, to imagine themselves to be mentally integrated into the cultures.

Initially 251 attempts were made with 18 subjects. A highly significant effect could be registered, and during the experimental phases the movements of the algae changed dramatically.

The experimenters themselves were very surprised by the results. Encouraged by the numbers, they undertook to confirm the effect in a second phase of the experiment. In scientific work it is regarded as correct procedure to confirm the results of an exploratory experiment by a further experiment. In order to achieve as impressive a confirmation as possible, Pleass and Dey proceeded with caution. Possible sources of error were identified and precautions were taken to eliminate them, including shielding from radio frequencies, improved temperature control in the room and better physical isolation of the containers with the microbe cultures. There was also overall control through comparative data gained by continuous recordings at other times. The University of Delaware considered the study to be so important that it contributed an elaborate temperature control system for the scientists' laboratory. To house the experiment in their lab, Pleass and Dey built a walk-in environmental chamber with grounded metal walls.

This time, 118 experimental runs with 14 subjects were conducted. Although an effect again appeared, to the despair of the scientists it was no longer significant. The hypothesis of mind interaction between man and microbes had to be rejected, even though the pilot study had provided such convincing proof.

How was this possible? Without having had this in mind, Pleass and Dey were able to answer this question by a second experiment. Inspired by Cleve Backster's work on the alleged 'primary perception' of plants (see Part 1, Chapter 2), they determined to find out whether micro-organisms can react to a 'psi signal' even without being influenced by the human mind. Backster had claimed that plants react to the killing of other organisms with an anomalous reaction.

For their experiment Pleass and Dey chose a colony of single-cell, motile marine algae (*Tetraselmis suecica*). The algal cultures were divided into two groups. One was placed inside the already proved measuring device, the other was put in a container above a tank with freshwater. The experimenters had devised a form of death particularly cruel to algae, so that any psi-transmitted pain signal could be registered by the sister cells in the measuring apparatus. Throwing saltwater algae into freshwater is the equivalent of hurling a human into a vacuum. The difference in osmotic pressure on the cell membrane is so enormous that the algae are literally blown apart.

The whole experiment was controlled by a computer program. Before the weekend, the scientists were able to set up the program and close the laboratory. At random intervals the computer would send an impulse to a valve beneath the colony of algae serving as 'victims'. The valve would open briefly and drop some of the algae into the freshwater tank. The measuring instruments for the second culture were also activated automatically shortly before every impulse for a 'sacrifice'.

Pleass and Dey scheduled the first complete pilot experiment for a day when their laboratory was expecting a visit from a very sceptical but still quite open-minded colleague. The two biologists were so excited at the thought of being able to demonstrate this elaborate experiment that they decided at short notice not to conduct an unobserved automatic run of the experiment but instead to carry out one in which the opening of the valve was directly controlled. Their guest pushed the decisive button and thereby sealed the fate of about 20 million *Tetraselmis*. After about 5 minutes, the guest again pushed the button in order to terminate the 'algae sacrifice'. Now everybody looked at the recordings with bated breath. The small group did not need to wait for a mathematical calculation of the effect, because the graph of the movements of the sister algae spoke volumes – before and after the decisive push of the button the colony of algae showed more or less the same constant high level of activity. Only during the 'sacrifice' had this mobility broken down at a stroke.

Pleass and Dey conducted five such pilot experiments that day. The results were so significant that they exceeded the limits of the statistics program that had been used. There could be no doubt that the activity of the algal culture under observation had diminished remarkably whenever other algae were being killed in a remote container. The Backster effect of a 'primary perception' appeared to have been impressively confirmed. At least for the moment.

Again, the formal, confirming experiments had to provide the corroboration of the assumption. These experiments were conducted according to the originally devised protocol in which the computer randomly selected 'sacrificial periods' in the absence of the scientists. During the 37 individual experiments, the probability of a real unknown effect having occurred diminished dramatically and could be called marginally significant at best. A third experiment was now required to clear the matter up. And now something strange occurred – the effect had disappeared, there was no significant result at all.

How could this be? Both experiments had been carefully designed and conducted with technically excellent equipment. Nevertheless, the 'dream results' in the pilot experiment collapsed like a house of cards the longer the experiments ran.

How can this be explained? The two scientists believe that the initially extraordinary results and the non-significant subsequent results are due to their own personal expectations and fears. There can be no doubt that there had been an effect that can be explained only in terms of an anomalous exchange of information between human consciousness and the algal cultures. In the second attempt there had also been a remarkable initial result in the presence of the experimenters, and this had occurred in periods when they knew that algae were being 'sacrificed'. This, too, can therefore be regarded as an anomalous artefact. The positive inner tension and the excitement about the new experiment led to a direct inter-action with the algal cultures, perhaps even with the sensitive optical instrument that measured the movement of the algae.

During the control experiments the psychological conditions of the experimenters had changed. While they had originally proceeded unin-hibitedly and with little thought to the consequences, now their egos were involved, and fear of failing or of having to defend a highly unusual result within the scientific community became part of the experiment. Such purely psychological conditions modified the original, naïve expectations and, according to Pleass and Dey, suppressed the possibility of an anomalous consciousness interaction.

The two biologists are left with the view that data can actually corre-late in an inexplicable manner with the expectations of the experimenter, as long as those expectations are free of any knowledge of the importance of the work. 'In a larger context, this suggests that the environment which an individual perceives may be a manifestation of their conscious and subconscious expectations. In engineering terminology, the individual and their environment may form an interactive feedback system.'[78]

Psi experiments are apparently particularly susceptible to anomalous influences of the experimenters themselves. They cause the effect in an initial result, but then they erase it in subsequent experiments. The thought is the seed that moves something in the material world. But success appears to be linked to a healthy measure of 'innocence'.

This strange observation runs through parapsychology like a thread in many different forms of manifestation. I call it the Parsifal effect. Parsifal is the 'pure innocent', who naïvely, unknowingly and without really want-ing to, attains what others vainly strive for, sight of the Holy Grail.

## MAKING SENSE OF THE EXTRASENSORY

The Parsifal effect suggests that naïvety favours psi. Our unconsidered intentions subtly shape our environment, but as soon as knowledge is drawn into the equation, as soon as we reflect on the sense of our actions, the interaction between mind and matter ceases to be effective. At times, this effect can choose strange paths.

Targ, Harary and White made their first round of predictions on the movements of the price of silver naïvely and with great expectations, and they were successful (see Part 2, Chapter 4). On the second attempt they had lost their innocence. Targ and White intended to become rich.

Suddenly, their psi method conveyed a certain specific meaning. Positive results ceased to appear, although in this case it was not because psi had disappeared, but because Harary's RV impressions were wrongly interpreted by Targ. It almost appears as if the impishness in psi, the rascal who appears so clearly in poltergeist cases, looks for strange ways to play his game of confusion.

The reality behind the anecdotes about 'beginner's luck' appears to be the Parsifal effect of psi. When we are uninhibited, when we decide quickly without stopping for second thoughts or analytical considerations, we gain the best entry into the fundamental psi function. We bypass the barriers that our knowledge of the importance of an act automatically erects. Such insights naturally also have their practical consequences. In general, intentions unfold their anomalous outcomes the more effectively the freer they are from (too much) meaning and significance.

Physicist Zha Leping reports that as a young student he and many of his friends were easily able, despite the application of fairly stringent conditions, to reproduce the exceptional functions of the human body (EFHB) phenomena that were so popular in China at the time.[79] These uninhibited experiments worked without any problems. As soon as innocence disappeared, psi was gone.

The sooner the answers to extrasensory impressions in the EFHB experiments with Chinese children appeared, the more distinct was the anomalous impression. If they answered within only a few minutes, they achieved very high hit rates. Sometimes the answer came within 3 to 4 seconds, and then they were mostly 100 per cent correct. If it took longer, the results were often wrong.[80] Ingo Swann had also discovered that the first quick reaction to an RV impression in the form of an 'ideogram' normally agreed with the target.

In the early psychokinetic experiments conducted by J.B. Rhine and his school in which rolling dice were to be influenced, a 'decline effect' was discovered. At the beginning of a session there were often high rates of success, but these declined with the duration of the experiment. This effect was attributed to a diminishing of interest in the often boring and tiring experiments. Over time, the initial motivation goes down and the changed psychological conditions mean that psychokinetic 'abilities' are no longer activated.

The scientists at the PEAR laboratory have recently also found a similar effect in their data.[81] The operators at Princeton showed a significant tendency to do best during the initial series, but their performance declined during the second and third series, sometimes even in the opposite direction to the intention, only to improve slightly from the fourth series on for the rest of the runs. The effect appears in various experimental designs and in local as well as in remote experiments.

It would appear that the data from the later series reflect the fundamental psi function – the constant, automatic interaction between mind and matter. Stimulated by something new, by a conscious alignment, by a decision in favour of an experiment or by a certain intention, the intensity of the interaction is briefly increased. Since it then soon decreases again strongly, there appears to be a process at work that prevents a lasting conscious control and availability of the effect. The interaction levels off on a 'determined' plane.

This could be the same effect as the rebounds Dean Radin observed in the anomalously influenced physical random processes. On a subtle level of consciousness the fundamental psi function rebounds in the opposite direction after an increased interaction, in order then to level off on an equilibrium. The statistical equilibrium that nature re-establishes on the micro-level must also be re-established in the mind. Perturbations that are introduced into a system lead to reactions by perturbations in the opposite direction in order to maintain the general state of statistical equilibrium. Is this an independent indicator for the assumption that matter and mind cannot be distinguished from each other on their most fundamental level?

I would dare to suggest that the rebounds in the fundamental psi function affect micro-physical processes in the brain, which cause interference in the mind, symptoms of exhaustion, diminishing concentration – in other words, those psychological factors that have traditionally been regarded as the causes for the drop in initially high psi performance.

How can we practise parapsychology at all if the Parsifal effect is constantly upsetting our calculations? Let us recall that Parsifal again reached the castle of the Holy Grail, but this time as a changed person, who understood the meaning of his search. It is possible, therefore, that there will be successes in that twilight zone where paradox appears to set the rules. The issue is how to re-establish freedom from knowledge and meaning at the very moment of understanding.

The science fiction novel *Macroscope*[82] involves a search for someone who can 'master' a clairvoyant telescope-microscope from a former highly developed civilization. Whoever knows how to look into this macroscope in the right way immediately obtains the non-communicable, universal knowledge of all things. When someone looks into it, a sequence of symbols unfolds before their eyes and becomes more and more complex. But it is impossible to escape from its logic. At some point reason no longer plays a part and the searcher is driven insane by the clarity of the mystery. In the end, there are more and more insane super-scientists and mathematicians who had dared to challenge the paradox wandering about. The inventors of the macroscope had built in a strange security device, because they had known how destructive knowledge can be in the hands of the 'wrong' person. In the end, an ordinary person succeeds in mastering the macroscope, because he approaches it with feeling, intuition, emotion and, above all, a willingness to undergo change, a true transformation.

Here we have a contemporary Parsifal figure. While parapsychology is not about metaphysics, it is about a reality that is protected by similar security devices to those in the macroscope. It is a field that can be approached only by those who are willing to undergo an inner transformation.

The Buddhist *Diamond Sutra* says: 'You should never let a clinging spirit rise. You should let a non-clinging spirit rise.' This instruction for the spiritual path is also appropriate for dealing with psi. It applies equally to the experiment, the subject in the laboratory and the psi researcher. We should approach psi with serenity – just like the test subject who achieves the effect only after releasing the conscious effort – without clinging to our knowledge, and we should be prepared to let ourselves be surprised. The passion for the subject and the desire to face the unfathomable must be deeply anchored in our consciousness, and if we succeed in pursuing our intentions with the necessary composure, they will be effective. We have to hold our wish fast in our mind, like a bird in our hand. If we grasp too firmly, we will kill it; if we hold too loosely, it will fly away.

To be able to deal with psi requires an approach such as is taught in the spiritual philosophies of the East. Only those who have a 'pure' heart, unencumbered by hidden intentions, will be successful. Those who pursue their intentions in this way face themselves and, with luck, will emerge transformed from the changes caused by confronting the extended view of the world that psi provides.

# EPILOGUE

With the potent new tool of the meta-analysis at its disposal, parapsychology entered a new, self-confident phase in the second half of the 1980s. The enormous amount of data collected in the laboratories during half a century successfully passed its scientific baptism of fire.

As Dean Radin put it: 'We are forced to conclude that when psi research is judged by the same standards as any other well-accepted scientific discipline, then the results are *as consistent* as those observed in the hardest of the hard sciences.'[83] The scientific recognition of paranormal phenomena is inevitable.

A major hurdle is still – temporarily – the lack of an appropriate theory. There are many promising areas for research, but few of them contain empirically testable propositions. The importance of theories for the everyday life of science can be illustrated by a simple example. In order to discover a certain particle, the omega minus particle, physicists conducted almost 200,000 experiments, in which they successfully detected the particle only twice. But those two occasions were sufficient for the physicists to be convinced that the particle actually exists.[84] This phenomenon is as good as being non-replicable. Imagine that parapsychologists would need to conduct 100,000 experiments in order to obtain a single indication of the existence of psi! They would have given this science up a long time ago and turned to more rewarding tasks.

Why was the particle accepted without argument, and why did psi research have to fight for recognition for so long? The secret lies not in empirical research, nor in the experiments, nor in the mountains of tangible proof. It lies in the lack of a theory. When it is based on a recognized theory, the replicability of a phenomenon becomes of secondary importance. The prediction made in the theory is the decisive factor.

In this sense, the science of anomalous mental phenomena has been dealt a poor hand. It must first prove the replicability of the phenomena it investigates, and that proof must be abundant. However, this has been achieved in a masterly way. Meta-analysis, the instrument of instruments for proof of the quality of replicability, has put an end to the discussion about the existence of psi, in psi's favour.

It is possible that we will never be able to present a practicable theory in the field of parapsychology, because there is an enormous difference between the ability required to understand a simple system and a complex one. Highly complex systems can easily exceed the limitations of man's comprehension. When this happens, the system can no longer be understood. Psi is such a highly complex system. But even if the development of a theory were to remain impossible, we have begun to understand the workings of psi.

The great philosophies of yoga, Buddhism and Zen do not actually have a 'theory' of consciousness, but they have nevertheless developed exercises that permit us to use our consciousness in special ways to activate its hidden potential. In the same way we might be able to develop means to begin to use the hidden potential of psi. The comparison suggests itself, because psi is an integral part of consciousness.

Parapsychology explores the interaction between mind and the physical world. Today it has found a place right in the heart of a new science: consciousness research. The unravelling of consciousness is currently being regarded as the last new frontier of science, and in recent years, consciousness research has been the subject of enormous interest from both the natural sciences and the humanities. Anomalous mental phenomena are seen as being decisive factors in our understanding of consciousness. But there are still innumerable unsolved tasks awaiting us. Physicist Nick Herbert appositely summarizes the problem: 'Science's biggest mystery is the nature of consciousness. It is not that we possess bad or imperfect theories of human awareness; we simply have no such theories at all. About all we know about consciousness is that it has something to do with the head, rather than the foot.'[85]

The most important thing we have to learn in the investigation of consciousness is something we have already learned from our insights into psi: thinking in categories of 'either ... or' leads to a dead end. We must begin to think in the categories of 'both ... and'. Just as a photon is both a particle and a wave, consciousness can have two complementary states. Normally consciousness more closely resembles a particle, localized in time and space. In this state a person experiences themselves as being an isolated, independent creature. In non-ordinary, altered states of consciousness, consciousness is more like a wave, not localized in time and space. In this state a person experiences boundlessness, identification, mystic unity and timelessness. Both ways of looking at the manifestations of consciousness are simultaneously valid. In between, both as mediator and as separator, is psi.

Psi is a phenomenon of the interface, of the transitions and changes. It is to be found wherever the continuous ceases to exist and the unknown can just be seen on the horizon; it is found where we lose our certainties and where the unfamiliar shows its face, on the borderline between waking and sleeping, between ordinary and non-ordinary states of consciousness, during moments of diminished attention. It is a phenomenon of the 'gap', the crack between the worlds, the window where we search for a glimpse at the unfathomable nature of our existence.

# NOTES

## Prologue

1. Jessica M. Utts, 'An Assessment of the Evidence for Psychic Functioning', in *Journal of Scientific Exploration*, 10, 1996, pp. 3–30

## Part 1
## Intelligence Services and Parapsychology: The History of Remote Viewing and the Psychic Spies

2. Jim Schnabel, *Remote Viewers: The Secret History of America's Psychic Spies*, Dell, New York, 1997, p. 7

## Chapter 1: Paranormal Rearmament

3. Compare Elmar R. Gruber, *Suche im Grenzenlosen. Hans Bender – ein Leben für die Parapsychology* ('Search in the Boundless. Hans Bender – A Life Devoted to Parapsychology'), Kiepenheuer & Witsch, Cologne, 1993, p. 109

4. Bernard Kazhinsky, 'Peredatsha mysslei' ('Transfer of Thoughts'), in *Izvestija Assotsiatsii Naturalistov*, Prilozhenije 2, Moscow, 1923

5. Leonid L. Vasiliev, *Experimentelle Untersuchungen der Mentalsuggestion* ('Experimental Investigation of Mental Suggestion'), Francke, Munich and Bern, 1965

6. Cited according to Martin Ebon, *Amplified Mind Power Research in the Former Soviet Union*, Internet 1996–7 (http://www.mindspring.com/~biomind/Pages/Ebon1.html)

7. Andrija Puharich, *The Sacred Mushroom: Key to the Door of Eternity*, Victor Gollancz, London, 1959

8. If the KGB had not wanted the film to reach the West, the somewhat clumsy John Gaither Pratt would not have succeeded in 'smuggling' it past customs. The film with Kulagina's famous experiment can be seen on my CD-ROM *Mysterium* ('Mystery'), United Soft Media, Munich, 1996

9. Sheila Ostrander and Lynn Schroeder, *Psychic Discoveries behind the Iron Curtain*, Prentice Hall, Englewood Cliffs, 1970

10. Documented in (the name of the author has not yet been released) 'Paraphysics R & D – Warsaw Pact (U)', DST–1810S–202–78, in *US Defense Intelligence Agency*, 30 March 1978

11. J.D. LaMothe, 'Controlled Offensive Behavior – USSR', US Defense Intelligence Agency. Prepared by the US Army, Office of the Surgeon General, *Medical Intelligence Office*, Washington, D.C., 1972 [#CT–CS–01–169–72]

## Chapter 2: Remote Viewing

12. Marilyn Schlitz and Elmar R. Gruber, 'Transcontinental Remote Viewing', in *Journal of Parapsychology*, 44, 1980, pp. 305–17; Marilyn Schlitz and Elmer R. Gruber, 'Transcontinental Remote Viewing. A Rejudging', in *Journal of Parapsychology*, 45, 1981, pp. 233–8. The experiment became one of the fundamental experiments of modern psi research and was included in the book by former director of the Institute for Parapsychology K. Ramakrishna Rao, *The Basic Experiments in Parapsychology*, McFarland, Jefferson, 1984
13. Gertrude R. Schmeidler, 'PK Effects upon Continously Recorded Temperature', in *Journal of the American Society for Psychical Research*, 67, 1973, pp. 325–40
14. Ingo Swann, *Remote Viewing: The Real Story*, Internet 1996–7 (http://www.mindspring.com/~biomind/Pages/RealStoryMain.html)
15. Ingo Swann, *ibid*.
16. Only in 1977, after it had become an open secret that Swann was now a 'psi spy' for the CIA, were the OBE experiments published, although in the *Journal* of the UK Society for Psychical Research
17. Harold E. Puthoff, 'CIA-Initiated Remote Viewing Program at Stanford Research Institute', in *Journal of Scientific Exploration*, 10, 1996, pp. 63–76

## Chapter 3: Stanford Research Institute and the CIA

18. Ingo Swann, *op. cit*.
19. Russell Targ, 'Remote Viewing at Stanford Research Institute in the 1970s: A Memoir', in *Journal of Scientific Exploration*, 10, 1996, pp. 77–88
20. Alpha waves are brain waves with a frequency of 8–13 Hz
21. Beta waves are brain waves with a frequency of 13–30 Hz; they are related to conscious wakefulness and attention
22. Russell Targ and Harold Puthoff, 'Information Transmission under Conditions of Sensory Shielding', in *Nature*, 252, 1974, pp. 602–607

23. Edwin C. May, Russell Targ and Harold Puthoff, 'EEG Correlates to Remote Light Flashes under Conditions of Sensory Shielding', in Charles Tart, Harold Puthoff and Russell Targ (eds), *Mind at Large: IEEE Symposia on the Nature of ESP*, Praeger, New York, 1979, pp. 127–36

24. Edwin C. May, Wanda Luke, Virginia Trask and Thane Frivold, 'Brain Responses and ESP', in *Research in Parapsychology*, 1990, Scarecrow, Metuchen, 1992

## Chapter 4: The Psychic Spies at Fort Meade

25. The Systems Exploitation Detachment (SED) was under the control of the office of the Assistant Chief of Staff for Intelligence (ACSI)

26. Even after this episode, the navy still remained true to its support for the investigation of electromagnetic mind control

27. Jim Schnabel, *op. cit.*, p. 50

28. Harold E. Puthoff and Russell Targ, 'A Perceptual Channel for Information Transfer over Kilometer Distances: Historical Perspective and Recent Research', in *Proceedings of the Institute of Electrical and Electronics Engineers*, 64, 1976, pp. 329–54

29. Joe McMoneagle, *Mind Trek*, Hampton Roads, Charlottesville, 1993

30. Russell Targ and Harold E. Puthoff in *Nature*, *op. cit.*; Puthoff and Targ in *Proceedings*, *op. cit.*

31. Harold E. Puthoff and Russell Targ, *Mind Reach*, Delacorte, New York, 1977; Russell Targ and Keith Harary, *The Mind Race: Understanding and Using Psychic Abilities*, Villard, New York, 1984

## Chapter 5: Swann's RV System

32. The abbreviation CRV (coordinate remote viewing) remained, but today Ingo Swann means 'controlled remote viewing'

33. René Warcollier, 'Fünfzig Jahre Telepathie' ('Fifty Years of Telepathy'), in *Neue Wissenschaft*, 11, 1962, pp. 49–57

34. Upton Sinclair, *Mental Radio*, Charles C. Thomas, Springfield, 1962 (original publication 1930)

## Chapter 6: Psychic Spying in Action

35. Walter Schellenberg, *Memoiren* ('Memoires'), Cologne, 1959, p. 301

36. Charles T. Tart, *Learning to Use Extrasensory Perception*, University of Chicago Press, Chicago, 1976

37. While Uri Geller's public demonstrations of 'spoon-bending' are very controversial and easy to copy by tricks, scientific investigations under controlled conditions with other subjects have produced proof that in rare cases 'spoon-bending' without any detectable physical influence is possible. See Bernhard Wälti, 'Die Silvio-Protokolle 1976–1977' ('The Silvio Protocols 1976–1977'), in *Zeitschrift für Parapsychologie und Grenzgebiete der Psychologie*, 20, 1978, pp. 1–46. John B. Hasted, *The Metal-Benders*, London, 1981

38. Harold E. Puthoff and Russell Targ, 'Perceptual Augmentation Techniques, Part 1, Executive Summary', in *SRI Project 3183, Final Report* (covering the period January 1974 to February 1975)

39. Jim Schnabel, *op. cit.*, pp. 284–6

40. John B. Alexander, 'The New Mental Battlefield: "Beam Me Up, Spock"', in *Military Review*, 9 (12), 1980, pp. 48–54

41. Friedrich Nietzsche, *Zu Zarathustra* ('On Zarathustra'), Kröner, Stuttgart, 1931, p. 446

42. See Elmar R. Gruber, *Was ist New Age?* ('What is New Age?'), Herder, Freiburg, 1987; Gruber, *Sanfte Verschwörung oder sanfte Verblödung? Kontroversen um New Age* ('Gentle Conspiracy or Gentle Stultification? Controversies about New Age'), Herder, Freiburg, 1989

43. John B. Alexander, Richard Groller and Janet Morris, *The Warrior's Edge*, William Morrow, New York, 1990, p. 9 ff.

44. 1 Hz equates to a frequency of one oscillation per second

45. Charles T. Tart, 'A Second Psychophysiological Study of Out-of-the-Body Experiences in a Gifted Subject', in *International Journal of Parapsychology*, 9, 1967, pp. 251–8; Tart, 'A Further Psychophysiological Study of Out-of-the-Body Experiences in a Gifted Subject, Robert A. Monroe', in W. Roll, R. Morris and J. Morris (eds), *Proceedings of the Parapsychological Association*, 1969, pp. 43–4

46. Compare Robert A. Monroe, *Journeys out of the Body*, Doubleday, Garden City, New York, 1971; Monroe, *Far Journeys*, Doubleday, Garden City, New York, 1985

47. Steven Emerson, *Secret Warriors*, G.P. Putnam's Sons, New York, 1988, pp. 103–4

48. National Research Council, *Enhancing Human Performance*, National Academy of Sciences, 1988, pp. 111–14

49. Joe McMoneagle, *op. cit.*

## Chapter 7: Decline of the RV Unit

50. David Morehouse, *Psychic Warrior*, St Martin's Press, New York, 1996

51. In 1996 May integrated the CSL into the Laboratories for Fundamental Research (LFR) in California. Included in the SAIC supervisory board were Admiral Bobby Inman, former director of the NSA and the CIA, Melvin Laird, Minister of Defense under President Richard Nixon, and General (ret.) Max Thurman, commander of the invasion in Panama. SAIC owns Network Solutions, a company that has controlled the allocation of the Internet domain names since September 1995.

52. Ray Hyman, 'Evaluation of a Program on Anomalous Mental Phenomena', in *Journal of Scientific Exploration*, 10, 1996, pp. 31–58, here p. 57

53. Mr X, Part 1: 'Bologna on Wry. A Review of the CIA/AIR Report "An Evaluation of Remote Viewing: Research and Applications"'; Part 2: 'A Second Helping. Further Reflections On the AIR/CIA Assessment on Remote Viewing'. Part 3: 'Scraps and Crumbs. Further Reflections on the AIR/CIA Assessment on Remote Viewing', Internet 1997 (http://www.mindspring.com/~biomind)

54. Jessica M. Utts, *op. cit.*

55. The rejection of psychokinesis is related to a presently controversial theory in parapsychology. It claims that certain PK effects on micro-processes can also be explained in terms of precognition. Ed May developed this theory together with Jessica Utts. It would go too far to discuss it in detail here. The further chapters in this book will provide enough proof that psychokinesis does, in fact, exist

56. Ray Hyman, *op. cit.*

57. Edwin C. May, 'The American Institutes of Research Review of the Department of Defense's Star Gate Program: A Commentary', in *Journal of Scientific Exploration*, 10, 1996, pp. 89–108

58. Courtney Brown, *Cosmic Voyage: A Scientific Discovery of Extraterrestrials Visiting Earth*, Dutton, New York, 1996

59. Accessible on the Internet under http://www.farsight.org/manual/html

## Part 2
## Contemporary Psi Research: Towards a New Understanding of Reality
## Chapter 1: Parapsychology in Russia: Legend and Fact

1. Ingo Swann made a contribution on the techniques of Scientology as a model for the development and exploration of psychic abilities: Ingo Swann, 'Scientological Techniques: A Modern Paradigm for the Exploration of Consciousness and Physics Integration', in *Proceedings of the First International Congress on Psychotronic Research*, Virginia, US Joint Publications Research Service, 6 September 1974, Document JPRS L/5022-1

2. Louis F. Maire and J.D. LaMothe, 'Soviet and Czechoslovakian Parapsychology Research'. in *US Defense Intelligence Agency*, prepared by the US Army, Medical Intelligence and Information Agency, Washington, D.C., 1975 [#DST-181OS-387-75]

3. Roger A. Baumont, 'C$^{nth}$? On the Strategic Potential of ESP', in *Signal*, 36 (5), 1982, pp. 39-45

4. Compare Martin Ebon, *Amplified Mind Power Research in the Former Soviet Union*, Internet 1996-7 (http://www.mindspring.com/~biomind/Pages/Ebon1.html)

5. Larissa Vilenskaya, *Psi Research in the Soviet Union: Are They Ahead of Us?*, in Russell Targ and Keith Harary, *The Mind Race*, Villard, New York, 1984, p. 256

6. Martin Ebon, *op. cit.*

7. Martin Ebon, *Psychic Warfare: Threat or Illusion*, McGraw-Hill, New York, 1983; compare also Ebon, 'Psi ist keine Geheimwaffe' ('Psi Is No Secret Weapon'), in *Zeitschrift für Parapsychologie und Grenzgebiete der Psychologie*, 27, 1985, pp. 246-52

8. Alexander P. Dubrow, 'Role of Parapsychology in the Change of the Paradigm of Modern Natural Science', in *Parapsychology and Psychophysics*, 23, 1997, p. 11

9. In contrast to this, in the West we use the term 'bioenergetics' for the body-orientated form of psychotherapy developed by Alexander Lowen

10. Edwin C. May and Larissa Vilenskaya, 'Overview of Current Parapsychology Research in the Former Soviet Union', in *Subtle Energies*, 3, 1992, pp. 45-67

11. There was no change in the problem-solving results when the mental interference was conducted intermittently – i.e., in assignments 2, 4 and 6

12. Juri S. Dolin, V.I. Dymow and N.N. Khatshenkov, 'Preliminary Study of a Human Operator's Remote Effect on the Psychophysiological State of Another Individual with EEG Recording', in *Proceedings of the 36th Annual Convention of the Parapsychological Association*, Toronto, Canada, 1993, pp. 24–40

13. Rupert Sheldrake, *A New Science of Life*, Blond & Briggs, London, 1981; Sheldrake, *Seven Experiments That Could Change the World*, Riverhead, New York, 1995

14. Edwin C. May and Larissa Vilenskaya, 'Anomalous Mental Phenomena Research in Russia and the Former Soviet Union: A Follow Up', in *Subtle Energies*, 4, 1993, pp. 231–50

15. Gabriel Veraldi, 'Les travaux récents de René Peoc'h. De la Psychophysique animale à une révision de la psychologie' ('The Recent Works of René Peoc'h. From the Psychophysics of Animals to a Revision of Psychology'), in *Bulletin de la Fondation Marcel et Monique Odier de Psycho-Physique*, 3, 1997, pp. 24–36

16. Juri S. Dolin, V.A. Davydov, E.V. Morozova and D.J. Shumow, 'Studies of a Remote Mental Effect on Plants with Electrophysiological Recording', in *Proceedings of the 36th Annual Convention of the Parapsychological Association*, Toronto, Canada, 1993, pp. 41–56

17. Radiaesthesis is the term introduced in 1930 by Abbé M.L. Bouly for the science and practice of dowsing and pendulum wielding

18. Charles T. Tart, *Transpersonal Psychologies*, Harper & Row, New York, 1975

19. Tõnu R. Soidla and S.I. Shapiro (eds), *Everything Is According to the Way: Voices of Russian Transpersonalism*, Bolda-Lok, Brisbane, 1997

20. Elmar R. Gruber, *Suche im Grenzenlosen. Hans Bender – ein Leben für die Parapsychology* ('Search in the Boundless. Hans Bender – A Life Devoted to Parapsychology'), Kiepenheuer & Witsch, Cologne, 1993, pp. 268–70.

21. Erlendur Haraldsson, 'Are Religiosity and Belief in an Afterlife Better Predictors of ESP Performance than Belief in Psychic Phenomena?', in *Journal of Parapsychology*, 57, 1993, pp. 259–73; also compare Erlendur Haraldsson and Joop M. Houtkooper, 'Meta-analysis of Ten Experiments on Perceptual Defensiveness and ESP', in *Journal of Parapsychology*, 59, 1995, pp. 251–71

## Chapter 2: Psychic Revolution in the Middle Kingdom

22. Ingo Swann, *Remote Viewing: The Real Story*, Internet 1996–97 (http://www.mindspring.com/~biomind/Pages/RealStoryMain.ht ml) Chapter III; according to Swann, a third copy was sold to an 'unstable nation in the Middle East', which, in turn, allowed an equally unstable neighbouring nation to look at the files

23. Chinese names are written with the family name preceding the given name

24. Harold Puthoff, 'Report on Investigations into "Exceptional Human Body Function" in the People's Republic of China', in *Research in Parapsychology 1982*, Scarecrow, Metuchen, 1983, pp. 275–8. The SRI team repeated the experiments whereby only a weak increase in photons appeared during correct remote viewing, which could not be clearly identified as being linked to the process

25. Chen Hsin and Mei Lei, 'Study of the Extraordinary Function of the Human Body in China', in *Research in Parapsychology 1982*, Scarecrow, Metuchen, 1983, pp. 278–82

26. Zha Leping and Tron McConnell, 'Parapsychology in the People's Republic of China 1979–1989', in *Journal of the American Society for Psychical Research*, 85, 1991, pp. 119–43

27. Zhu YiYi in Alexander Imich (ed.), *Incredible Tales of the Paranormal: Documented Accounts of Poltergeists, Levitations, Phantoms and Other Phenomena*, Bramble, Bearsville, 1995, p. 203

28. *Ibid.*, p. 206

29. P. Dong, *The Four Major Mysteries of Mainland China*, Prentice Hall, Engelwood Cliffs, 1984, pp. 90–91

30. Cited in Zha Leping and Tron McConnell, *op. cit.*, p. 125

31. Qian Xuesen, 'Is It an Unborn Scientific Revolution? (original in Chinese), in *Renti Teyigongneng Yanjiu* ('EFHB Research'), 1, 1983, pp. 3–8

32. Lin Shuhuang *et al.*, 'PK Experiments: Objects Moved In and Out of Sealed Containers' (original in Chinese), in *Renti Teyigongneng Yanjiu* ('EFHB Research'), 1, 1983, pp. 110–18

33. Song Kongzhi, Lan Rongliang, Li Xianggao and Zhou Liangzhong, 'Research on Breaking Through Spatial Barriers' (original in Chinese), in *Chinese Journal of Somatic Science*, 1990, pp. 22–31

34. Qian Cheng and Zhou Xin (eds), 'Yan Xin and Qigong' (original in Chinese), Workers' Publishing House, Beijing, 1988, p. 241

35. We differentiate between *jinggong* (exercises at rest) and *donggong* (exercises in movement)

36. Yan Xin, Li Shengping, Yu Jianyuan, Li Baike and Lu Zuying, 'The Effect of Qigong on the Raman Spectrum of Tap Water, Salt and Glucose Solutions' (original in Chinese), in *Ziran Zazhi*, 11, 1988, pp. 567–71; Lu Zuying, Zhao Nanming, Li Shengping, Zheng Changxue and Yan Xin, 'Observations on Qi Emission Effects on the Structure and Properties of Some Substances' (original in Chinese), *Shengwu Wuli Xuebao* (*Acta Biophysica Sinica*), 3, 1987, pp. 93–4

37. Cited according to Qian Cheng and Zhou Xin (eds), *op. cit.*, p. 315

38. Cited according to Zha Leping and Tron McConnell, *op. cit.*, p. 132

39. In Chinese tradition yin and yang are the fundamental opposites that become visible in any and all forms of existence. Yang stands for the active, male, dynamic, light principle; yin stands for the passive, female, dark principle

## Chapter 3: Anomalous Cognition: Tracking Down the Mystery

40. Dream phases can be detected by physiological recordings, for example by rapid eye movement

41. Montague Ullmann, Stanley Krippner and Alan Vaughan, *Dream Telepathy*, Macmillan, New York, 1973, p. 123

42. Herman A. Witkin and Helen B. Lewis, 'The Relation of Experimentally Induced Pre-sleep Experiences in Dreams: A Report on Method and Preliminary Findings', in *Journal of the American Psychoanalytical Association*, 13, 1963, pp. 819–49

43. Compare Richard Broughton, *Parapsychology: The Controversial Science*, Ballantine, New York, 1991, pp. 99–101

44. Charles Honorton and Ephraim Schechter, 'Ganzfeld Target Retrieval with an Automated Testing System: A Model for Initial Ganzfeld Success', in *Research in Parapsychology 1986*, Scarecrow, Metuchen, 1987

45. Charles Honorton, 'Response to Hyman's Critique of Psi Ganzfeld Studies', in *Research in Parapsychology 1982*, Scarecrow, Metuchen, 1983, pp. 23–6

46. Gene V. Glass, 'Primary, Secondary and Meta-analysis of Research', in *Educational Researcher*, 5, 1976, pp. 5–8

47. Steering Committee of the Physicians' Health Study Research Group, Preliminary Report: Finding from the Aspirin Component on the Ongoing Physicians' Health Study, in *New England Journal of*

*Medicine*, 318, 1988, pp. 262–4; compare C. Mann, 'Meta-analysis in the Breech', in *Science*, 249, 1990, pp. 476–80

48.  Robert Rosenthal, *Meta-analytic Procedures for Social Research*, rev. ed., Sage, Beverly Hills, 1991, p. 324

49.  Ray Hyman, 'The Psi Ganzfeld Experiment: A Critical Appraisal', in *Journal of Parapsychology*, 49, 1985, pp. 3–49

50.  Charles Honorton, 'Meta-analysis of Psi Ganzfeld Research: A Response to Hyman', in *Journal of Parapsychology*, 49, 1985, pp. 51–91

51.  Robert Rosenthal, 'Meta-analytic Procedures and the Nature of Replication: The Ganzfeld Debate', in *Journal of Parapsychology*, 50, 1986, pp. 315–36

52.  Ray Hyman and Charles Honorton, 'A Joint Communiqué: The Psi Ganzfeld Controversy', in *Journal of Parapsychology*, 50, 1986, pp. 351–64; here p. 351

53.  Jessica M. Utts, 'Replication and Meta-analysis in Parapsychology', in *Statistical Science*, 6, 1991, pp. 396–403

54.  Ray Hyman, 'Comment', in *Statistical Science*, 6, 1991, pp. 389–92; here p. 392

55.  Ray Hyman, 'Evaluation of a Program on Anomalous Mental Phenomena', in *Journal of Scientific Exploration*, 10, 1996, pp. 31–58; here p. 55

56.  Robert L. Morris, Kathy Dalton, Deborah Delanoy and Caroline Watt, 'Comparison of the Sender/No Sender Condition in the Ganzfeld', in *Proceedings of the 38th Annual Parapsychological Association Convention*, 1995, pp. 244–59

57.  Daryl J. Bem and Charles Honorton, 'Does Psi Exist? Replicable Evidence for an Anomalous Process of Information Transfer', in *Psychological Bulletin*, 115, 1994, pp. 4–18

58.  Daryl J. Bem, 'The Ganzfeld Experiment', in *Journal of Parapsychology*, 57, 1993, pp. 101–10

## Chapter 4: In Search of the Ideal Conditions for Psi

59.  M. Carlyn, 'An Assessment of the Myers–Briggs Type Indicator', in *Journal of Personality Assessment*, 41, 1977, pp. 461–73

60.  Charles Honorton and Ephraim Schechter, *op. cit.*

61.  Richard Broughton and Cheryl Alexander, 'Auto-ganzfeld II: The First 100 Sessions', in *Proceedings of the 38th Annual Parapsychological Association Convention*, 1995, pp. 53–61

62. A.R. Lawrence, 'Gathering in the Sheep and Goats: A Meta-analysis of Forced-Choice Sheep–Goat ESP Studies, 1947–1993', in *Proceedings of the 36th Annual Convention of the Parapsychological Association*, 1993, pp. 75–86

63. Charles Honorton, Diane C. Ferrari and Daryl J. Bem, 'Extroversion and ESP Performance: A Meta-analysis and a New Confirmation', in *Research in Parapsychology 1990*, Scarecrow, Metuchen, 1992, pp. 35–8

64. Henri Bergson, 'Presidential Address', in *Proceedings of the Society for Psychical Research*, 24, 1913, pp. 462–79

65. Compare Elmar R. Gruber, *Tranceformation: Schamanismus und die Auflösung der Ordnung* ('Tranceformation: Shamanism and the Dissolution of Order'), Sphinx, Basle, 1982; Gruber, *Traum, Trance und Tod* ('Dream, Trance and Death'), Herder, Freiburg, 1985

66. There is disagreement about the age of the *Yoga Sutras*. Today science believes that they date back only to the second or third century AD. The greater part of the original Yoga literature in the tradition of Patañjali was not written until the fourth century AD. Compare *Yoga Sutra – Der Yogaleitfaden des Patañjali* ('Yoga Sutra – Patañjali's Yoga Guideline'), original in Sanskrit–German, Papyrus, Hamburg, 1987

67. Rhea A. White, 'A Comparison of Old and New Methods of Response to Targets in ESP Experiments', in *Journal of the American Society for Psychical Research*, 58, 1964, pp. 21–56

68. Peter L. Nelson, 'The Technology of the Praeternatural: An Empirically Based Model of Transpersonal Experiences', in *Journal of Transpersonal Psychology*, 22, 1990, pp. 35–50

69. Charles Honorton, R. Davidson and P. Bindler, 'Shifts in Subjective State Associated with Feedback-Augmented EEG Alpha', in *Psychophysiology* 9, 1972, pp. 269–70; Honorton *et al.*, 'Feedback-Augmented EEG Alpha Shifts in Subjective State, and ESP Cardguessing Performance', in *Journal of the American Society for Psychical Research*, 65, 1971, pp. 308–23

70. Edgar S. Wilson, 'The Transits of Consciousness', in *Subtle Energies*, 4, 1993, pp. 171–86

71. Masahiko Hirasawa, Mikio Yamamoto, Kimiko Kawano and Akira Furukawa, 'An Experiment on Extrasensory Information Transfer with Electroencephalogram Measurement', in *Journal of the International Society of Life Information Sciences*, 14, 1996, pp. 43–5

72.  In the hind part and in the top lobe of the cerebral cortex.

73.  Masahiko Hirasawa *et al., op. cit.*, part II, pp. 185–95

74.  Mikio Yamamoto, Masahiko Hirasawa, Hideyuki Kokubo, Kimiko
     Kawano, Tomoko Kokado, Tsuyoshi Hirata and Nakashiro Yasuda,
     'EEG-Change in Anomalous Perception Task Related to Somatic
     Sensation', in *Journal of the International Society of Life Information
     Sciences*, 15, 1997, pp. 88–92

75.  D.H. Lloyd, 'Objective Events in the Brain Correlating with Psychic
     Phenomena', in *New Horizons*, 1, 1973, pp. 69–75

76.  Jacobo Grinberg-Zylberbaum, M. Delaflor, M.E. Sanchez Arellano,
     M.A. Guevara and M. Perez, 'Human Communication and the
     Electrophysiological Activity of the Brain', in *Subtle Energies*, 3,
     1992, pp. 25–44

77.  Charles A. Warren, Bruce E. McDonough and Norman S. Don,
     'Event-Related Brain Potential Changes in a Psi Task', in *Journal of
     Parapsychology*, 56, 1992, pp. 1–30

78.  Hideyuki Kokubo, Tsuyoshi Hirata, Masahiko Hirasawa, Masayuki
     Hirafuji, Takaaki Ohtay, Shinya Ito, Tomoko Kokado and Mikio
     Yamamoto, 'A Study of Remote Anomalous Cognition with
     Judgement and Measurement of Auditory Evoked Potential and
     EEG', in *Journal of the International Society of Life Information Sciences*,
     15, 1997, pp. 97–102

79.  Julie Milton, 'Ordinary State ESP Meta-analysis', in *Proceedings of the
     36th Annual Convention of the Parapsychological Association*, Toronto,
     Canada, 1993, pp. 87–104

80.  Rex G. Stanford and Adam Stein, 'A Meta-analysis of ESP Studies
     Contrasting Hypnosis and a Comparison Condition', in *Journal of
     Parapsychology*, 58, 1994, pp. 235–70

81.  The original instrument was called a ten-choice trainer. The
     advanced version is known as an 'advanced decimal extrasensory
     perception trainer' (ADEPT)

82.  Charles T. Tart, *The Application of Learning Theory to ESP Performance*,
     Parapsychology Foundation, 1975; Tart, 'Toward Conscious
     Control of Psi through Immediate Feedback Training: Some
     Considerations of Internal Processes', in *Journal of the American
     Society for Psychical Research*, 71, 1977, pp. 375–408

83.  James C. Carpenter, 'Toward the Effective Utilization of Enhanced
     Weak-Signal ESP Effects', presentation at the conference of the *American
     Association for the Advancement of Science*, New York, January 1975

84. Stephen Schwartz, *The Alexandria Project*, Delacorte, New York, 1983

85. Keith Harary, 'Response to Reply of Schwartz and De Mattei to "On the Discovery of an American Brig"', in *Journal of the American Society for Psychical Research*, 86, 1992, pp. 257–90

86. Russell Targ also attempted to apply the technique for the discovery of natural resources; see Russell Targ, 'Proposed Application of Associational Remote Viewing to Oil and Natural Resource Recovery', in *Research in Parapsychology 1982*, Scarecrow, Metuchen, 1983, pp. 264–6

87. Keith Harary, 'The Goose That Laid the Silver Egg: A Criticism of Psi and Silver Futures Forecasting', in *Journal of the American Society for Psychical Research*, 86, 1992, pp. 375–409

88. Russell Targ, Jane Katra, Dean Brown and Wenden Wiegand, 'Viewing the Future: A Pilot Study with an Error-Detecting Protocol', in *Journal of Scientific Exploration*, 9, 1995, pp. 367–80

## Chapter 5: Mental Influence on Living Systems

89. Elmar R. Gruber, 'Conformance Behavior Involving Animal and Human Subjects', in *European Journal of Parapsychology*, 3, 1979, pp. 36–50; Gruber, 'A Study of Conformance Behavior Involving Rats and Mice', presentation at the *3rd Conference of the Society for Psychical Research*, Edinburgh, 1979

90. William G. Braud and Marilyn J. Schlitz, 'Consciousness Interactions with Remote Biological Systems: Anomalous Intentionality Effects', in *Subtle Energies*, 2, 1991, pp. 1–46

91. William G. Braud, 'Allobiofeedback: Immediate Feedback for a Psychokinetic Influence upon Another Person's Physiology', in *Research in Parapsychology 1977*, Scarecrow, Metuchen, 1978, pp. 123–34

92. Marilyn J. Schlitz, 'Intentionality and Intuition and Their Clinical Implications: A Challenge for Science and Medicine', in *Advances: The Journal of Mind–Body Health*, 12, 1996, pp. 58–66

93. Compare Elmar R. Gruber, *Dream, Trance and Death*, Herder, Freiburg, pp. 60–75

94. William G. Braud, Donna Schafer and Sperry Andrews, 'Reaction to an Unseen Gaze (Remote Attention): A Review with New Data on Autonomic Staring Detection', in *Journal of Parapsychology*, 57, 1993, pp. 373–90; Braud *et al.*, 'Further Studies of Autonomic

Detection of Remote Staring: Replication, New Control Procedures, and Personality Correlates', in *Journal of Parapsychology*, 57, 1993, pp. 391–410

95. Keisuke Kobayashi and Yoshiko Itagaki, 'Experiments on Subconscious Information Transfer in Sleeping Infants', in *Journal of the International Society of Life Information Sciences*, 14, 1996, pp. 124–30

96. Edwin C. May and Larissa Vilenskaya, 'Overview', *op. cit.*, pp. 45–67; V.I. Kartsev, 'Lethal Gamma-Irradiation and Bioenergy Therapy', in *Parapsychology and Psychophysics*, 9, 1993, pp. 44–8

97. Masatake Yamauchi, Toshiyuki Saito, Mikio Yamamoto and Masahiko Hirasawa, 'Attempts to Develop an in Vitro Experimental System for Detecting the Effect of Stimulant Emission Using Cultures Human Cells', in *Journal of the International Society of Life Information Sciences*, 14, 1996, pp. 266–71

98. Robert N. Miller, P.B. Reinhart and A. Kern, 'Scientists Register Thought Energy', in *Ernest Holmes Research Foundation Research Report*, July 1974, pp. 12–16

99. L.N. Pyatnitsky and V.A. Fonkin, 'Human Consciousness Influence on Water Structure', in *Journal of Scientific Exploration*, 9, 1995, pp. 89–105

100. G.N. Dulnev, V.T. Prokopenko and O.S. Polyakova, 'Optical Methods for the Study of Psi Phenomena', in *Parapsychology and Psychophysics*, 1, 1993, pp. 39–44

101. Edwin C. May and Larissa Vilenskaya, 'A Follow Up', *op. cit.*

102. Glen Rein, 'A Psychokinetic Effect on Neurotransmitter Metabolism: Alterations in the Degradative Enzyme Monoamine Oxidase', in *Research in Parapsychology 1985*, Scarecrow, Metuchen, 1986, pp. 77–80

103. William G. Braud, 'Distant Mental Influence of Rate of Hemolysis of Human Red Blood Cells', in *Research in Parapsychology 1988*, Scarecrow, Metuchen, 1989

104. Brenio Onetto and Gita H. Elguin, 'Psychokinesis in Experimental Tumorgenesis', in *Journal of Parapsychology*, 30, 1966, p. 220

105. The study is reported in William G. Braud, Gary Davis and Robert Wood, 'Experiments with Matthew Manning', in *Journal of the Society for Psychical Research*, 50, 1979, pp. 199–223

106. Frans Snel, 'PK Influence on Malignant Cell Growth', in *Research Letter No. 10*, Parapsychology Laboratory, University of Utrecht, 1980

107. Daniel J. Benor, *Healing Research*, vol. I, Helix, Munich, 1992

108. Justa M. Smith, 'Paranormal Effects on Enzyme Activity', in *Human Dimensions Institute*, professional paper, 1972; Smith, 'Paranormal Effects on Enzyme Activity', in *Journal of Parapsychology*, 32, 1968, p. 281. Smith used enzymes because they act as catalysts for metabolic reactions of cells. Many illnesses can be traced to the lack or dysfunction of enzymes. Trypsin, which is produced by the human and animal pancreas, is a protease that breaks down proteins into polypeptides

109. Tatsutaka Yamamoto, Akira Seto, Seiki Nakazato and Tadashi Hisamitsu, 'Biophysical Study on the Phenomenon of Human Extremely Strong Magnetic Field Emission from a Healer', in *Journal of the International Society of Life Information Sciences*, 14, 1996, pp. 162–70; Yamamoto *et al.*, 'Emission of Extremely Strong Magnetic Fields from the Head and Whole Body during Oriental Breathing Exercises', in *Acupuncture and Electro-therapeutics Research*, 21, 1996, pp. 219–27

110. David J. Muehsam, M.S. Markov, Patricia A. Muehsam, Arthur A. Pilla, Ronger Shen and Yi Wu, 'Effects of Qigong on Cell-Free Myosin Phosphorylation: Preliminary Experiments', in *Subtle Energies*, 5, 1994, pp. 93–108

111. Fritz Albert Popp, *Die Botschaft der Nahrung* ('The Message in Nutrients'), Fischer, Frankfurt, 1993

112. Liu Yaning, Zhao Xinhus, Cao Jie, Hu Yulan and Zhao Yungsheng, 'The Effects of Taoist Qigong on the Photon Emission from the Body Surface and Cells', in *Proceedings of the First World Conference for Academic Exchange of Medical Qigong*, Beijing, October 1988

113. Marco Bischof, *Biophotonen. Das Licht in unseren Zellen* ('Biophotons. The Light in Our Cells'), Zweitausendeins, Frankfurt, 1995

114. Elmer E. Green, 'Mind over Matter: Volition and Cosmic Connection in Yogic Theory', in *Subtle Energies*, 4, 1993, pp. 151–70

115. Mikio Yamamoto *et al.*, 'Study on Analysing Methods of Human Body Functions Using Various Simultaneous Measurements (VSM)', in *Journal of the International Society of Life Information Sciences*, 15, 1997, pp. 351–8

116. Mikio Yamamoto, Masahiko Hirasawa, Kimiko Kawano, Nakashiro Yasuda and Akira Furukawa, 'An Experiment on Remote Action against Man in Sense Shielding Condition', in *Journal of the International Society of Life Information Sciences*, 14, 1996, pp. 97–9

117. Mikio Yamamoto, Masahiko Hirasawa, Kimiko Kawano, Hideyuki Kokubo, Tomoko Kokado, Tsuyoshi Hirata, Nakashiro Yasuda, Akira Furukawa and Nobuo Fukuda, 'An Experiment in Remote Action against Man on Sensory-Shielding Condition (Part II)', in *Journal of the International Society of Life Information Sciences*, 14, 1996, pp. 228–39

118. Yoshio Machi, Liu Chao and Wu Ren Zhao, 'Physiological Measurements for Static Qigong "Xiao Zhou Tian"', in *Journal of the International Society of Life Information Sciences*, 15, 1997, pp. 200–6

119. Kimiko Kawano, J.M. Shi and L.Y. Duan, 'The Frequency Change in a-Waves and the Appearance of q-Waves during Qigong and Meditation', in *Journal of the International Society of Life Information Sciences*, 14, 1996, pp. 22–7

120. Masatoshi Itoh, Hiroshi Miyazaki and Yasuo Takahashi, 'Imaging of Mind Using Positron Emission Tomography', in *Journal of the International Society for Life Information Sciences*, 14, 1996, pp. 67–80

121. Kimiko Kawano, Hidemi Koito, Takeo Fujiki and Yoshiya Shinagawa, 'EEG Topography during Chinese "Qigong" Training', in *Neurosciences*, 16, 1990, pp. 503–8

**Part 3**
**A Self-Aware Universe?: Silent Revolution in the Psi Laboratories**
**Chapter 1: The Physics of Consciousness**

1. Rex G. Stanford, R. Zenhausen, A. Taylor and M. Dwyer, 'Psychokinesis as Psi-Mediated Instrumental Response', in *Journal of the American Society for Psychical Research*, 69, 1975, pp. 127–33

2. Dean I. Radin and Diane C. Ferrari, 'Effects of Consciousness on the Fall of Dice: A Meta-analysis', in *Journal of Scientific Exploration*, 5, 1991, pp. 61–85

3. Robert G. Jahn and Brenda J. Dunne, *Margins of Reality*, Harcourt Brace Jovanovich, New York, 1987; Jahn and Dunne, 'Science of the Subjective', in *Journal of Scientific Exploration*, 11, 1997, pp. 201–24

4. Robert G. Jahn, York H. Dobyns and Brenda J. Dunne, 'Count Population Profiles in Engineering Anomalies Experiments', in *Journal of Scientific Exploration*, 5, 1991, pp. 205–32; here p. 206

5. Brenda J. Dunne, Roger D. Nelson and Robert G. Jahn, 'Operator Related Anomalies in a Random Mechanical Cascade', in *Journal of*

*Scientific Exploration*, 2, 1988, pp. 155–79

6. Brenda J. Dunne and Robert G. Jahn, 'Experiments in Remote Human/Machine Interaction', in *Journal of Scientific Exploration*, 6, 1992, pp. 311–32

7. Roger D. Nelson, G.J. Bradish, Robert G. Jahn and Brenda J. Dunne, 'A Linear Pendulum Experiment: Effects of Operator Intention on Damping Rate', in *Journal of Scientific Exploration*, 8, 1994, pp. 471–89

8. Dean I. Radin and Roger D. Nelson, 'Evidence for Consciousness-Related Anomalies in Random Physical Systems', in *Foundations of Physics*, 19 (12), 1989, pp. 1499–514; compare Deborah L. Delanoy, 'Experimental Evidence Suggestive of Anomalous Consciousness Interactions', in Dhanjoo N. Ghista (ed.), *Biomedical and Life Physics*, Proceedings of the Second Gauss Symposium, August 1993, Vieweg, Brunswick, Munich, 1996, pp. 398–410

9. York H. Dobyns, 'Selection versus Influence Revisited: New Methods and Conclusions', in *Journal of Scientific Exploration*, 10, 1996, pp. 253–68

10. Russian scientists presented an independent confirmation of the ordering influence of consciousness on random systems. In their investigations of the effect of operators on REGs, they observed with an oscillograph that certain segments in the recordings of electric noise appeared to be structured. See Georgi K. Gurtovoy and Alexander G. Parkhomov, 'Experimental Study on a Person's Remote Influence on Physical and Biological Systems', in *Parapsychology and Psychophysics*, 6, 1992, pp. 31–51

11. Robert G. Jahn, York H. Dobyns and Brenda J. Dunne, 'Count Population Profiles', *op. cit.*, p. 226

12. Roger D. Nelson, 'Multiple FieldREG/RNG Recordings during a Global Event', in *Princeton Engineering Anomalies Research*, Princeton University, Princeton, N.J., 1997

13. Roger D. Nelson, 'FieldREG Anomalies in Group Situations', in *Journal of Scientific Exploration*, 10, 1996, pp. 111–41

14. Dean I. Radin, *The Conscious Universe: The Scientific Truth of Psychic Phenomena*, Harper Edge, San Francisco, 1997, chapter 11

15. Roger D. Nelson, 'Wishing for Good Weather: A Natural Experiment in Group Consciousness', in *Journal of Scientific Exploration*, 11, 1997, pp. 47–58

16. *Ibid.*, p. 50

## Chapter 2: Subtle Connections

17.  Michael A. Persinger and G.F. Lafreniere, *Space–Time Transients and Unusual Events*, Nelson-Hall, Chicago, 1977; compare Sarada Subrahmanyam, P.V. Sanker Narayan and T.M. Srinivasan, 'Effect of Magnetic Micropulsations on the Biological Systems: A Bioenvironmental Study', in *International Journal of Biometeorology*, 29, 1985, pp. 293–305

18.  Edmund Gurney, Frederick Myers and Frank Podmore, *Phantasms of the Living*, 2 vols, Trübner, London, 1886

19.  Michael A. Persinger, 'Spontaneous Telepathic Experiences from Phantasms of the Living and Low Global Geomagnetic Activity', in *Journal of the American Society for Psychical Research*, 81, 1987, pp. 23–36

20.  G.B. Schaut and Michael A. Persinger, 'Geophysical Variables and Behavior: XXXI. Global Geomagnetic Activity during Spontaneous Paranormal Experiences: A Replication', in *Perceptual & Motor Skills*, 61, 1985, pp. 412–14; M.A. Arango, 'Spontaneous Crisis-Evoked Telepathic Phenomena from the Sidgwick Collection of 1922 and Low Global Geomagnetic Activity', unpublished dissertation, Laurentian University, Ontario, Canada, 1988

21.  R.E. Berger and Michael A. Persinger, 'Geophysical Variables and Behavior: LXVII. Quieter Annual Geomagnetic Activity and Larger Effect Size for Experimental Psi (ESP) Studies over Six Decades', in *Perceptual & Motor Skills*, 73, 1991, pp. 1219–23

22.  Michael A. Persinger and Stanley Krippner, 'Dream ESP Experiments and Geomagnetic Activity', in *Journal of the American Society for Psychical Research*, 83, 1989, pp. 101–16; Persinger and Krippner, 'Evidence for Enhanced Congruence between Dreams and Distant Target Material during Periods of Decreased Geomagnetic Activity', in *Journal of Scientific Exploration*, 10, 1996, pp. 487–93

23.  Kathy Dalton and Paul Stevens, 'Geomagnetism and the Edinburgh Automated Ganzfeld', in *European Journal of Parapsychology*, 12, 1996, pp. 23–34

24.  Erlendur Haraldsson and Loftur Reimar Gissurarson, 'Does Geomagnetic Activity Affect Extrasensory Perception?, in *Personality and Individual Differences*, 8, 1987, pp. 745–7

25.  William G. Braud and S.P. Dennis, 'Geophysical Variables and

Behavior: LVIII. Autonomic Activity, Hemolysis and Biological Psychokinesis: Possible Relationships with Geomagnetic Field Activity', in *Perception & Motor Skills*, 68, 1989, pp. 1243–54; Loftur Reimar Gissurarson, 'The Psychokinesis Effect: Geomagnetic Influence, Age and Sex Differences', in *Journal of Scientific Exploration*, 6, 1992, pp. 157–65

26. Stanley Krippner, Michael Winkler, Amyr Amiden, Robert Crema, Ruth Kelson, Harbans Lal Arora and Pierre Weil, 'Physiological and Geomagnetic Correlates of Apparent Anomalous Phenomena Observed in the Presence of a Brazilian "Psychic"', in *Journal of Scientific Exploration*, 10, 1996, 281–98

27. S. James P. Spottiswoode, 'Geomagnetic Activity and Anomalous Cognition: A Preliminary Report of New Evidence', in *Subtle Energies*, 1, 1990, pp. 65–77; Michael A. Persinger, 'Geophysical Variables and Behavior: XXX. Intense Paranormal Experiences Occur during Days of Quiet Global Geomagnetic Activity', in *Perceptual & Motor Skills*, 61, 1985, pp. 320–22; Persinger, 'Intense Paranormal Experiences Occur during Days of Quiet Global Geomagnetic Activity', in *Research in Parapsychology 1985*, Scarecrow, Metuchen, 28, 1986, p. 32

28. Anne Schienle, Rudolf Stark, R. Kulzer, R. Klöpper and Dieter Vaitl, 'Atmospheric Electromagnetism: Individual Differences in Brain Electrical Response to Simulated Sferics', in *International Journal of Psychophysiology*, 21, 1996, pp. 177–88

29. Michael A. Persinger, 'Religious and Mystical Experiences as Artifacts on Temporal Lobe Function: A General Hypothesis', in *Perceptual & Motor Skills*, 57, 1983, pp. 1255–62

30. Susan Blackmore, 'Alien Abduction: The Inside Story', in *New Scientist*, 1119, 1994, pp. 29–31

31. Norman Geschwind, 'Behavioural Change in Temporal Lobe Epilepsy', in *Psychological Medicine*, 9, 1979, pp. 217–19

32. Anthropological studies provide some indications that shamans, indigenous healers and participants in possession cults experience unusual electrical discharges in the temporal lobes; see Michael J. Winkelman, *Shamans, Priests and Witches: A Cross-cultural Study of Magico-religious Practitioners*, Arizona State University, Tempe, 1992

33. Vernon M. Neppe, 'The Relevance of the Temporal Lobe to Anomalous Subjective Experience', in *Research in Parapsychology 1983*, Scarecrow, Metuchen, 1984, pp. 7–10

34. James F. McHarg, 'An Uncanny Temporal Lobe Epilepsy Apparition', in *Research in Parapsychology 1976*, Scarecrow, Metuchen, 1977, pp. 120–22

35. Masatoshi Itoh, Hiroshi Miyazaki and Yasuo Takahashi, 'Imaging of Mind Using Positron Emission Tomography', in *Journal of the International Society of Life Information Sciences*, 14, 1996, pp. 67–80

36. Manabu Tashiro, Hiroyuki Ishizaki, Nobuyuki Okamura, Hiroshi Miyazaki, Keizo Ishii and Masatoshi Itoh, 'Brain Activation during Visual (Subliminal) Stimulation of Ultra-short Duration', in *Journal of the International Society of Life Information Sciences*, 15, 1997, pp. 18–26

37. Compare Elmar R. Gruber, *Suche im Grenzenlosen. Hans Bender – ein Leben für die Parapsychology* ('Search in the Boundless. Hans Bender – A Life Devoted to Parapsychology'), Kiepenheuer & Witsch, Cologne, 1993, p. 41

38. Michael A. Persinger and G.B. Schaut, 'Geomagnetic Factors in Subjective Telepathic, Precognitive and Postmortem Experiences', in *Journal of the American Society for Psychical Research*, 82, 1988, pp. 217–35

39. Edgar S. Wilson, 'The Transits of Consciousness', in *Subtle Energies*, 4, 1993, pp. 171–86

40. Johanna Paungger and Thomas Poppe, *Vom richtigen Zeitpunkt. Die Anwendung des Mondkalenders im täglichen Leben* ('The Right Point in Time. Application of the Moon Calendar in Daily Life'), Hugendubel, Munich, 1991

41. Andrija Puharich, *Beyond Telepathy*, Anchor Books, Garden City, 1973, pp. 281–9

42. Dean I. Radin, *The Conscious Universe*, op. cit., chapter 12

43. http://hrcweb.lv-hrc.nevada.edu/cogno/index3.html; Dick Bierman also offers controlled on-line psi experiments, for example on precognition, on his website, http://www.psy.uva.nl/resedu/pn/EXOMNTS/PRE/PUBLIC/prece p2.3html, as does the Koestler Parapsychology Unit in Edinburgh, http://moebius.psy.ed.ac.uk/~psi-ping/

44. René Peoc'h, 'Psychokinèse animale et humaine' ('Human and Animal Psychokinesis'), in *Bulletin de la Fondation Odier*, 2, 1994, pp. 23–8

45. René Peoc'h, 'Psychokinetic Action of Young Chicks on the Path of an Illuminated Source', in *Journal of Scientific Exploration*, 9, 1995,

pp. 223–30

46. Michael Levin, 'On the Lack of Evidence for the Evolution of Psi as an Argument against the Reality of the Paranormal', in *Journal of the American Society for Psychical Research*, 90, 1996, pp. 221–30; here p. 225

47. As an example of many books on this topic see Alan Gauld and Anthony D. Cornell, *Poltergeists*, Routledge & Kegan Paul, London, 1979

48. Elmar R. Gruber, 'Four German Poltergeists', in *Theta*, 8, 1980, pp. 6–7; Gruber, 'On the Track of the Poltergeists, in *ASPR Newsletter*, 7, 1981, pp. 1–2

49. On the basis of this theoretic assumption, poltergeist phenomena are (in my opinion wrongly) called recurrent spontaneous psychokinesis (RSPK); compare Elmar R. Gruber, 'Spuren zum Spuk' ('Tracks to the Poltergeist'), in *Unter dem Pflaster liegt der Strand*, 6, 1979, pp. 159–76

50. William G. Roll and Elson A. de Montagno, 'Psi and the Brain', in *Research in Parapsychology 1983*, Scarecrow, Metuchen, 1984, pp. 4–7

51. A study by scientists of the University of Illinois in Springfield recently contradicted this opinion; James Houran, T.M. Harte and Rense Lange, 'Haunting Phenomena as an Experience of Accumulated Contexts: A Process Model', presentation at the conference *Towards a Science of Consciousness II*, Tucson, Arizona, 1997

52. Michaeleen C. Maher and George P. Hansen, 'Quantitative Investigation of a Reported Haunting Using Several Detection Techniques', in *Journal of the American Society for Psychical Research*, 86, 1992, pp. 347–74; Maher and Hansen, 'Quantitative Investigation of a "Haunted Castle" in New Jersey', in *Journal of the American Society for Psychical Research*, 89, 1995, pp. 19–50

53. Johan L.F. Gerding, Rens Wezelman and Dick J. Bierman, 'The Druten Disturbances: Exploratory RSPK Research', unpublished manuscript, 1997

54. In my CD-ROM, *Mysterium*, United Soft Media, Munich, 1996, I have compiled and described in detail many cases with this poltergeist pattern

55. Dean I. Radin and William G. Roll, 'Investigation of Two Haunted Castles in Scandinavia', in *Electronic Journal for Anomalous Phenomena*, 4, 1996
(http://www.psy.uva.nl/ResEdu/PN/eJAP/1996.4/1996-4.html)

56. The English and Scandinavian equivalent of the 'White Lady' in German-speaking countries

## Chapter 3: The Fingerprint of Consciousness

57. Dean I. Radin, 'Searching for "Signatures" in Anomalous Human–Machine Interaction Data: A Neural Network Approach', in *Journal of Scientific Exploration*, 3, 1989, pp. 185–200
58. Dean I. Radin, 'Neural Network Analysis of Consciousness-Related Patterns in Random Sequences', in *Journal of Scientific Exploration*, 7, 1993, pp. 355–73
59. Dean I. Radin, 'Environmental Modulation and Statistical Equilibrium in Mind–Matter Interaction', in *Subtle Energies*, 4, 1993, pp. 1–30

## Chapter 4: Through the Time Barrier

60. William E. Cox, 'Precognition: An Analysis, II', in *Journal of the American Society for Psychical Research*, 50, 1956, pp. 99–109
61. Charles Honorton and Diane C. Ferrari, ' "Future Telling": A Meta-analysis of Forced-Choice Precognition Experiments, 1935–1987', in *Journal of Parapsychology*, 35, 1989, pp. 281–308
62. Holger Klintman, 'Is There a Paranormal (Precognitive) Influence in Certain Types of Perceptual Sequences? Part I and II', in *European Journal of Parapsychology*, 5, 1983, pp. 19–49; 5, 1984, pp. 125–40
63. Benjamin Libet, Elwood W. Wright, Bertram Feinstein and Dennis K. Pearl, 'Subjective Referral of the Timing for a Conscious Sensory Experience: A Functional Role for the Somatosensory Specific Projection System in Man', in *Brain*, 102, 1979, pp. 193–224; Libet, 'Subjective Antedating of a Sensory Experience and Mind–Brain Theories: Reply to Honderich', in *Journal of Theoretical Biology*, 114, 1985, pp. 563–70
64. A. Bechara, H. Damasio, D. Tranel and A.R. Damasio, 'Deciding Advantageously before Knowing the Advantageous Strategy', in *Science*, 275, 28 February 1997, pp. 1293–5
65. Dean I. Radin, 'Unconscious Perception of Future Emotions. An Experiment in Presentiment', in *Proceedings of the 39th Parapsychological Association Convention*, San Diego, 1996, pp. 171–85
66. Dean I. Radin, 'Autonomic Physiological Reactions to Future Emotional Targets', project 66 10 10, project report to the Institut für Grenzgebiete der Psychologie und Psychohygiene, Consciousness

Research Division, Harry Reid Center for Environmental Studies, University of Nevada, Las Vegas, 1997; Radin's experiment was based on previous successful demonstrations of this effect. See Dick J. Bierman and Dean I. Radin, 'Anomalous Anticipatory Response on Randomized Future Conditions', in *Perceptual & Motor Skills*, 84, 1997, pp. 689–90

67. Dick J. Bierman, 'Emotion and Intuition I, II, III, IV, & V: Unravelling Variables Contributing to the Presentiment Effect', unpublished manuscript, University of Utrecht and Amsterdam, 1997

68. A. Bechara *et al.*, *op. cit.*

## Chapter 5: Cosmic Connections: Psi, the Earth and the Sky

69. S. James P. Spottiswoode, 'Association between Effect Size in Free Response Anomalous Cognition Experiments and Local Sidereal Time', in *Journal of Scientific Exploration*, 11, 1997, pp. 109–22

70. Charles T. Tart, 'Effects of Electrical Shielding on GESP Performance', in *Journal of the American Society for Psychical Research*, 82, 1988, pp. 129–45; Tart, 'Electrical Shielding, ESP, and the Earth's Magnetic Field', in T.M. Srinivasan, *Energy Medicine around the World*, Gabriel, Phoenix, 1988, pp. 325–38

71. People with access to the Internet can have local time at any chosen spot converted into local sidereal time by the Institut für Geodäsie of the University of the Bundeswehr in Munich, http://habicht.bauv.unibw-muenchen.de/ex-scherer/ast1-UTST.html

72. S. James P. Spottiswoode and Edwin C. May, 'Anomalous Cognition Effect Size: Dependence on Sidereal Time and Solar Wind Parameters', in *Proceedings of the Parapsychological Association 40th Convention*, Brighton, 1997

73. S. James P. Spottiswoode, 'Geomagnetic Fluctuations and Free Response Anomalous Cognition: A New Understanding', in *Journal of Parapsychology*, 61, 1997, pp. 3–12

## Chapter 6: The Parsifal Effect

74. D.J. West and G.W. Fisk, 'A Dual ESP Experiment with Clock Cards', in *Journal of the Society for Psychical Research*, 37, 1953, pp. 185–9

75. Marilyn J. Schlitz and Richard Wiseman, 'Experimenter Effects and the Remote Detection of Staring', in Edwin C. May (ed.), *Proceedings of the 39th Annual Convention of the Parapsychological Association*, San Diego, 1996

76. Harald Walach and Stefan Schmidt, 'Empirical Evidence for a Non-classical Experimenter Effect: An Experimental, Double-Blind Investigation of Unconventional Information Transfer', in *Journal of Scientific Exploration*, 11, 1997, pp. 59–68

77. C.M. Pleass and N. Dean Dey, 'Conditions That Appear to Favor Extrasensory Interactions between *Homo sapiens* and Microbes', in *Journal of Scientific Exploration*, 4, 1990, pp. 213–31

78. *Ibid.*, p. 230

79. Zha Leping and Tron McConnell, 'Parapsychology in the People's Republic of China: 1979–1989', in *Journal of the American Society for Psychical Research*, 85, 1991, pp. 119–43

80. *Ibid.*, p. 123

81. Brenda J. Dunne, York H. Dobyns, Robert G. Jahn and Roger D. Nelson, 'Series Position Effects in Random Event Generator Experiments', in *Journal of Scientific Exploration*, 8, 1994, pp. 197–215

82. Piers Anthony, *Macroscope*, New York, 1969

## Epilogue

83. Dean I. Radin, *The Conscious Universe: The Scientific Truth of Psychic Phenomena*, Harper Edge, San Francisco, 1997, chapter 4

84. V. Barns *et al.*, 'Confirmation of the Existence of the Omega-Minus Hyperon', in *Physics Letters*, 12, 1964, pp. 134–6

85. Nick Herbert, *Quantum Reality: Beyond the New Physics*, Anchor Books, Garden City, 1985, p. 249

# GLOSSARY

**Anomalous cognition** (AC) A a new collective term for extrasensory perception.

**Anomalous mental phenomena** (AMP) A new collective term for all paranormal phenomena.

**Anomalous perturbation** (AP) A new collective term for psychokinesis. See also MMI.

**Apparition** In the terminology of parapsychology, a paranormal manifestation; a visual paranormal impression (in the form of an hallucination, for example) or a (possible) material 'phantom'.

**Backster effect** The electric reactions of plants that are interpreted as being a form of rudimentary perception (primary perception).

**Biophotons** Photons (the physically smallest unit of light with coherent wavelength) emitted by cells in a living system.

**Bio-PK** Anomalous perturbation in biological systems (organisms, animals, humans). See also DMILS.

**Clairvoyance** The obtaining of information about remote objects or situations without transmission by the normal senses.

**Conformance behaviour** A further development of the PMIR model, according to which random systems have the tendency to 'conform' to ordered systems that enter into an anomalous relationship with them.

**Déjà vu** (French 'already seen') The feeling of already being familiar with previously unknown surroundings or of having already experienced a new situation.

**Direct hit** The subsequent correct selection of the target by the subject out of all the possible targets when employing the free-response method.

**DMILS** (direct mental influence of living systems) A term for experiments in which biological systems are influenced by intentions from a distance. See also bio-PK.

**EFHB** (exceptional functions of the human body) A term used by Chinese scientists to designate paranormal abilities.

**Extrasensory perception** (ESP) The reception of information by other means than the known senses. This includes telepathy, > clairvoyance, and > precognition.

**Forced-choice method** A technique in experiments in anomalous cognition in which predetermined target symbols have to be 'guessed'.

**Free-response method** A technique in experiments in anomalous cognition, in which impressions of unknown target images or objects are described in the subject's own words.

**Fundamental psi function** (FPF) A model of a reciprocal, autonomous process between an organism and the environment, in which its consciousness and the physical reality mutually affect each other. This interaction is based on a mechanism in which the immediate space–time environment of the organism is scanned constantly via psi.

**Ganzfeld** A technically induced state of altered consciousness favouring the appearance of hypnagogic hallucinations.

**Hallucination** (from Latin *alucinari*, 'blathering', 'dreaming') A delusion of the senses that is not triggered by a sensual stimulus.

**Macro-PK** Anomalous perturbation in macro-physical processes that can be observed with the naked eye.

**Meta-analysis** A type of statistical analyses in which the importance and replicability of effects is analysed.

**Micro-PK** anomalous perturbation in micro-physical processes.

**MMI** (mind-matter interaction) A new collective term for psychokinetic effects.

**Out-of-body experience** (OBE) A state of consciousness in which the subject experiences being outside of the physical body.

**Paranormal** The characteristic of phenomena being investigated by parapsychology.

**Parapsychology** The science that investigates the phenomena of anomalous cognition and anomalous perturbation.

**PEAR** (Princeton Engineering Anomalies Research) A psi research laboratory at Princeton University.

**Percipient** The receiver of telepathic information.

**PK** See psychokinesis.

**PMIR** (psi-mediated instrumental response) A model based on the concept that organisms constantly subconsciously employ anomalous mental phenomena in order to optimize their interaction with their environment.

**Precognition** (from Latin *prae*, 'in advance' and *cognescere*, 'to know') Information about future events, without this information having been gained by normal means.

**Presentiment** A vague, emotionally charged precognitive impression.

**Presentiment reflex** A reaction by the autonomous nervous system to a presentiment.

**PRL** (Psychophysical Research Laboratories) A psi research laboratory at Princeton University which existed between 1980 and 1989.

**Psi** The twenty-third letter of the Greek alphabet and the collective term for all paranormal phenomena. Introduced in 1943 by Robert Thouless and H.P. Wiesner.

**Psi phenomena** See anomalous mental phenomena.

**Psi research** See parapsychology.

**Psi-missing** The employment of psi in order to avoid hits in a psi experiment.

**Psychic** A person with paranormal talents.

**Psychokinesis** (PK) Mental influence on material systems that can at present still not be explained by the natural sciences.

**Qi** (also ch'i) According to traditional Chinese concepts, the life energy that permeates the human body and the universe.

**Qigong** Mental–physical exercises to bring the life energy qi into circulation. The external emission of qi can bring about paranormal effects.

**REG** (random-event generator) A machine that produces completely random sequences of states.

**Remote viewing** (RV) A new term for anomalous cognition, originally based on a specific experimental technique.

**RSPK** (recurrent spontaneous psychokinesis) A specialist term for poltergeist phenomena.

**Sender** A person who transmits information during telepathy.

**Significance** (from Latin *significare*, 'to signal') In statistics, the designation of a result that cannot have come about by chance but is the result of some sort of influence.

**Spontaneous phenomenon** A paranormal phenomenon that was neither provoked nor expected.

**SRI** (Stanford Research Institute) A research centre in Menlo Park, California.

**Subtle energy** A hypothetical energy as carrier for anomalous effects, particularly bio-PK.

**Telepathy** (Greek 'to feel from afar') The exchange of information from person to person without the aid of the normal senses.

# ABBREVIATIONS

| | |
|---|---|
| AC | anomalous cognition |
| AIR | American Institutes for Research |
| AMP | anomalous mental phenomena |
| AOL | analytical overlay |
| AP | anomalous perturbation |
| ASPR | American Society for Psychical Research |
| CIA | Central Intelligence Agency |
| CRV | coordinate remote viewing |
| CSICOP | Committee for the Scientific Investigation of the Claims of the Paranormal |
| CSL | Cognitive Sciences Laboratory |
| DIA | Defense Intelligence Agency |
| DMILS | direct mental influence of living systems |
| EEG | electroencephalograph, electroencephalogram |
| EFHB | exceptional functions of the human body |
| ERV | extended remote viewing |
| ESP | extrasensory perception |
| FPF | fundamental psi function |
| INSCOM | Intelligence and Security Command |
| ISME | Institute of Space Medico-Engineering, Beijing |
| LST | local sidereal time |
| MBTI | Myers–Briggs type indicator |
| MCG | magnetocardiograph, magnetocardiogram |
| MEG | magnetoencephalograph, magnetoencephalogram |
| MMI | mind–matter interaction |
| NPIC | National Photographic Interpretation Center |
| NSA | National Security Agency |
| OBE | out-of-body experience |
| ONR | Office of Naval Research |
| OPSEC | Operations Security Group |
| OTS | Office of Technical Service (part of the CIA) |
| PEAR | Princeton Engineering Anomalies Research Program |
| PET | positron emission tomography |
| PK | psychokinesis |
| PMIR | psi-mediated instrumental response |
| REG | random-event generator |
| RMC | random mechanical cascade |
| RV | remote viewing |
| SAIC | Science Applications International Corporation |
| SCANATE | scanning by coordinate |
| SRI | Stanford Research Institute |
| TLE | temporal lobe epilepsy |
| WRV | written remote viewing |

# ACKNOWLEDGEMENTS

Many people helped me in the preparation of this manuscript and made valuable suggestions for my work. I am especially grateful to Dr Dean Radin, Professor Dr Dick Bierman and James Spottiswoode, who put their newest and still unpublished works at my disposal. Many colleagues discussed important experiments and psi research in their countries with me, and I would like to thank them for this: Carlos Alvarado, Dr Richard Broughton, Dr Keith Harary, Dr Kimiko Kawano, Hideyuki Kokubo, Hong Zhang, Dr Stanley Krippner, Professor Dr Andrei Lee, Li Zhi Nan, Professor Dr Yoshio Machi, Leszek Matela, Dr Edwin May, Professor Dr Robert Morris, Alejandro Parra, Tom Porter, Dr Hal Puthoff, Yoichiro Sako, Paul Smith, Dr Toñu Soidla, Ingo Swann, Professor Dr Charles Tart, Dr Wei Nengrun and Dr Mikio Yamamoto.

My special thanks go to my friend Marco, who with great care and enthusiasm contributed many valuable suggestions and ideas to the manuscript. As ever, my wife Dagmar was able not only to contribute important suggestions to the content of the book but to organize my daily life so perfectly that I was able to deliver the manuscript on time.

# INDEX

# Index